To - Mark Roberto

From - Peace Lutheran
Sunday School

1968

The Question Box

THE

QUESTION

BOX

by William N. Emch

THE WARTBURG PRESS

Columbus, Ohio

FOREWORD

For many years The Question Box, conducted by Dr. William N. Emch, has been a regular feature of the *Lutheran Standard*. With the more than one hundred thousand readers of the *Lutheran Standard* The Question Box has proven to be a most popular feature.

From time to time requests have been received by the editor and by the publisher to have The Question Box appear in a more permanent form. In response to these many requests the files of the *Lutheran Standard* for a period of more than twenty-five years were carefully examined, and the more interesting of the questions and answers from The Question Box were compiled. The examination disclosed such a plethora of material, such a variety of subjects, and such a broad scope of inquiries that the task of making a final selection proved to be a formidable one indeed. But the work was completed, and the results are herewith presented in book form in the hope that the many friends of the editor of The Question Box will welcome them and find as much pleasure and profit in their perusal as they did when the questions were first submitted and answered.

To know Dr. Emch from his writings is to become interested in him. To know him in person, is to love him. He is one of the grand old men of the Christian ministry who never seems to grow old. After successful and fruitful pastorates in various parts of Ohio he is now, in his eightieth year, serving the Lutheran Old Folks' Home, Toledo, as resident chaplain.

In the evening of his life he seems busier than ever. Besides the voluminous correspondence which he carries on as editor of the Question Box he ministers to the men and the women residents of the home and radiates a genuine Christian optimism and joy through his ministry. He is also in almost constant demand as a supply pastor in near-by pulpits and still preaches with vigor and vitality.

Truly, Dr. Emch is one of God's magnificent men. He has served his Lord and his church faithfully and well. We are confident that these contributions from his facile pen will also serve the Lord and His church.

PAUL W. NESPER

CONTENTS

III. The Christian Life, Attitudes, Convictions

IV. Home, Family, Marriage

V. Beliefs, Customs, Traditions

VI. Health, Sickness, Death, Burial

PART ONE

THE BIBLE

1. *About Its Books, Versions, Sources, and Subjects*

The Apocryphal Books

Why do we not accept the apocryphal books as a part of our Bible as do the Roman Catholics?

It is because we do not believe they were divinely inspired. These books did not form a part of the ancient Hebrew Scriptures. Paul affirms that unto the Jews "were committed the oracles of God," Rom. 3:2. These books thus were evidently not a part of those oracles of God. They originated in a period of time after the last of the Hebrew prophets. Christ and His apostles never quote from nor refer to these apocryphal books. The apostolic church refused to accept them as a part of the canon of Scripture. St. Jerome, the translator of "the authentic Latin version of the Bible, called the Vulgate," rejected the apocryphal books as uninspired.

The Origin of the Bible

Will you, please, give us a brief account of the origin of the Bible? We are asking for nothing in detail. Just a brief outline that we may consider in our Sunday school class.

When Jesus said to the unbelieving Jews of His day: "Search the scriptures; for in them ye think ye have eternal life: and they are they which testify of Me," every intelligent man before Him understood what He meant by the Scriptures. There were other important writings in that day, but "the Scriptures" were a collection of unique scrolls especially sacred and authoritative because they were written by Moses and the prophets at the express command of God.

The history of these books (scrolls) can be traced from their origin down through the centuries. In Exodus 17:14 we read: "And the Lord said unto Moses, Write this for a memorial in a book, and rehearse it in the ears of Joshua." We know that Moses heeded this injunction, for in Deuteronomy 31:9 we are told: "And Moses wrote this law and delivered it unto the priests, the sons of Levi, which bear the ark of the covenant of the Lord." In verse 24 of the same chapter we read: "And it came to pass when Moses had made an end of writing the words of this law in a book, until they were finished, that Moses commanded the Levites which bare the ark of the covenant of the Lord, saying, Take this book of the law and put it in the side of the ark of the covenant of the Lord your God, that it may be there for a witness against thee." The book of the law was accordingly put by the side of the ark of the covenant for safekeeping.

This same book of the law or a copy of it appears again many years later, namely, in the reign of Josiah, the good king of Judah. In II Kings 22:8, 10 we find this statement: "And Hilkiah the high priest said unto Shaphan the scribe, I have found the book of the law in the house of the Lord. And Hilkiah gave the book to Shaphan and he read it. . . . And Shaphan read it before the king." The reading of this book caused quite a stir, proving that the king and his helpers knew that it was the authoritative Word of God.

In the days of Ezra this book was publicly read and explained in the presence of great multitudes. "And all the people gathered themselves together as one man into the street . . . and they spake unto Ezra the scribe to bring the book of the law of Moses, which the Lord had commanded to Israel. And Ezra the priest brought the law before the congregation both of men and women, and all that could hear with understanding. . . . And he read therein, . . . and the ears of the people were attentive unto the book of the law. And Ezra the scribe stood upon a pulpit of wood, which was made for the purpose. . . . And Ezra opened the book in the sight of all the people . . . and when he opened it, all the people stood up. And Ezra blessed the Lord, the great God. And all the people answered, Amen, Amen, with lifting up their hands: and they bowed their heads and worshipped the Lord with their faces to the ground. . . . So they read the book of the law of God distinctly, and gave the sense and caused them to understand the reading," Nehemiah 8:1-8.

The various books of the Old Testament were assembled with great care at the time of Ezra. They were written in Hebrew, but a translation of the entire Old Testament into Greek (called the Septuagint) was

2

made over two hundred years before the birth of our Savior. Jesus put His stamp of approval upon this Old Testament, which we have to this day. To these Old Testament books He and the apostles ever appealed as the authoritative Word of God. Hundreds of times they refer to and quote from these Old Testament Scriptures.

The New Testament books were not definitely assembled until quite a number of years after the death of the apostles. It would take us far afield for me to attempt even briefly to go into the history of the assembling of the books included in the New Testament. Suffice it, therefore, to say that we have proof sufficient to believe and to teach that:

1. The Bible is a book written at the express command of God. Recall His words to Moses. Think how often we find statements like these: "Thus saith the Lord." "Hear the word of the Lord." "The word of the Lord came unto me saying. . . ." "The Lord spake unto me again saying. . . ." A voice said to John on the isle of Patmos, "What thou seest write in a book, and send it unto the seven churches." And again the voice enjoined: "Write the things which thou hast seen, and the things which are, and the things which shall be hereafter."

2. The Bible is a book written at the express command of God under the guidance of God. "All scripture is given by inspiration of God," II Timothy 3:16. "Holy men of God spake as they were moved by the Holy Ghost," II Peter 1:21. "We . . . know the things that are freely given to us of God. Which things we speak, not in the words which man's wisdom teacheth, but which the Holy Ghost teacheth," I Cor. 2:12, 13.

3. The Bible is a book marvelously preserved by the providential care of God. We have stated above how He cared for the preservation of the early books of the Old Testament. "Heaven and earth shall pass away, but My words shall not pass away," Matthew 24:35. "The word of the Lord endureth forever. And this is the word which by the gospel is preached unto you," I Peter 1:25. The Bible is complete for all ages and for all people to the end of time (see Revelation 22:18, 19; Psalm 119:105; John 8:31, 32). This is the challenge of the Bible, "Supplant me or supplement me if you can."

The Douay Version

What difference is there between the Douay Version of the Bible and the King James Version?

The Douay Bible is the official Roman Catholic English translation of the Latin Bible (the so-called Vulgate) which was made in 1582 at

Rheims, France. The King James Version is a retranslation of the Hebrew Old Testament and the Greek New Testament into English. This work was done in England in 1611. The Douay Bible includes the Apocrypha, the King James Version does not. Different scholars do not translate a sentence or a verse in exactly the same way. The wording of a translation is, therefore, bound to be somewhat different though the meaning is practically the same. We could accept the Douay Bible without changing one major doctrine of our church. The difference between Roman Catholicism and Lutheranism is not a difference in the Bibles we use but a difference of ignoring or accepting the Bible as man's only infallible norm and guide. To the question, "What, then, must a Christian believe?" the Roman Catholic catechism by Pastor Joseph Deharbe, S.J., gives the following answer: "A Christian must believe all that God has revealed and the Catholic Church teaches, whether it is contained in Holy Scripture or not."

The Numbering of the Ten Commandments

Discuss the numbering of the Ten Commandments.

1. The Bible repeatedly speaks of "Ten Commandments" (see Exod. 34:28; Deut. 4:13; 10:4), hence there is no doubt as to the number "ten." But the commandments are not numerically divided in Scripture, so we cannot say positively which is the first, which is the second, etc. Four different ways of dividing the commandments have prevailed at some time or other among Jews and Christians.

1. *Talmudical.* According to this division the First Commandment consists of the words, "I am the Lord thy God, which have brought thee out of the land of Egypt," etc. (Exod. 20:2). The second, "Thou shalt have no other gods before Me. Thou shalt not make unto thee any graven image," etc. (Exod. 20:3-6). The third, "Thou shalt not take the name," etc., to the end (Exod. 20:17). This was the division of the ancient Jews.

2. *Origenian.* This division is named after the church father Origen. According to this method of division the First Commandment is, "Thou shalt have no other gods before Me" (Exod. 20:3). The second, "Thou shalt not make unto thee any graven image," etc., (Exod. 20:4-6). The tenth, "Thou shalt not covet," etc., to the end (Exod. 20:17). This division is accepted by the Greek Catholics and by all Protestants except the Lutherans.

3. *First Masoretic.* The commandment concerning the worship of the one true God also forbids the bowing down before some graven image or likeness. Hence in this method of division the First Commandment

4

in its full and extended form includes Exod. 20:3-6. The Ninth Commandment reads, "Thou shalt not covet thy neighbor's house." The tenth, "Thou shalt not covet thy neighbor's wife," etc., to the end (Exod. 20:17). This division is accepted by the Roman Catholics and the Lutherans.

4. *Second Masoretic,* also called the Augustinian. This division differs from the former merely in this that it follows Deut. 5:21 instead of Exod. 20:17. Hence the Ninth Commandment reads, "Thou shalt not covet thy neighbor's wife," and the tenth, "Thou shalt not covet thy neighbor's house," etc., to the end, as found in Deut. 5:21. No church denomination of the present time to my knowledge divides the Ten Commandments in this way.

I shall not enter into the arguments which are given in favor of the one or the other division. Since Moses himself in Deut. 5:21 places the commandment, "Neither shalt thou desire thy neighbor's wife," before the precept, "neither shalt thou covet thy neighbor's house," it seems to me that the method of dividing the Ten Commandments is immaterial. The church of Luther's day divided the Ten Commandments in the same way as the Roman Catholics and the Lutherans still divide them. What Luther found in the church of his time he continued to keep if it was not directly contrary to Scripture. It is doubtless mainly for this reason that we continue to divide the Ten Commandments as we do. It was John Calvin who revived the Origenian way of dividing the Decalogue.

The Book of Jonah

Is the book of Jonah a parable?

Jonah is as historical a character as were Isaiah, Jeremiah, or any of the prophets of old. If you turn to the latter part of the fourteenth chapter of Second Kings you will find the father of Jonah named, thus giving his genealogy. You will find the place of his residence given. We also learn the name of the king who ruled in the days of Jonah. History also attests that some of his prophecies were fulfilled in the reign of that king. Thus we see also from this historic book of the Old Testament that Jonah was a real person.

On two different occasions Jesus referred to Jonah as a historic character. And He quotes from the story of Jonah as from authentic history and not as from fiction. He gives the experience of Jonah as a type of His own burial and resurrection (Matthew 12:39, 41; 16:4). And Jesus says that the men of Nineveh shall rise up in judgment against the generation of His day because they repented at the preaching of Jonah;

and, behold, they would not repent when the Messiah Himself preached to them (Luke 11:32). From the authority of Jesus we have it that Jonah was a historic character, and the narrative given in the book of Jonah is history and not fiction or parable.

The Order of the Ten Commandments

I have a neighbor who claims that the Lutheran Church is guilty of having changed the order of the Ten Commandments. Is this true?

The record of the giving of the divine law on Mt. Sinai is found in Exodus, chapter 20, and is repeated in the fifth chapter of Deuteronomy. But in neither of these records are we told that this God-given law is to be divided into ten separate commandments. However, we do elsewhere in Scripture read that this divine law, written on two tables of stone, consists of "ten commandments" (see Exodus 34:28; Deut. 4:13; 10:4).

But the Bible nowhere attaches a number to any of these commandments. In other words, although there are ten commandments, the Scriptures never numerically divide them. The Bible nowhere tells us, for instance, which is the third, the sixth or the tenth commandment.

Moreover, the two records, Exodus 20 and Deuteronomy 5, do not give the commandments in exactly the same order. In Exodus 20 we read: "Thou shalt not covet thy neighbor's house, thou shalt not covet thy neighbor's wife, nor his manservant," etc. But in Deuteronomy we find: "Neither shalt thou desire thy neighbor's wife, neither shalt thou covet thy neighbor's house, his field, or his manservant."

We, indeed, number the commandments for convenience' sake, and it leads to confusion when all denominations do not divide and number them in the same way. But where is the authority that is going to tell us just how they are to be divided and numbered? No divine authority tells us how to divide and to number or even in what order to cite the Ten Commandments.

Strange as it may seem, since the days of Moses the Ten Commandments have been divided and numbered in four different ways. I cannot go into detail on this point. Suffice it to say that the Western Church in the centuries just preceding the Reformation considered the precept: "Thou shalt have no other gods before Me," as the first commandment. The words, "Thou shalt not make unto thee any graven image, or any likeness," etc., were taken to be merely a further explanation of the First Commandment just as the words, "Six days shalt thou labor, and do all thy work: but the seventh day is the sabbath of the Lord thy

God: in it thou shalt not do any work," etc., are only an explanation of the commandment: "Remember the sabbath day, to keep it holy."

"Thou shalt not covet thy neighbor's house," was taken as the Ninth Commandment, and the words, "Thou shalt not covet thy neighbor's wife, nor his manservant," etc., as the Tenth Commandment. Luther and his co-laborers, being conservative reformers, accepted this way of dividing and numbering the Ten Commandments because it was not directly contrary to the Word of God. It remained for a more radical reformer, namely, John Calvin, in 1536 to revive the mode of division approved by Origen and hence known of the Origenian. The denominations known as the Reformed group followed the leadership of Calvin. They consider the words: "Thou shalt not make unto thee any graven image, or any likeness," etc., as the Second Commandment. The words, "Thou shalt not covet thy neighbor's house, thou shalt not covet thy neighbor's wife," etc., are combined into one and numbered as the Tenth Commandment.

Now, in the end, what is the difference? Except this that John Calvin and his followers by insisting on a different way of dividing and enumerating the Ten Commandments have brought about a lot of confusion.

The Gospel in the Old Testament

Are there any parts of the Old Testament that can be called gospel? If so, what parts?

Certainly! Law and gospel are interspersed throughout the Bible. What is the law? Our catechism answers: "Every part of the Bible which forbids and condemns sin." What is the gospel? "Every part of the Bible which offers and gives me Jesus Christ and the forgiveness of sins." What is the chief difference between the law and the gospel? "The law condemns the sinner because of his sins. The gospel frees the sinner from his sins through faith in Jesus Christ."

Every announcement of God's love for fallen humanity is sweet gospel. "I will put enmity between thee [Satan] and the woman, and between thy seed and her seed; it shall bruise thy head, and thou shalt bruise his heel." This is the first gospel message of the Bible, and it is found in Genesis 3:15. It promises hope through the coming "Seed of the woman." This promised Victor over Satan, sin, and death is our blessed Redeemer and Savior, Christ Jesus. "When the fulness of time was come, God sent forth His Son, made of a woman, made under the law; to redeem them that were under the law, that we might receive the adoption of sons," Galatians 4:4, 5.

7

Every promise concerning the Messiah who was to come, every announcement of God's grace and pardon to the penitent and believing is cheering gospel. The Book of Leviticus is especially filled with gospel because it tells us of mercy and forgiveness through atonement. All those prescribed bloody sacrifices of old point to and have their fulfillment in the spotless "Lamb of God which taketh away the sin of the world."

There is salvation for us only in the gospel. The Old Testament believers looked forward to the Redeemer who was to come even as we trust in that same God-sent Redeemer who gave Himself as the atoning sacrifice on Calvary for all people and for all time.

2. About Persons, Places, Problems and Promises

Cain

It is evident that Cain must have taken a sister as his wife. This does not cause me any difficulty. What puzzles me is how Cain "builded a city" when there was no one "in the land of Nod" but Cain and his wife and their son Enoch (Genesis 4:16, 17). Can you solve this puzzle for me?

It is usually taken for granted that Adam and Eve's first two children were Cain and Abel. After the tragic death of Abel, do you suppose there was no one left but Adam and Eve and Cain? If so, where did Cain get his wife? When Adam was one hundred and thirty years of age, Seth was born (Genesis 5:3). "And the days of Adam after he had begotten Seth were eight hundred years: and he begat sons and daughters." If Adam and Eve had children after they were 130 years old, have we not reason to believe that they had many sons and daughters before that age?

Remember, Adam and Eve were in full vigor of manhood and womanhood as they came from the creative hand of God. And keep in mind, too, that God had expressly given them the command: "Be fruitful, and multiply and replenish the earth." Only three of their children are mentioned by name, but we have reason to believe that they had many children. Doubtless, Cain and Abel had numerous brothers and sisters at the time of Abel's death. This is indicated, it would seem to me, by the fact that "Cain was a tiller of the ground," and "Abel was a keeper of sheep." If there were only four human beings on earth, there would be little need of farming and sheep-raising.

Perhaps there were several generations on earth already by the time of the killing of Abel. There could have been a half dozen generations when Seth was born to his 130-year-old parents. Thus by that time the human population on earth could have been several thousand. It has been estimated that, when Adam died at the age of 930, there were at least twenty million people in the world. The Bible does not say that Cain at once builded a city when he went to the land of Nod. Other people, no doubt, followed him to that part of the country, and in time there was a city there.

The Children of Light and the Children of this World

I have difficulty with Luke 16:8–12. Will you be kind enough to make these words of our Lord clear to me?

In this parable of the unjust steward Jesus is contrasting "the children of this world," i.e., the worldlings who know no treasures and hence have no interests other than those of this world and life; and "the children of light," i.e., those who at least pretend to set their affections on the things above and, therefore, have their highest interests in the heavenly treasures which abide forever.

Now Jesus makes the amazing statement that in a certain sense the children of this world are wiser than the children of light. They are not wiser in that they ignore the spiritual treasures and make no provision for the life to come. In this they are the greatest of fools, "for what shall it profit a man, if he shall gain the whole world, and lose his own soul?" "Thou fool, this night thy soul shall be required of thee: then whose shall those things be which thou hast provided?" The children of this world *are in their generation* wiser. They choose to have their portion in this life, and they are very solicitous about their welfare in this world. The children of light claim to believe in a life to come, but they show little real concern about making provision for that life.

"The Lord commended the unjust steward." Not the Lord of heaven and earth but that "certain rich man" who had hired this rascal to be his manager, he praised him for his shrewdness. Herein this dishonest worldling was wise, that he so shrewdly went about to attain his goal—namely, that when he is thrown out of his job he will have friends who will take him in. We cannot but detest his method, but we must admit that he acted shrewdly.

Note the craftiness of this unjust steward. He was in possession of great wealth. He did not own it, but he had the control of it. He knew, however, that this wealth was going to be in his possession but a very short time. Now it was up to him to provide for the future, when this wealth would be taken from him. And the only way that he could provide for the coming days was with the wealth which he as yet had under his control because he was too proud to beg and he had never learned to work. The application that Jesus desires to make is this, The children of light have in their possession certain wealth, which they control but do not own. Everything belongs to the Lord, but He has entrusted to every individual certain talents and gifts of body, mind, and spirit, as well as certain material possessions. These material possessions are here especially emphasized. The true riches do not consist of money and material wealth, but our attitude toward money, and the way we use our material possessions, are a fair index of our standing with God and our relationship to Him. These things will soon be taken from us. Death will wrench every copper from our clinched fists. Our duty is to provide for the future, not merely for our remaining few days in this world—that is the height of folly, merely to do that—but for life everlasting.

"Make to yourselves friends by means of the mammon of unrighteousness; that when it shall fail, they may receive you into the eternal tabernacles" (Revised Version). When money and material wealth are here referred to as "the mammon of unrighteousness," it does not necessarily imply that it has all been dishonestly acquired, but that it is perishable and hence deceptive and disappointing to those who put their trust in it and make it their chief treasure. Use your possessions to the honor of God to whom they belong and for the temporal and spiritual welfare of the needy, but especially of God's true servants. And when you leave this world, those whom you have befriended will arise and call you blessed and welcome you in the home above, where God's reward of grace awaits you.

The worldling chooses "that which is least," namely, money, that which is of little value, that which always remains the property of God. If he is unfaithful in the use of this entrusted wealth, "which is another man's," this minor, earthly wealth; who would commit to his trust "the true riches," the abiding, heavenly wealth which is of infinite value?

The Days of Creation

Were the creation days 24-hour days or periods?

Some believe that the days of creation were days of twenty-four hours. The words of Scripture in their literal and ordinary sense would seem clearly to indicate this. Others contend that the term "day" need not necessarily be taken in its ordinary sense since the sun, which at least now governs the day, was not created until the fourth day.

What is considered demonstrated scientific truth today may be proven absolutely false by the scientists of tomorrow. Most conservative Lutheran theologians believe that as yet true science has proved nothing that would compel them to conclude that their time-honored way of interpreting Genesis 1 is false.

St. Peter says, "One day is with the Lord as a thousand years," II Peter 3:8. Some use this passage to prove that "day" in Genesis means a long period of time. The connection of this passage plainly shows that St. Peter is here refuting the scoffers who were saying: "Where is the promise of His coming?" They claimed that the Lord had not kept His promise. They evidently misinterpreted Christ's prediction concerning the time of His return and the day of judgment. They thought that Jesus meant that He would return after a few years or a decade or two at most. And, lo, now at the time of the writing of this epistle almost a half-century had passed, and still that prediction had not yet come true. Now, to refute these scoffers and to strengthen the faith of the Christians, St. Peter says: "Beloved, be not ignorant of this one thing, that one day is with the Lord as a thousand years, and a thousand years as one day." From this I conclude that we better not lay too much stress on our interpretation of time. The apostle certainly wants to say that God does not reckon time as we do. A brief space suffices for Him to accomplish what we think would require a very long period of time. But, on the other hand, what we reckoned to be a day may in reality with Him mean a thousand years.

The essential thing for us to hold fast is this: In the beginning (wherever that may have been) God created the heaven and the earth. By His almighty Word He called all things into being, and by His almighty power He still sustains and governs all things. Someday—God alone knows when that day will be—Christ will come again to judge the living and the dead.

The Fruit of the Forbidden Tree

Gen. 3:6 says the woman ate of the "fruit." Why do people say it was an apple?

We do not know what kind of tree it was that God used as "the tree of the knowledge of good and evil." It could have been a fruit tree of any species since it was simply to serve as a test of obedience. It was, no doubt, a tree of beauty with attractive fruit, but nothing is told us as to what kind of fruit or tree it was. Early painters represented this tree as an apple tree, and this doubtless gave rise to the prevalent idea that it was an apple tree.

The Tree of Life and the Tree of Knowledge

If Adam and Eve had eaten of the "tree of life" instead of the "tree of the knowledge of good and evil," would that have put them on a level with the good angels? Gen. 2:9.

There are, no doubt, many who answer this question with an unqualified "yes." Most of our theologians, both ancient and modern, have held to this supposition. But I fear it is merely a conjecture that amounts to little. The truth is, our first parents ate of the forbidden tree, and God in mercy prevented them from eating of the "tree of life" after they had fallen into sin.

Jesus has regained for us our lost Paradise, and he who remains true to Him will someday eat of the "tree of life which is in the midst of the Paradise of God," Rev. 2:7. This is the one thing needful.

The Descendants of Ham

What is your interpretation of Genesis 9:20—25? Does it possibly indicate that Ham's misbehavior in connection with his father's drunkenness and the resultant curse for his descendants were the origin of the Negro race? If so, Christians should have a more sympathetic understanding of the segregated Negro, should they not?

The old theory that the Negro race is the result of a curse pronounced by Noah on Canaan, the fourth son of Ham, because of a misdemeanor of his father's should certainly be discarded. Notice, Ham, the one who did the wicked deed, is not cursed, but only Canaan, the youngest of his four sons. Ham had four sons (see Genesis 10:6). Why were not Cush, Havilah, and Phut, sons of Ham, also cursed as well as Canaan, the youngest son? I am convinced that Dr. H. C. Leupold is right when, in his *Exposition of Genesis,* he says that Noah, though filled with righteous indignation, here "speaks a word of prophecy. This prophetic word is to serve as a guide for the human race as well as for a solemn warning for all times to come."

Dr. Leupold translates verse 25 thus: "And he said: Cursed *is* Canaan; servant of servants shall he be to his brethren." Noah is not wishing or pronouncing a curse on his grandson and his descendants, but he is pronouncing the prophetic truth that they will be an accursed people because of their exceptional wickedness. He does not say, "May he be a servant of servants to his brethren," but "servant of servants shall he be to his brethren."

The whole human race sprang from one couple, Adam and Eve. "God hath made of one blood all nations of men," Acts 17:26. Who knows of what complexion Adam and Eve were? Were they both blonds? Were they both brunettes? Did they both have curly hair? Did the one have blue eyes and the other brown eyes? The Mendelian law of heredity has proved that all the varieties of dogs, of cattle, of roses, of chickens, etc., have sprung from one pair of that species. And thus the human race, too, with all the various shades of color and variety of peculiarities could have sprung from one human pair.

If you are in need of a transfusion of blood, the blood of a Negro, an Indian, or a Jap, if it is of your type, can serve you just as well as the blood of a white person. Science can distinguish human blood from animal blood, but it cannot tell you whether that human blood is from the body of a Negro, a Chinaman, or a very fair white person.

God is no respecter of persons. The black man is as dear to Him as is the white man. It is unchristian to mistreat, to look down upon, and to be uninterested in the bodily and the spiritual welfare of any person because of his race or color.

Gog and Magog

What is the significance of "Gog and Magog" in Ezekiel 38 and 39 and Revelation 20?

The prophet Ezekiel is enjoined to set his face "against Gog, the land of Magog, the chief prince of Masheck and Tubal, and prophesy against him." Gog seems to have been the king, and Magog the kingdom. This wicked king, together with his many confederates, undertook to destroy, or at least to capture and enslave, Israel. This took place sometime after Israel's return from the Babylonian captivity. However, though this formidable force came against Israel it met with a crushing defeat. God fought for Israel even as He had predicted through the prophet (see Ezekiel 38:22).

This Old Testament event is brought into prominence because it is referred to in Revelation 20. There in verses 7 to 10 we read: "And when the thousand years are expired, Satan shall be loosed out of his prison and shall go out to deceive the nations which are in the four corners of the earth, Gog and Magog, to gather them together to battle; the number of whom is as the sand of the sea. And they went up on the breadth of the earth, and compassed the saints about, and the beloved city: and fire came down from God out of heaven, and devoured them. And the devil that deceived them was cast into the lake of fire and brimstone."

Wickedness on earth just before the end shall abound, and the number of true believers will be few in comparison with the many who are in the camp of the enemy. Satan will make his dupes believe that by one united, supreme effort Christianity can be utterly banished from the earth. He is pictured as gathering his hordes from every nook and corner of the earth and encircling the saints in their capital city. But God intervenes in behalf of His people, and Satan and his whole camp are utterly crushed, for "fire came down from God out of heaven and devoured them."

We believe that "Gog and Magog" stand as representatives of all opposition to Christ and the church. As in the days of Ezekiel these enemies of God met with utter defeat, so Satan and all his cohorts will on the last great day meet their utter and final doom. We are not expecting the devil and all his hellish forces to meet their Waterloo in a fierce battle fought with material weapons like the conflict which overthrew Napoleon.

The Age of Methuselah

Was Methuselah 969 years old according to our reckoning of years?

A year is a complete revolution of the earth around the sun. Or we may also say that a year is a complete course of the seasons. The exact year, we are told, consists of 365 days, 5 hours, 48 minutes, and 46 seconds. It is not likely that the ancients had this exact knowledge. But we do read of years from the very beginning of the human race. "Adam lived an hundred and thirty years and begat a son, . . . and called his name Seth," Gen. 5:3. The length of the year was determined variously by the nations of antiquity. The earliest method was, no doubt, that of making it include a certain number of lunar months. (From one "new moon" to the next is a lunar month). Twelve lunar months give a year of 354 days. It was soon found that such a year was defective because it was not true to the course of the seasons. It became necessary, therefore, to intercalate an extra month quite often. In other words, some years consisted of twelve months and others of thirteen. In this way men kept the year in a constant relative position to the seasons. We have, therefore, from the very earliest times an approximation of the true solar year.

Methuselah died just before the Flood. If we study the dates mentioned in the narrative of the Flood (Gen. 7 and 8), it becomes quite apparent that the year of the Flood consisted of twelve months.

If you intend to ask, "Did they in the days of Methuselah have common years consisting of 365 days and leap years consisting of 366 days?" my answer is, "No." But I do believe that the average year of those days was the same as it is now.

The Millennium

Do we Lutherans believe in a millennium? Why or why not?

There are Lutherans who believe in a millennium, but the Lutheran Church as such does not. In the 17th Article of the Augsburg Confession our church teaches that "at the consummation of the world [at the last day], Christ shall raise up all the dead." Again: "They condemn others also, who now scatter Jewish opinions that, before the resurrection of the dead, the godly shall take possession of the kingdom of the world, the ungodly being everywhere suppressed." These quotations from the Augsburg Confession make plain that the Lutheran Church rejects the gross, material idea of a millennium that was held by some at the time the Confessions were adopted and is still held by some today.

In the Apostolic Creed we profess to believe that the ascended Christ now "sitteth at the right hand of God the Father Almighty, from whence He shall come [not to establish a glorious earthly kingdom, but] to judge the quick and the dead." And in the explanation of the Third Article of the Creed we with Luther confess that Christ "will at the last day [not a thousand years before the last], raise up me and all the dead." And He will raise up "me" as a believer in Christ and an heir of heaven. But "all the dead," alas, are not saints of God. Thus we there profess to believe that all the dead will be raised at the same time. This great truth is also taught and confessed by all who accept the other two ancient creeds of Christendom, the Nicene Creed and the Athanasian Creed.

Those who believe in a millennium think that they find proof for their teaching in many passages of Scripture. But their chief proof passages are found in the prophetical books of the Old Testament and especially in the very difficult and obscure prophetical book of the New Testament, The Revelation of St. John. We cannot accept an explanation of these obscure passages which directly contradicts the plain statements of other portions of Scripture.

The millennialists teach that all the dead will not arise at the same time, but that the resurrection of the saved will be at least a thousand years before the resurrection of the lost. Jesus, however, says: "The hour is coming in which all that are in their graves shall hear His voice and come forth; they that have done good, unto the resurrection of life; and they that have done evil, unto the resurrection of damnation," John 5:28, 29. This "hour" is certainly one and the same time because in the very next chapter Jesus says: "And this is the Father's will which hath sent Me, that of all which He hath given Me I should lose nothing, but raise it up again at the last day." That Christ will raise up His people "at the last day" He tells us four times in chapter six of the Gospel according to St. John. (See verses 39, 40, 44, 54.) Martha of Bethany believed in the resurrection of the just at the last day. "I know that he [Lazarus] shall rise again in the resurrection at the last day," John 11:24. "The word that I have spoken, the same shall judge him in the last day," John 12:48. The resurrection of the just, as well as of the wicked, and the judgment will take place on the same day.

St. Peter, warning, writes: "Be sober, be vigilant; because your adversary the devil, as a roaring lion, walketh about, seeking whom he may devour," I Peter 5:8. Will the time ever come as long as this wicked world stands that it will not be true that the devil goeth about seeking to devour? "We wrestle not against flesh and blood, but against principalities, against powers, against the rulers of the darkness of this world, against spiritual wickedness in high places," Eph. 6:12. Paul knew of no time this side of eternity and no place this side of heaven when and where Christians would not have the devil to wrestle with. There will never come a time as long as this world stands that the devil will not attempt and succeed in sowing tares among the wheat. And the tares and the wheat will grow side by side "until the harvest." The harvesttime is not a thousand years before the day when Christ says to the reapers: "Gather ye together first the tares, and bind them in bundles to burn them: but gather the wheat into my barn," Matthew 13:30.

Most millennialists of our day (the kind that are making extensive use of the radio and in their literature consider nothing quite so important as the second coming of Christ) teach that a thousand years before the last day Christ shall visibly appear upon earth and establish a glorious earthly kingdom. The departed saints, or at least the martyrs, will be raised. Christ and His risen and transformed saints (those still living when He comes) shall rule over the earth. The Jews, after having been converted to Christ, will again flock back to Palestine, and Jerusalem will be the capital city of Christ's kingdom. At the close of this period there shall be a great falling away again, for Satan shall be loosed. Then shall follow the destruction of the ungodly, the raising of the rest of the dead, the final judgment, and the new heavens and the new earth. This form of millennialism we reject. Christ said: "In this world ye shall have tribulation." And the inspired St. Paul tells us: "We must through much tribulation enter into the kingdom of God." "Yea, and all that will live godly in Christ Jesus shall suffer persecution." Will there ever come a time before we reach heaven that this will not be true?

The Jews of old were always dreaming of a glorious earthly kingdom. This we believe is the serious mistake which the millennialists of our day are still making. As for me, I shall, like Paul, seek the things which are above and never look for great things in this world. "If ye then be risen with Christ, seek those things which are above, where Christ sitteth on the right hand of God. Set your affection on things above, not on things on this earth," Col. 3:1, 2.

The Son of Perdition

Please give me an explanation of II Thessalonians 2:3, 4, and 9. Thanks.

The verses to which you refer read: "Let no one deceive you in any way; for that day will not come, unless the rebellion comes first, and the man of lawlessness is revealed, the son of perdition, who opposes and exalts himself against every so-called god or object of worship, so that he takes his seat in the temple of God, proclaiming himself to be God. . . . The coming of the lawless one by the activity of Satan will be with all power and with pretended signs and wonders" (Revised Standard Version).

The congregation at Thessalonica was deeply disturbed about a reported early return of the Lord Jesus. Communications, faked as coming from Paul, had caused great excitement and filled some with nervous fear. The apostle assures his people that there is no truth to this claim and begs them to pay no attention to it. The Lord may return at any moment, and the child of God should not be forgetful and indifferent about this. But it is wholly unbecoming that he should become unduly excited or even panicky about it.

The apostle assures his readers that the second advent of the Lord will not occur until the rebellion (the apostasy) has first come, and the man of lawlessness (or the man of sin), the son of perdition, has been revealed. This apostasy does not refer to the ordinary falling away of some who at one time vowed allegiance to Christ. It must refer to a future sad mass's falling away from revealed truth under the leadership of one who is here called the man of lawlessness or the man of sin, the son of perdition.

The apostle further describes this son of perdition, who is the leader of this sad rebellion or apostasy, as one who exalts himself against every so-called god, the true God as well as all false gods, and seats himself in the very temple of God and declares himself God, the supreme authority to whom all must bow in slavish obedience. Though the mystery of this "iniquity" or lawlessness was already at work at the time of the apostle, something was restraining this man of sin and the mass apostasy which he was leading. In time this restraining power would be taken out of the way, then this "lawless one" shall be revealed, "and the Lord Jesus will slay him with the breath of His mouth and destroy him by His appearing and His coming."

Now who is this "man of sin"? That is a hard question. The great church father Augustine answered that question in the words, "I confess that I am entirely ignorant what the apostle meant." Of course, Augustine lived before the rise of the Roman papacy. Most Lutheran theologians believe that we have here a description of the Antichrist, and that this passage refers to the papacy. "The history of the church during these hundreds of years presents only one phenomenon of this type—the papacy" (Lenski).

The arrogance of the bishop of Rome, the self-appointed master of the whole world who claimed authority over all nations in temporal as well as in spiritual matters, was held in check for several centuries. But in time this opposition melted away. And, lo, during the middle ages we find the pope of Rome the absolute master of the world. His will was law in the church, and all kings and princes, too, were under his sway. It was the Reformation that exposed him as the man of sin, the son of perdition. The everlasting gospel reveals him as such. "The Lord Jesus will slay him by the breath of His mouth"—His Word.

Others are today finding in Communism the marks of the Antichrist. But however or whatever the Antichrist is, and however terrible his power, the child of God has in Christ one who is mightier than he. And at the appearing and coming of Christ the Antichrist and all that opposes Christ will be destroyed.

The Law of Sin

I am puzzled about the meaning of Romans 7:23.

The passage you refer to reads thus: "But I see another law in my members, warring against the law of my mind, and bringing me into captivity to the law of sin which is in my members." Read this passage in its connection and you will find that the apostle wants to say that there is a continual struggle going on within him. He earnestly desires to do the right, for he is a child of God, but he cannot entirely rid himself of his old wicked nature. This inborn tendency toward sin is ever and again tripping him and causing him to do that which he does not want to do. He himself, the converted child of God, delights in the law of God, but, alas, in his members there dwells still another law, the law of sin, which is ever trying to keep him from doing what he himself wants to do.

You and I feel this same struggle within us. We want to be pure in thought, but do what we please, we are often impure. We do not want to be envious or selfish and egotistic, but we do have to fight these evil tendencies, this "law of sin" which still lures us into evil. Every truly converted man is a new man, yet there is always some of the "old man of sin" that he has not yet gotten fully rid of. No wonder that Paul in agony cries out: "O wretched man that I am; who shall deliver me from the body of this death?" He will, indeed, someday be fully delivered by his Savior, and in the meantime God in mercy for Jesus' sake pardons these failures.

The End of the Earth

Will the earth abide forever, cf. Matt. 24:35 with Eccles. 1:4?

The earth will come to an end. It will someday pass away.

Some take these words of Jesus to mean that this earth or planet on which we live will be utterly annihilated, that is, snuffed out of existence. As the material that composes this earth was created and brought into existence by almighty power, so the Lord will by fire someday utterly destroy it.

Others hold that the present condition of the earth will pass away. The earth is now under the curse of God and has been ever since the fall of man into sin. This curse with all its blighting influence and result will be removed. Thus by fire God will someday thoroughly purge, renovate, and transform this world. It will then be an earth wherein dwelleth righteousness, a fit home for the blessed made perfect.

"Heaven and earth" literally means the heavens or sky above us together with the earth of which it is a part. The new heavens and the new earth refer either to an entirely new planet, which God will create after He has utterly destroyed the present earth together with the heavens that surround it; or these new heavens and new earth refer to the cleansed, purified, and perfectly transformed earth, which is prepared as a bride adorned for her husband. A place made fit for the "holy Jerusalem," which shall descend out of heaven upon it.

Solomon, the writer of Ecclesiastes, is speaking of the vanity and perishableness of everything earthly. Man's life is very brief. One generation must pass away to make room for the next. But while we pass on, the earth continues. It exists age after age. One generation passeth, and another generation cometh, but it is not so with the earth. It continues on and on until the end of time. Perhaps, as we have seen above, it may, in a perfectly purified state, even continue throughout eternity.

The New Heaven and the New Earth

Please explain the passage: "For as the new heaven and the new earth which I will make shall remain before Me, saith the Lord, so shall your seed and your name remain," Isaiah 66:22.

We read repeatedly of the "new heavens and a new earth, wherein dwelleth righteousness," II Peter 3:13. John was given a vision of this new heaven and new earth, and he tells us about it in chapter 21 of the last book of the Bible:

"And I saw a new heaven and a new earth: for the first heaven and the first earth were passed away; and there was no more sea. And I John saw the holy city, new Jerusalem, coming down from God out of heaven, prepared as a bride adorned for her husband. And I heard a great voice out of heaven saying, Behold the tabernacle of God is with men, and He will dwell with them, and they shall be His people, and God Himself shall be with them, and be their God. And God shall wipe away all tears from their eyes; and there shall be no more death, neither sorrow nor crying, neither shall there be any more pain: for the former things are passed away," Rev. 21:1–4.

From this it would seem that the ultimate home of the blessed will be right here on earth. This earth shall not be absolutely annihilated on the last great day but thoroughly purged from all sin and sin's curse. So thorough and complete will be this renovation that it may be called a re-creation. "For, behold, I create new heavens and a new earth; and the former shall not be remembered, nor come into mind," Isaiah 65:17. This new heaven and new earth shall exist forever, and the same is true of those who dwell there. This is the meaning of the passage you refer to.

This newness of the new heaven and the new earth will be like the newness of ourselves when we are taken to that blessed abode. We shall be the same persons we now are, with the same body and the same soul, but made entirely new, as perfect as were Adam and Eve before the fall. This newness begins when we receive the birth from above. Already then we become new creatures in Christ Jesus (Gal. 6:15). After body and soul are glorified, we shall be re-created beings indeed but still the same beings. Man is the creature for whom the first heaven and the first earth were created. That same human being, thoroughly remade, shall occupy that same earth, completely freed from sin and every trace of its curse.

The Gift of the Holy Spirit

Will you, please, explain Acts 2:38.

Acts 2:38 reads as follows: "Then Peter said unto them, Repent, and be baptized every one of you in the name of Jesus Christ for the remission of sins, and ye shall receive the gift of the Holy Ghost."

This passage is part of Peter's sermon on the day of Pentecost. By referring to Old Testament predictions which were fulfilled in Jesus he had proved to his hearers that Jesus was indeed "both Lord and Christ." This Savior, promised from of old, they rejected and finally crucified. Many in Peter's audience came to a realization of the deep guilt that thus rested upon them, and in alarm they asked: "Men and brethren, what shall we do?" There is only one thing that awakened and frightened sinners can do, namely, penitently to admit their guilt and throw themselves on the mercy of God offered to us through Jesus Christ. Therefore Peter said to them: "Repent and be baptized every one of you in the name of Jesus Christ for the remission of sins, and ye shall receive the gift of the Holy Ghost."

Thus to those who are truly penitent and baptized God graciously imparts full and complete pardon and at the same time bestows upon them the gift of the Holy Spirit, that is, the Holy Spirit enters their heart with His saving grace. We know that mercy is offered only because of the atonement made in our behalf by Christ Jesus. When Peter enjoins his hearers to be baptized "in the name of Jesus Christ" he certainly does not want to change the formula for baptism or give to the church an additional formula for the sacrament. The risen Lord had given the command to "make disciples of all nations, baptizing them in the name of the Father and of the Son and of the Holy Ghost."

There are some who think they find in this verse a proof against infant baptism. How that is possible is beyond me, for any true minister of the gospel who believes in infant baptism would have spoken as did St. Peter on this occasion. He was addressing those guilty people standing before him; and there was only one thing for them to do in order to find pardon. They must realize and acknowledge their deep guilt, which they did by the question they asked. And in true repentance and faith they must yield themselves to Jesus Christ as their Redeemer and Savior. This they did by accepting baptism. Do not separate this verse from that which follows. In order to draw these guilty people to repentance and baptism, Peter assuringly continues: "For the promise is unto you and to your children." To them first as Jews, the chosen people of God, is this gracious promise of forgiveness given. Of course, also to those who as yet "are afar off," the Gentiles. But first to the lost sheep of the house of Israel was the gospel to be proclaimed. And please note the significant statement, "and to your children." The children were always a part of the Old Testament people of God, received into covenant relation with Him by a divinely enjoined rite when but eight days of age (Genesis 17:12–14). Is the New Covenant to exclude these little ones, or are they to be received without any prescribed rite? That which is born of the flesh must be born also of the Spirit, says the Master. We know no way of giving small children the spiritual birth except by "the washing of regeneration" which took the place of the Old Testament circumcision.

The Sabbath

In Exodus 31:12–18 God says the Sabbath is a sign between Him and His people, and that it is a "*perpetual* covenant." By what right, then, do we observe the first day of the week instead of the seventh day?

What do we find in Exodus 31:12–18? "And the Lord spake unto Moses, saying, Speak thou also unto the children of Israel, saying, [note well, *the children of Israel*], Verily My sabbaths ye shall keep; for it is a sign between Me and you throughout your generations; that ye may know that I am the Lord that doth sanctify you. Ye shall keep the sabbath therefore; for it is holy unto you: every one that defileth it shall be put to death; for whosoever doeth any work therein, that soul shall be cut off from among his people. Six days may work be done; but in the seventh is the sabbath of rest, holy to the Lord: whosoever doeth any work in the sabbath day, he shall surely be put to death. Wherefore *the children of Israel* shall keep the sabbath, to observe the sabbath throughout their generations for a perpetual covenant. It is a sign between Me and the children of Israel forever." The Sabbath is often referred to from the days of Moses onward, but always in language that limits it to Israel.

Prompted by the Spirit of God, the early church, under the leadership of the apostles, chose the first day of the week as an appropriate day for rest and the public worship required by God. The Sabbath was never changed from Saturday to Sunday; it was abolished. The Lord's Day is an altogether different institution. The keeping of the seventh day of the week with all its many regulations was a part of the ceremonial law. Paul tells us this very plainly when he says: "Let no one pass judgment on you in questions of food and drink or with regard to a festival or a new moon or a sabbath. These are only a shadow of what is to come; but the substance belongs to Christ," Colossians 2:16, 17, R.S.V. You and I are no more bound to the observing of the Sabbath than we are to the observing of the new moon or abstaining from ham because it comes from a hog. Study also carefully, in their connection, Galatians 4:10, 11 and Romans 14:5, 6.

To us Christians every day is sacred and holy. We observe the first day of the week in a special way, not because of any direct command of God, but because good order demands that we have a certain time for the public worship required by God, and because Sunday has been kept since the days of the apostles (see Acts 20:7; I Cor. 16:1, 2; Rev. 1:10). The Jewish Christians naturally could not at once break away from the custom of ages, but the Gentile Christians never felt bound to the Sabbath. And when the Judaizers tried to compel them to observe the Sabbath and the other ceremonial laws, including circumcision, Paul met them with an emphatic "no." "Stand fast in the liberty wherewith Christ hath made us free, and be not entangled again with the yoke of bondage," Galatians 5:1.

On the cross the shadow gave way to the substance (Col. 2:16, 17). Jesus became the believer's rest. The Christian's rest is now not a day but a person. The day was the shadow, the body is Christ. Paul, "a Hebrew of the Hebrews," never once enjoined the Christians to keep the Sabbath. There is no warning against Sabbath-breaking in any of the New Testament epistles. The first conference of the leaders of the New Testament Church met in Jerusalem. It was to settle the question about the Old Testament ceremonial law—circumcision, distinction of meats, the Sabbath, etc.: Are these things still necessary? The conclusion of the meeting was thus summarized by James, the president of the assembly: "It seemed good to the Holy Ghost and to us, to lay upon you no greater burden than these necessary things; that ye abstain from meats offered to idols, and from blood, and from things strangled, and from fornication: from which if ye keep yourselves, ye shall do well," Acts 15:28, 29. Sabbath observance is not mentioned.

To insist on Saturday as the day of rest and worship, or to think of Sunday as a continuation of the Sabbath, is to mix Judaism and Christianity and to introduce a false legalism into Sunday observance.

Permit another thought. The Sabbath of old began at sundown on Friday and ended with sundown on Saturday. "From even to even shall you celebrate your sabbath," Leviticus 23:32. This very fact that the Sabbath was to be from the evening of one day to the evening of the next day certainly indicates that this arrangement was never intended to be for all ages and for all places on earth. Such a Sabbath is impossible within the Arctic and the Antarctic Circle, for there we have no sunrise and no sunset during parts of the year. What about the "midnight sun" that is sometimes seen in the northern tip of Norway? Do that sunrise and that sunset also govern the Sabbath?

The Lord of the Sabbath

How do you understand the words of Jesus found in Mark 2:27, 28: "The sabbath was made for man, and not man for the sabbath. Therefore the Son of man is Lord also of the sabbath"?

The Pharisees accused Jesus of permitting His disciples to do that which is unlawful on the Sabbath Day. "One sabbath He was going through the grainfields; and as they made their way His disciples began to pluck ears of grain," verse 23, R.S.V. St Matthew tells us that the disciples were hungry, and that they ate the grain which they plucked as they went on their way. This was the awful sin the disciples committed, and Jesus did not so much as reprove them for it. The Pharisees were not accusing the disciples of stealing but of threshing grain on the Sabbath.

Jesus reminds the Pharisees of what David and his men did when they were in need of food. They went to the Tabernacle, and the priest in charge gave them of the sacred "showbread" which no one but the priests were to eat. This was God's own law. Therefore the priest as well as David and his men did that which was "not lawful." Still Jesus sanctioned the act under the circumstances. This proves that even the divine ceremonial law was not intended to be absolute in its application, much less these invented Pharisaic notions about Sabbath observance. God cares more for the proper spiritual condition of the heart than for the outward observance of His own ceremonial regulations.

Jesus then states a fundamental principle about Sabbath observance: "The sabbath was made for man, and not man for the sabbath." The Sabbath was intended as a blessing for man, as a needful day of rest and spiritual edification. The fanatic Pharisees treated man as if he had been created for the express purpose of keeping the strict Sabbath laws. The Sabbath had to be kept, even according to their false notions, no matter what became of man whereas God clearly meant that man should be blessed by the Sabbath even, if necessary, at the expense of some regulation regarding the Sabbath.

"Therefore the Son of man is Lord also of the sabbath." This certainly does not mean that He is going to do as He pleases on the holy day. Jesus kept the Sabbath even as He perfectly kept all of God's laws. But He correctly understood the meaning and the purpose of the Sabbath and was the authoritative interpreter of the Sabbath. Jesus did not "come to destroy the law, or the prophets: I am not come to destroy, but to fulfil." He did fulfil perfectly all divine law. And then the entire ceremonial law with all the forms of Jewish worship, including the Sabbath with its many regulations, was forever put away. All these regulations, including the Sabbath, were to help to prepare Israel, and through Israel the world, for the coming Savior of humanity.

The Person of Satan

Is Satan a person, or are we to think of him as merely the personification of an evil principle in ourselves that tempts us to wickedness?

Satan is certainly a person. Every mention of him and of his work in Scripture shows this. The Bible always refers to him as a cunning, subtle, crafty, powerful enemy who attacks us from without. He even tried to mislead our Savior, and there was certainly no evil principle in the Sinless One. The knowledge of Satan is great, and he uses it with subtle thought and shrewdness. Behind his crafty actions there is thought. Only a thinker can produce intelligent thought. A thinker must necessarily be an individual person. To delude, Satan can appear "as an angel of light." At other times to intimidate and overwhelm he "walketh about as a roaring lion, seeking whom he may devour." Jesus called Satan "the prince of this world," John 12:3.

The personality of the devil is assumed in Scripture. The Bible does not try to prove his existence but infers, accepts, and takes it for granted. Satan is not the personification of an evil principle as some would have us believe. He is the arch evil personality who brought all evil into this world. He is not merely an evil influence emanating from man's own wicked heart, he is an evil intelligence. It is a clever move on the part of this "father of lies" to suggest that he is not a person who really exists. He who believes that lie underestimates the foe whom he must encounter and is defeated even before the battle is begun.

The Savior Foretold

In Genesis 3:15 we read: "It shall bruise thy head, and thou shalt bruise his heel." Many claim this foretells the coming of the Savior. I cannot understand this and would appreciate your explanation.

Genesis 3:15 is universally referred to as the first evangel, i.e., the first gospel message of the Bible. Punishment always follows in the wake of sin. The sad fall of our first parents is described in the opening verses of this chapter. Then follows the arraignment, the confession of guilt on the part of Adam and Eve, and the meting out of punishment. In passing sentence (see verse 14) God began with the serpent, who lent himself as an agent to the devil in the bringing about of the fall. In the verse that is under consideration God is dealing with Satan, who used the serpent as his subtle vehicle of approach. He it was who spoke in the disguise of a serpent. He is "that old serpent" as he is repeatedly referred to in the New Testament. To him God says: "I will put enmity between thee and the woman, and between thy seed and her seed; it shall bruise thy head, and thou shalt bruise his heel."

A perpetual strife is here predicted between Satan and the human race and especially between Satan and the "seed of the woman," who is Christ. The Redeemer and Savior of humanity is truly a man, born of a woman. But he was born of a virgin, without a human father. He is, therefore, properly designated, not the seed of the man, but "her seed," the seed of the woman. We have here a gracious promise that this Child of the woman will finally overcome Satan and utterly crush him. Jesus came to destroy the works of the devil and to enable us to overcome the wicked one. But in redeeming us our Savior had to suffer. This is figuratively referred to and predicted by the words, "thou [Satan] shalt bruise His [the Savior's] heel."

The Gift of Tongues

Please explain Acts 2:4. Thank you.

The passage you refer to reads: "And they were all filled with the Holy Ghost, and began to speak with other tongues, as the Spirit gave them utterance." This took place on the day of Pentecost. All the disciples, men and women, old and young, doubtless over a hundred in number, were assembled "with one accord in one place." Suddenly two supernatural manifestations occurred. They heard a sound as the coming of a great storm, and presently they saw cloven tongues, like as of fire, which sat upon the head of each of them. These were only the outward manifestations of the real miracle that was taking place, namely, the outpouring of the Holy Spirit in New Testament fullness upon the disciples of Jesus. It was the realization of the Savior's promise, "Ye shall be baptized with the Holy Ghost not many days hence," Acts 1:5. John the Baptist had already said of the Savior, "He shall baptize you with the Holy Ghost and with fire," Luke 3:16.

The Holy Spirit, of course, worked upon and in the hearts of the people of God before that marvelous day of Pentecost, but never before had the divine Spirit been given to mankind in such measure and power. And it was a permanent gift to the church. Jesus promised that this "Comforter," this "Spirit of truth," would abide with His disciples forever (John 14:16, 17). We need not pray for a new, miraculous outpouring of the Holy Spirit upon the church, we need but pray God to enable us to use and to lay hold on the Spirit's power as He dwells in, and operates through, the Word of God and the sacraments.

The Spirit of God on that occasion enabled the disciples to speak in languages which before were entirely unknown to them. Perhaps the disciple himself did not understand what he was saying. But the various nationalities represented in Jerusalem on that day heard this or that disciple speak the language wherein he was born. It is not likely that the disciple could make use, after Pentecost, of the strange language which the Spirit empowered him to use on that day.

The miraculous gift of tongues was never promised nor bestowed upon the church of all ages. This marvelous gift (like the gift of healing and other miraculous gifts) has served its purpose. It was to attest visibly and unmistakably the fulfillment of the promised baptism of the Holy Ghost at a time when such proof was needed. This gift and all the other miraculous gifts are no longer needed as they were in the pioneer days of the church. Hence these gifts gradually disappeared when the church had grown to such proportions that its very presence and moral power witnessed to its divine character.

The Weeping Women

Luke 23:28—31 was never clear to me. Does this latter passage mean that those who are mothers and mothers-to-be at the end of the world will not be saved?

Jesus, a condemned man, was being led out to the place of execution. He was compelled to bear the cross on which He was soon to die. An ever-increasing throng of people attended this sad procession. The common people, especially the women, as a rule befriended the Master and heard Him gladly. They knew that He had been wrongly condemned and was being cruelly mistreated. This filled them with pity and moved them to tears, and they gave expression to their compassion. Jesus, no doubt, deeply appreciated their sympathy and good will, but He could not help but direct their attention to the fact that there was much more reason for them to bewail their own fate and that of their children than His. The sympathy of the daughters of Jerusalem was but a natural, temporary emotion, it did not spring from their sorrow because of sin. Sin was the cause of Christ's suffering and death, and it will be our eternal undoing unless we find pardon. So Jesus turns to them and says: "Weep not for Me, but weep for yourselves and for your children." Your sins have brought all this about. Your nation has rejected its Messiah, and the wrath of God is resting upon the people of Israel because of it.

The day is not far off when this proud city will be utterly destroyed and the obstinate children of Israel scattered to the four winds. In the midst of these untold sufferings and privations many a woman will deem herself happy, indeed, because she has no children, for in those days mothers were to see their children starving to death or brutally murdered or sold into slavery. So terrible will be the siege and overthrow of Jerusalem that the suffering people will want the hills to fall on them, and the mountains to cover them. For if God so severely deals with Jesus—the green tree, the holy and righteous One, full of spiritual life and ever fruitful, because He took the sinner's place—how will He in righteous indignation deal with the dry tree—spiritually dead and unfruitful Israel and all who reject His mercy and die in their sins? This, in brief, I believe to be the meaning of the verses in St. Luke's Gospel to which you refer.

The Nature of Temptation

In James 1:13 we read: "Let no man say when he is tempted, I am tempted of God: for God cannot be tempted with evil, neither tempteth He any man." Yet in the Lord's Prayer He has taught us to say: "Lead us not into temptation." Please explain.

Scripture interprets Scripture. This fundamental rule in Bible interpretation must ever be kept in mind. James tells us plainly that evil in no way allures God. He is incapable of being tempted by anything that is wrong. Now, can such a God lure us into sin; does He entice, attract, solicit, and thus attempt to induce us to commit some wickedness? That is simply impossible.

In verses two and three of this very chapter James says: "My brethren, count it all joy when ye fall into divers temptations; knowing this, that the trying of your faith worketh patience."

We are now ready to look at that Sixth Petition of the Lord's Prayer. Luther's explanation as given in his catechism surely is correct: "God indeed tempts no one." God tries to lure no one into sin. The trinity of evil, "the devil, the world, and our flesh," try to do this, but not our God.

What do we mean when we pray: "Lead us not into temptation"? We are not asking God never to permit us in any way to be tempted. Under present conditions that is impossible. Moreover, it is good for us to meet and to withstand temptation, for by God's sustaining grace we grow in ability to resist and to overcome temptation. Here in this petition of the Lord's Prayer we ask our Father in heaven in His providence to take charge of us and not permit us to go where we may be unduly tempted, lured to our fall and disgrace. And if He does see fit to permit the devil, the world, and our flesh to tempt us, we pray Him to enable us to resist the attack and come forth as victors.

The Baptism of John

How do you harmonize the statement: "We believe that John's baptism or that of Jesus before His death was practically the same as the baptism we now have," with Acts 19:1–6? Would Paul have re-baptized those Ephesians if John's baptism had been "practically the same" as the baptism Christ commanded in Matthew 28?

You, of course, believe that the "baptism of John" was of God and not of men. "There was a man sent from God, whose name was John," John 1:6. "The baptism of John, whence was it? from heaven, or of men?" Matthew 21:25. John's baptism was of divine origin as was the baptism commanded in Matthew 28.

John indeed baptized with water. But this baptism could not have been destitute of spiritual blessing, for it was "the baptism of repentance for the remission of sins," Mark 1:4. There is no repentance without faith, and no remission of sins without repentance and faith. And there can be neither repentance, faith, nor pardon apart from the gracious work of the Holy Spirit. Thus John's baptism was not a mere "water baptism" as some slightingly speak of all baptism with water but "a gracious water of life and a washing of regeneration in the Holy Ghost." It was "the washing of water by the word," the same as the baptism enjoined by Christ in Matthew 28.

If we now turn to Acts 19:1–6 we wonder why these twelve men were re-baptized. This is not an easy question. These men are referred to as disciples and believers before this re-baptism. Paul, therefore, accepted them as brethren in the faith. When he asked them the question, "Have ye received the Holy Ghost since ye believed?" he was not referring to baptism. He doubtless meant to say, "Have you been given any special outward manifestation of the divine Spirit?" In other words, "Have you been granted any charismatic gift of the Holy Spirit?" Their answer was, "We have not so much as heard whether there be any Holy Ghost." In astonishment the apostle asks, "Unto what then were ye baptized?" They reply, "Unto John's baptism." Paul then explained to them the real meaning and significance of the baptism of John. In fact, he gave them considerable instruction in fundamental truths they had never heard of. After hearing Paul they doubtless explained the manner of their baptism, and the apostle could not accept their baptism as a valid and genuine baptism. Therefore they were given a true Christian baptism.

Note that Paul asked, "Unto what then were ye baptized?" "How then were you baptized?" is the way Goodspeed translates Paul's question. Is it possible that the name of the Holy Ghost was not even mentioned when these men were baptized? It would seem so. Some Bible students suggest that some follower of John had baptized these men with these words, "I baptize you with John's baptism," or in some other way or manner that Paul could not accept as a valid formula for Christian baptism. We should have an analogous case in our day if some person who had been baptized in a non-Trinitarian church would ask for membership in our church. We could not accept him as a baptized person. It must have been that the baptism these twelve men of Ephesus had received was not John's real baptism.

When Apollos came to Ephesus he, too, knew "only the baptism of John," Acts 18:25. Though he was "mighty in the Scriptures" (the Old Testament), and "was instructed in the way of the Lord," he yet needed far more instruction about the things that happened after John's imprisonment and his death. Aquila and Priscilla privately gave him this instruction. But we are not told that he was re-baptized. So we must conclude that he had received John's real baptism, and that it was considered valid and sufficient.

Those Who Create Divisions

Please explain Romans 16:17, 18.

The verses you refer to are thus translated in the Revised Standard Version: "I appeal to you, brethren, to take note of those who create dissensions and difficulties, in opposition to the doctrine which you have been taught; avoid them. For such persons do not serve our Lord Christ, but their own appetites, and by fair and flattering words they deceive the hearts of the simple-minded." God certainly wants us to be united in the truth, the whole truth as it was taught to the early Christians at Rome, and as we have it today in the revealed, written Word. "Sanctify them through Thy truth: Thy word is truth," John 17:17, is the prayer of Jesus for His disciples. "The truth shall make you free," John 8:32. The truth saves, but all error tends to lead astray. This underlies the Bible's emphasis on holding truth and avoiding error.

Truth is one; it is a unit, and it unifies. Errors are many, and they lead to divisions. Many well-meaning people counsel that these errors be overlooked and ignored. The apostle, on the contrary, appeals to us that we take note of those who teach contrary to the truth and, if need be, avoid them lest we encourage them in their error and become partakers of their guilt.

To enforce his earnest warning, St. Paul describes these false teachers and tells us of the subtle method which they employ to carry out their design. They "do not serve our Lord Christ," they serve "their own appetites" (Greek, their own belly). Their interests are not the glory of Christ and the advancement of His kingdom; their interests are base, secular, and even carnal. "By fair and flattering words they deceive the hearts of the simple-minded," the innocent, trustful souls who are not on their guard.

In Acts 15:5 we read: "But there rose up certain of the sect of the Pharisees which believed, saying, that it was needful to circumcise them, and to keep the law of Moses." Their claim was untrue as the early church, led by the Holy Spirit, decided and ever taught. But it shows that Christians, "believers," may go astray and thus be errorists in certain respects and therefore must be warned against and, perhaps, finally even avoided. All falsehood is sin, and it eats "as doth a canker." But we have reason to fear that the passage under consideration is sometimes quoted where it is not in place and applied to those to whom it does not apply.

3. About Teachings, Concepts, and Interpretations

The Descent into Hell

What is the significance of the clause: "He descended into hell"? Why is it in the Apostolic Creed and not in the Nicene?

This article of faith is based on several passages of Scripture, notably, I Peter 3:18, 19; Colossians 2:15; Ephesians 4:9, 10. Jesus did not descend into hell at the time of His death. He said: "Father, into Thy hands I commend My spirit." He promised the penitent thief, "Today shalt thou be with Me in Paradise." His descent into hell, therefore, did not take place on Good Friday. Neither did He descend into hell to suffer. His sufferings ended when He said, "It is finished," and body and soul separated. Christ's descent into hell must have taken place very early on Easter morning because it was after He had been "quickened by the Spirit," that is, after body and soul were reunited, but before His reappearance on earth.

Why did Jesus descend into hell? Here is the answer given to this question by our catechism: "That He might show Himself to the spirits in hell as their conqueror and mightily triumph over them."

Why this article of faith is found in the Apostolic Creed but not in the Nicene, I do not know. I have often wondered why the Apostolic Creed says nothing about either of the sacraments. Such a brief summary cannot contain even all of the more important articles of the Christian faith.

Time of the Descent into Hell

Taking into consideration the events in Jesus' death and resurrection, when did He descend into hell?

It was not on Good Friday, for on that day He commended His spirit into the hands of His Father. He also promised to be with the penitent thief on that day in Paradise. The descent into hell took place early on Easter morning, but before Jesus visibly came forth from the tomb. According to I Peter 3:18, 19 Jesus was "put to death in the flesh, but quickened [made alive] by the Spirit: by which also He went and preached unto the spirits in prison." Thus it was the revived Christ who descended into hell to triumph over Satan as his conqueror. By His descent into hell Jesus proclaimed His victory there; by His coming forth from the grave He proclaimed His victory on earth, and by His ascension forty days later He proclaimed it in heaven. For to Jesus every knee must bow, of things in heaven, and things on earth, and things under the earth. And every tongue must confess that Jesus Christ is Lord, to the glory of God the Father.

Foot Washing

Why is the practice of the Savior in St. John 13:14, 15 not continued in many churches of today? What is the attitude of the Lutheran Church toward such practice?

The custom of washing the feet of one's guest was among the Oriental people one of the common courtesies of hospitality. It was regarded as a mark of respect to one's guest and a token of humility and affectionate attention on the part of the entertainer. This custom grew out of the fact that the climate was warm, and the people either went barefooted or simply wore soles of some kind bound under the feet. These "sandals" were ordinarily put aside on entering a house.

Foot washing as a religious rite was observed by some of the professed followers of Christ from the earliest days of the Christian Church. It is still so observed by the Dunkards and a few others. With some foot washing is rather a ceremony than a service and is performed at appointed seasons. At Rome on Holy Thursday twelve poor men are brought in from the streets, and in the Clementine Chapel, while others look on in feigned astonishment, the Holy Father in great condescension washes their feet. This, too, was customary among some of the former kings of Europe. Such pretense of humility and service is certainly naught but a travesty of the noble deed of Jesus.

If we carefully study John's account of Jesus washing the disciples' feet and compare it with Luke 22:24–26 and I Tim. 5:10 we shall find that the Savior wanted to give the disciples through this act: 1. Another proof of His undying love for them; 2. An object lesson of their need of His spiritual washing; 3. An impressive example of true humility and kindly service.

We wash each other's feet when at all times we manifest a spirit of true humility and are ever ready to do for each other kindly and helpful service, not hesitating even as occasions arise to do the most menial of tasks.

The Second Coming of Christ

Will the second coming of Christ, the resurrection of the dead, good and evil, and the final judgment take place on one and the same day?

That is my conviction. I have always so understood the Word of God and have hence always so taught. This is certainly in agreement with the doctrine of the Lutheran Church as set forth in the Seventeenth Article of the Augsburg Confession. There are, indeed, many Christian people who believe in two bodily resurrections, the one—that of the righteous—a thousand years before the last day, the other—that of the wicked and unbelieving—on the last day. This doctrine is based primarily on the literal interpretation of a single highly symbolic passage in the prophetic book of Revelation (chapter 20:1–6).

Jesus nowhere tells us that He will come again in visible form to reign with His saints as an earthly King over the nations of the earth for a thousand years before the final judgment comes. On the contrary, both He and the apostles plainly and repeatedly state that the second coming of Christ, the bodily resurrection of all those who are in the grave, and the final judgment of all mankind will take place on what is called "the last day." "This is the will of Him that sent Me, that every one which seeth the Son, and believeth on Him, may have everlasting life, and I will raise him up at the last day," John 6:40. Here it is plainly stated that the righteous will be raised *at the last day,* and this fact is reiterated four times in this same chapter (see verses 39, 40, 44, 54). When Jesus said to Martha: "Thy brother shall rise again," Martha's reply was, "I know that he shall rise again in the resurrection at the last day," John 11:23, 24. Martha was not expecting her brother Lazarus, "he whom Thou lovest," to be raised a thousand years before the last day.

Christ is the "first fruits of them that slept," they that are Christ's are to be raised up "at His coming" (I Cor. 15:20, 23). What also is to take place when He comes? "Behold I show you a mystery; we shall not all sleep, but we shall all be changed. In a moment, in the twinkling of an eye, at the last trump: for the trumpet shall sound and the dead shall be raised incorruptible, and we [those still living on that day] shall be changed," I Cor. 15:51, 52. "Our conversation [citizenship or commonwealth] is in heaven; from whence also we look for the Savior, the Lord Jesus Christ, who shall change our vile body, that it may be fashioned like unto His glorious body," Phil. 3:20, 21. "When the Son of man shall come in His glory, . . . then shall He sit upon the throne of His glory: and before Him shall be gathered all nations" for the final judgment (Matt. 25:31, 32).

The disciples one day asked Jesus the question: "What shall be the sign of Thy coming, and of the end of the world?" Matt. 24:3. The disciples manifestly expected Christ's coming and the end to occur at the same time, and so it shall be. "The general judgment will immediately succeed the general resurrection of the dead. The resurrection will occur on the last or latest of all days, and will place an end to the vicissitudes of worldly things, and therefore to time itself" (Quenstedt).

Faith to Remove Mountains

Please explain Matthew 21:22, and kindly do so in a way that a layman can understand it.

Verses 21 and 22 read thus: "Jesus answered and said unto them, Verily I say unto you, If ye have faith, and doubt not, ye shall not only do this which is done to the fig tree, but also ye shall say unto this mountain, Be thou removed, and be thou cast into the sea; it shall be done. And all things whatsoever ye shall ask in prayer, believing, ye shall receive." Christ had cursed the barren, disappointing fig tree. When the disciples expressed surprise and marvelled at the power Jesus manifested when

He merely spoke the word, He assured them that they would be able to do even greater things if they had the faith fully to trust and thus to lay hold on the power of their almighty Lord.

"With God nothing shall be impossible." And the impossible would become possible for us if we could only fully and unreservedly take God at His word. This power is promised to those who ask with unwavering faith. But we must remember that God does no silly things, nor does He do that which is useless—merely to amuse and astonish humanity. Yet He does promise the humanly impossible in answer to the prayer of unwavering faith when the disciple is on the manifest path of duty. It must also be kept in mind that, when praying for bodily and temporal gifts, the Christian has been taught to ask conditionally, "Nevertheless, Father, not my will, but Thine, be done."

Christ's reference to the removing of a mountain is doubtless figurative language. It is a supreme example of the humanly impossible becoming easily possible through God's answer to believing prayer when that disciple is about the work which Christ has laid upon him as His disciple.

The Fatherhood of God and the Brotherhood of Man

I have a good friend who says his religion is all summed up in the first two words of the Lord's Prayer, "Our Father." On these two words he bases his favorite and to him all-important statement: "The fatherhood of God and the brotherhood of man." Does this catchy statement express a divine truth?

This is, indeed, a catchy phrase. It sounds quite musical, and the sentiment it expresses is beautiful, broad, and humanitarian. There is a sense in which this statement is true. "We are the offspring of God," says St. Paul, for He "hath made of one blood all nations of men." We form one human family. We are blood relatives, for we spring from one ancestry. There are no two human beings exactly alike, yet we are all very, very much alike . . . from the most cultured and enlightened human being to the most ignorant and degraded pagan. In a comparatively short time the descendants of a cultured people may degenerate into the lowest type of barbarians, or the offspring of savages may be advanced physically, mentally, and morally to the height of noble, intelligent, Christian manhood and womanhood.

All the races of the human family belong to one and the same genus, Homo. Hence, from the standpoint of ancestry, nature, and general characteristics there is a brotherhood of all mankind, and we are all the creatures of one benign Creator.

In this sense there is a fatherhood of God and a brotherhood of man. If every human being would acknowledge God as Father and treat Him as such and by word and deed regard every man and women as brother or sister, we should have heaven on earth.

Strange as it may sound at first thought, there is a very important sense in which God is not the Father of everybody, and every man is not my brother. All people, irrespective of faith or unbelief, Christian, Jew, or Hottentot, cannot alike claim to be children of God in the true and intimate sense of the term "child." Jesus, speaking to the unbelieving Jews of His day, said: "Ye are of your father the devil, and the lusts of your father ye will do," John 8:44. That is a different father, and hence an altogether different set of children. In Scripture we read of "children of the kingdom" and "children of the evil one," of "children of the world" in contradistinction to "children of light."

To be brief, these are the facts. Because of sin man has forfeited his sonship, and he cannot again come into this blessed relationship to God except he be reinstated as a child. In the fulness of time God sent forth His Son, and through Him we can again receive the adoption of sons and daughters, Galatians 4:4, 5. "As many as received Him [Christ], to them gave He power to become the sons of God, even to them that believe on His name," John 1:12. What about those who do not accept Jesus in true faith as their Savior? They "shall not see life, but the wrath of God abideth on them," John 3:36.

Without Christ the proud boast of a universal brotherhood of all men as sons of God is a snare and a delusion of Satan to lure men to their destruction. So long as Christ's atoning blood is ignored, it is a brotherhood of sin and condemnation, bearing the impress of the father of lies. The Father of our Lord Jesus Christ "hath begotten us again [new birth] unto a lively hope by the resurrection of Jesus Christ from the dead," I Peter 1:3. Not by natural generation but by spiritual regeneration do we become sons of God. "Ye must be born again." Only through faith in Christ Jesus do we become children and heirs of eternal glory.

The Lord's Prayer was taught to the disciples. Not until we have been brought into proper relation with God through Christ Jesus can we properly say, "Our Father." Creatures of God we are by nature, but we are children only through the new birth from above.

It is sad and misleading to have well-meaning people talk about the fatherhood of God and the brotherhood of man in the sense we are now speaking of. They thus encourage unconverted people to think they are on the direct road to the Father's house because they are good, moral people though they indifferently pass by "the Lamb of God," without whom no man cometh to the Father. To claim sonship without regeneration is a delusion. To say "Our Father" aright we must be new creatures in Christ Jesus. "Whosoever denieth the Son, the same hath not the Father," I John 2:23.

The Will of God

How can we tell just what God's will is at all times and in all things?

"I delight to do Thy will, O my God," exclaims the Psalmist. I am convinced that the more one surrenders himself to God and prayerfully seeks His guidance because he is desirous of knowing and of acting in accordance with his Lord's will, the more clearly the Lord will at all times and under all circumstances manifest His will unto him. But "to err is human," and though we seek wisdom from above and plead for divine guidance, who is ready to affirm that he has never made a mistake in interpreting God's guidance? As long as we are fallible beings, we shall, no doubt, in weakness at times also fail in this respect. Hence, I believe that no man can infallibly know just what God's will is at all times and in all things. But if one lives close to God and truly delights to do His will he is not apt to go far astray, and God in mercy will overrule even his mistakes and make them work together in some way for his good. But you and I do know assuredly that it is the Lord's will that none perish, but that all come to a knowledge of the truth and be saved through Christ Jesus, the world's Redeemer. And this is the one thing needful, that must ever come first in all our thinking and doing.

A Jealous God

I have difficulty with the phrase, "a jealous God," in Exodus 20:5. I would appreciate an explanation.

There is such a thing as a godly jealousy. Paul says to the believers of Corinth: "I am jealous over you with godly jealousy: for I have espoused you to one husband, that I may present you as a chaste virgin to Christ," II Cor. 11:2. Through the preaching of the gospel Paul had won these people for Christianity. Through repentance and faith, the Spirit's fruit of Paul's work among them, Paul had espoused or married them to Christ, and he is zealously anxious that no false teacher mislead them and thus separate them from their divine Spouse. Was not this a righteous jealousy?

"I the Lord, thy God, am a jealous God." God is very jealous of His

37

authority, very tender as to His honor and His right, zealous to maintain it. He can tolerate no rival. "I am the Lord; that is My name; and My glory will I not give to another, neither My praise to graven images." He demands our fullest love and devotion. "Thou shalt love the Lord thy God with all thy heart, and with all thy soul, and with all thy mind." He will not tolerate a rival to whom we give that love, devotion, and service which we owe to Him alone. He threatens dire punishment upon all those who disobey His commandments, and we have all reason to fear His righteous wrath and not act contrary to His commandments. This is a holy zeal for the maintenance of His honor and authority, which our English Bible designates as jealousy.

You say: "To me jealousy is always sin." In this you are mistaken, and that has led to your difficulty. The word jealousy is used in both a good and a bad sense. "I was jealous for Zion with great jealousy," Zech. 8:2. "I have been very jealous for the Lord God of hosts," I Kings 19:10. But the word jealousy as commonly used among us does refer to a sin of the deepest dye. It is that morbid fear of rivalry in love, unduly suspicious and mistrustful of the fidelity of a loved one. This "green-eyed monster" is the source of untold misery and crime and must be prayerfully guarded against with all earnestness.

The Pride of Life

Will you, please, interpret for me I John 2:16: "For all that is in the world, the lust of the flesh, and the lust of the eyes, and the pride of life, is not of the Father, but is of the world"? Please explain every word and phrase, especially the phrase, "the pride of life."

We must, of course, study this passage in its connection. The apostle exhorts us not to love the world. The word "world" has various meanings as it is used in Scripture. Sometimes it refers to the earth on which we dwell. "The earth is the Lord's and the fulness thereof, the world, and they that dwell therein." Sometimes the "world" refers to all mankind. "God so loved the world that He gave His only-begotten Son." Again, by the "world" is meant the kingdom of darkness over which Satan rules; everything that is detrimental to the kingdom of our Lord Jesus Christ. "If the world hate you, ye know that it hated Me before it hated you. If ye were of the world, the world would love his own: but because ye are not of the world, therefore the world hateth you." In the passage before us it manifestly has this latter meaning.

We are not to set our affection on the perishable things of this world, much less on the wicked things which our depraved nature naturally craves. If the heart of man is filled with love for the wicked world it is so occupied that the love of the Father cannot dwell there. Why? Because "all that is in the world, the lust of the flesh, and the lust of the eyes, and the pride of life, is not of the Father, but is of the world," I John 2:16. The Revised Version translates: "The lust of the flesh and the lust of the eyes, and the vainglory of life." Professor Goodspeed gives it thus: "For all that there is in the world, the things that our physical nature and our eyes crave, and the proud display of life—these do not come from the Father, but from the world; and the world with its cravings is passing away, but whosoever does God's will will endure forever."

On the "lusts of the flesh," compare passages like Phil. 3:19; I Cor. 6:18; Gal. 5:19-21. "The lust of the eyes" reminds us of Matt. 5:28. Feasting the eyes on unseemly sights, vile pictures, sensual movies. Doubtless this lust of the eyes also includes the glitter of gold and thus refers also to the root of all evil—avarice, greed, covetousness. By "the pride of life" the apostle, no doubt, designates that haughty, puffed-up arrogance so prevalent among the worldly-minded, who love to glory in their possessions and attainments. Their heart is set on the riches of this world and the honors of this life. To gratify these cravings they will stoop to any means; anything to indulge their vanity. But all this vainglory will come to an early, ignominious end, for "the world passeth away, and the lusts thereof: but he that doeth the will of God abideth forever."

Our Iniquities Covered

Please explain the two following passages: "Thou hast forgiven the iniquity of Thy people, Thou hast covered all their sin," Psalm 85:2; and "As far as the east is from the west, so far hath He removed our transgressions from us," Psalm 103:12.

Your letter reveals plainly to me that you have the correct understanding of these and similar passages. Do not doubt the Lord's mercy. He means what He says, and He will do what He promises. When we accept Jesus as our Redeemer and Savior; when we depend on Him and look to Him for every blessing and give ourselves over to His care and keeping we become children of God, we are His people. And what the inspired Psalmist says is true: "Thou hast forgiven the iniquity of Thy people, Thou hast covered all their sin." Out of pure grace, for the sake of what Jesus did for us, God freely and fully forgives all those who accept this mercy by entrusting themselves to Christ Jesus as the

God-sent Savior. God charges not their sins against them, they are blotted out, to be remembered against them no more forever. God treats such believers as though they were not sinners, as though they had never done an evil thing. Jesus answered for those sins, He suffered the penalty of them as though He Himself had been the one who committed every one of them.

As a child of God your sins are removed from you as far as the east is from the west. What can this mean but that you and your pardoned sins are separated, never to meet again? "Come now, and let us reason together, saith the Lord: though your sins be as scarlet, they shall be as white as snow; though they be red like crimson, they shall be as wool," Isaiah 1:18. God washes us whiter than snow. He blots out our sins like a cloud, that never appears again; He casts them into the depths of the sea, from which they never arise. God uses these various expressions in order to emphasize and make clear to us the fullness and completeness of our forgiveness.

There is no condemnation to them who are in Christ Jesus (Romans 8:1). But such people do not walk after the flesh, but after the Spirit. They have been changed; they stand in a new relationship to their God and Savior; they have been born again, and they have new thoughts, aims, and desires. They have chosen Jesus as their divine Friend and Master, and they travel with Him the homeward way. They love Him because He first loved them, and in love and gratitude they serve Him and try to please Him and become more and more like Him.

You are right, the pardoned children of God are not indifferent toward sin; they do not sin wilfully. The "old Adam" in them does not rule but is suppressed. They hunger and thirst after righteousness and seek the things which are above. "As many as are led by the Spirit of God, they are the sons of God," Rom. 8:14, and these are the ones who stand in grace and have full and complete pardon.

How God Speaks to Us

Does God actually now speak to us and to all mankind through the Bible, or is the Bible only a record of a revelation of God made to people thousands of years ago, while He now speaks to us really only through the church or through the ministry?

God speaks to you and to me personally and directly in the Bible, as much so as He ever did to any individual that ever existed. "Thou shalt not steal" is a direct command to you as truly as if God had never spoken these words to any individual but you. You and I are to put our own name in the place of that "thou."

"Be thou faithful unto death, and I will give thee a crown of life." God is speaking to you as an individual, personally and directly. He is making this promise to you as truly as if He had never made a like promise to any other individual.

Where does the church get its message which it is to deliver to me? If the church brings me not the Word of God as contained in the Bible, I have no use for it. Such a church would cease to be the church of which Christ is both Foundation and Head.

The minister is to be an ambassador of Christ. An ambassador has no message of his own. He only carries the message of another which he has been sent to deliver. If a minister brings me not the divine truth as contained in the Bible, he is not an ambassador of Christ, he is not a minister of the gospel, no matter by what title he is known among men.

The Voice of God

Do we hear God's voice *only* in the Bible?

In a sense God speaks to us through nature. "The heavens declare the glory of God; and the firmament showeth His handywork." We have the "world-book" as well as the "Word-book," and our heavenly Father is the author of both. God speaks to us in the visitations which He sends or which He permits to come upon us. In no uncertain terms He sometimes tells us of His righteous indignation and then again of His loving-kindness and tender mercy. Conscience has been called the voice of God, and rightly so. God certainly speaks to us through the promptings of His Spirit. "As many as are led by the Spirit of God, they are the sons of God." The apostle lifts his voice in warning and says: "Quench not the Spirit." "The Spirit of God will not always strive with men," we are told; but this certainly implies that He does strive. He is sent to guide us into all truth, and "He shall testify of Me," promises the Savior. "The Spirit itself beareth witness with our spirit that we are the children of God," affirms St. Paul.

But while all this is most certainly true, it is also an undeniable fact that the book of nature alone cannot make us wise unto salvation. Conscience, too, and all the voices within us are not a sufficient guide. Conscience is dependent on knowledge, and one's knowledge may be very imperfect and defective. "Beloved, believe not every spirit, but try the spirits whether they are of God." "Prove all things, hold fast that which is good." By what are we to test the voices within us and round about us? "If ye continue in My Word then are ye My disciples indeed, and ye shall know the truth." "Sanctify them through Thy truth, Thy Word is truth," is the prayer of Jesus for His disciples.

We are sure of our position only when we are building on the written Word. The Spirit of truth never teaches us anything contrary to the revealed Word. "Howbeit when He, the Spirit of truth, is come, He will guide you into all truth. . . . He shall glorify Me, for He shall receive of Mine, and show it unto you." "He shall testify of Me." The divine Spirit never contradicts the teachings of Jesus. "The Comforter, which is the Holy Ghost, whom the Father will send in My name, He shall teach you all things, and bring all things to your remembrance whatsoever I have said unto you."

When in meditation and prayer the voice within you assures you of the love of your heavenly Father and the atoning merits of your Redeemer; when you are reminded of the promises of your Savior, and the thought of them draws you closer to Him and breathes peace into your soul, you may be assured that because of the merit of your Savior, whose you are and whom you serve, you have found favor with God, and the voice within you bears witness with your spirit that you are again reinstated as a child and hence also as an heir of God, you may be certain that it is the Comforter whom Jesus promised, who is communing with your soul. But when the divine Spirit beareth witness with our spirits and assures us of being children of God and joint heirs with Christ, it is not an immediate extraordinary revelation but an illumination and confirmation of that which comes to us through the medium of the revealed written Word. The testimony of the Holy Spirit is always in agreement with the written Word. We are never sure of our ground except when we have a written "thus saith the Lord" to back us up. To this we must hold fast, otherwise we are apt to run off into all manner of error and fanaticism. Ultimately, therefore, we can be sure of the voice of God only in the written inspired Word. It is in this sense, no doubt, that the minister you refer to meant his words when he said: "The one and only way we can hear the voice of God is in the Bible."

Man's Will

Could God not make us righteous without the death of His Son?

God did make man righteous in the first place. But He did not make it impossible for him to sin. God made Adam and Eve human personalities; He gave them a will. And that meant the possibility of willing to do wrong as well as willing to do right. Had Adam and Eve been made without this freedom of will and choice, they would have been automata—machines—and not free personalities, made in the image of

God Himself. They were given every encouragement and incentive to obey God and thus develop their God-given powers. When the test came, they were fully equipped to meet the test. But they failed to use the strength that God had given them; they allowed themselves to entertain a doubt of God's goodness and His love; and soon they had used their will to rebel against their Creator.

Do you ask: "Why should God have made man such a free moral agent? Why didn't He just make him a mechanical creature that could do no wrong because he was without the power to make a moral choice?" Emerson answers that question briefly:

> For He that ruleth high and wise,
> Nor pauseth in His plan,
> Will tear the sun out of the skies
> Ere freedom out of man.

Would you rather be a "happy automaton" than a personality, corrupted indeed by sin, but gloriously redeemed by the Savior of sinners? Someday we shall fully understand that men, created in the image of God, endowed with free will, redeemed from the curse of sin by the Son of God's love, are the finest justification for the way in which God created the race. God's ways are always right.

Water Into Wine

In our Sunday school class last Sunday we studied Jesus' first miracle, the changing of water into wine. Here are some questions that were puzzling to us. Did Jesus make real, i. e., intoxicating wine? If so, did He not condone drunkenness since the guests had already drunk freely? Why did He make wine in the first place; why did He not advise the guests to drink water since they had all had enough wine? We await your reply.

I shall begin with your last question. I am not so audacious as to find fault with the actions of my Savior. He saw fit to make wine, lots of wine, and the very best of wine, at that marriage in Cana, and He thus manifested His Messianic glory and goodness, and His disciples to this day are drawn to Him in faith because of what He did there. If it would have been at your wedding or at mine, He would, perhaps, have made lemonade or orangeade. But, please note this, Jesus never apologizes for what He has done. In all His years He never admitted having made a mistake. Therefore He made no mistake when He performed His first miracle.

The six waterpots had a capacity of two or three firkins each. We are not absolutely certain as to the exact size of a firkin of that day. "The Attic metretes is estimated at over 8½ gallons (Josephus), and answers in general to the Hebrew bath. The Rabbinists, however, make the bath equal to a little less than 4½ gallons" (Lenski). Take either measurement, and you have a large supply of wine. All, of course, was not used on that occasion. Here was Jesus' generous wedding present to that young couple.

There can be no doubt as to the quality of the wine that Jesus made, for it is pronounced "good wine." The text does not say that the guests at that wedding had already drunk freely. The governor of the feast told the bridegroom that he had made a mistake, that he was acting contrary to custom. He had served the poorer grade of wine first and kept the excellent grade until last. The rule of that day was that, when two grades of wine are used at a festive occasion, the better quality grade wine would be served first, then, if need be, that of an inferior grade. This custom was doubtless for the very purpose of counteracting excess in drinking. Now, did the governor want to reprove the bridegroom for encouraging excess in drinking by keeping the good wine until toward the end of the feast? I think not. Neither can I imagine Jesus as the honored guest in the midst of a carousing, half-tipsy crowd. Such a scene is read into the story, for it is not there.

The Lord's Prayer

What is the meaning of the Lord's Prayer?

Jesus taught His disciples to address God as Father. How close and intimate He would have us feel toward Him! With confidence and even with boldness He would have us come "in His name," i. e., trusting in what He has done for us and ask for everything we need just as children go to a dear earthly parent. Creatures of God we are by nature, but we receive the status and rights of children through faith in Christ Jesus. We say "our" and not my Father because all of God's children are brethren, and we pray for each other.

"Hallowed be Thy name." This means, holy and sacred be to us Thy name. May we reverence, respect, and bring honor upon it by teaching Thy Word aright and living according to it. As the name of God stands for God Himself, we may also give this petition thus: "Holy be to us our God. Holy be to us His name, His Word, His church, all that is near and dear to Him. May we not profane or bring shame in any way upon Thy holy name by teaching or living contrary to Thy Word."

"Thy kingdom come." To us come Thy kingdom. We are asking God to bless the preaching of His Word and extend the borders of His church. May Satan's kingdom diminish and God's kingdom grow. Help the church to grow in grace and in numbers; bring all nations into it. And finally may we be transferred from Thy kingdom of grace here on earth to Thy kingdom of glory in heaven.

Thou art King, and we want to be of Thy kingdom, therefore, help us to do Thy will even as it is being done by the angels and blessed ones in heaven. Enable us to resist the wish and will of the devil, the wicked world, and our own perverse nature, but to do and gladly submit ourselves to Thy holy will as we find it recorded in Scripture. Thy will is that we accept Jesus as our Savior, live in obedience to Thy commandments, and trustfully submit ourselves to Thy wise and merciful providence even though at times it may seem dark and strange to us. Thy will, not ours, be done.

The first three petitions refer only to spiritual things. "Seek ye first the kingdom of God." But as long as we are in the body we shall have also bodily needs. Hence we are taught next to plead: "Give us this day our daily bread." The word bread as here used embraces all that we need to support this body and life. But note that we are not asking for luxuries, pie, cake, etc., but only for the necessities of life. We pray only for a supply of the needs of this day. We are not to distrust the divine Father and have anxious worries about the future. In this petition we acknowledge God as the giver on whom we are dependent, and we desire to receive all His gifts with thanksgiving. Give us health, give us a job, and enable us through honest toil and effort to earn and thus to eat our own daily bread.

Forgive us our sins as we forgive those who sin against us. We here have a *confession,* a *petition,* and a *promise.* Our confession is that we sin daily and deserve naught but punishment, and that God alone can pardon us. Hence we come to Him with our petition, and our plea is, "Forgive us, merciful Father." And as disciples of Jesus we come in His name and trust in His merits. Our promise is that we will from the heart pardon those who wrong us. We need mercy, and we ask for it, and as Spirit-led followers of Christ we will also show mercy.

As children of God we not only seek pardon for past offenses, but we are desirous of avoiding sin in the future. We now look forward, and when we think of our many weaknesses and the cunning and power of the enemy, our prayer is, "Lead us not into temptation." The dear Lord, indeed, does not tempt anyone to sin, for His wish is that we do good and not evil. Test us not too severely, dear Lord, subject us not unduly to temptation. Permit not Satan, the world, or our flesh

45

to tempt us to our fall. If we are assailed by them enable us to resist and come forth from the conflict as victors.

"But deliver us from evil." In mercy free us from everything that is harmful to the *body*, to the *soul*, to our *property*, and to our *honor*, our good name and standing in the community. As long as we are in this world, some evils will have to be endured for our chastening, but our prayer is that God will overrule them all and make them a blessing in disguise for us. And finally, in His own good time, we ask Him to take us out of this vale of tears and give us entrance to that home where evils shall never be known.

The conclusion is a word of praise in which we express our confidence that our Father in heaven can and will hear our prayer. Thine is the kingdom for the growth of which we pray. Thou art King and Lord of all. Thine is the power to give us abundantly above all that we ask or think. And Thine is the glory. To Thee alone will redound all honor and praise if Thou dost hear and answer our prayer. And forever and ever the kingdom, the power, and the glory will be Thine.

Amen means yea or verily. Amen, that is, it shall be so. I will cease from further pleading, for my heavenly Father hears. Or it is the answer of our God saying: "Yes, yes, My child, I hear. It shall be so."

Holy Spirit's Assistance in Prayer

In Romans 8:26, 27 we read: "Likewise the Spirit also helpeth our infirmities: for we know not what we should pray for as we ought: but the Spirit itself maketh intercession for us with groanings which cannot be uttered. And He that searcheth the hearts knoweth what is the mind of the Spirit, because He maketh intercession for the saints according to the will of God." Does this mean that we are not to voice our petitions to God in prayer but to leave it to the Spirit to pray for us? Or are we to be led and assisted by the Holy Spirit in our prayers?

Certainly, we are to pray, but even the best of us often show great weaknesses in prayer. We lack fervor or confidence in prayer; we lay undue emphasis on the wrong thing, we do not pray according to the will of God. Here the Spirit of God comes to our assistance. These deficiencies in our prayers the Spirit Himself makes good. He intercedes, He pleads in behalf of the saints and enables them more and more to pray for those things which are for their eternal good.

What a comforting thought: Jesus is not only our advocate with the Father, but here we are assured that the Holy Spirit also comes to our rescue and intercedes for us in a way that lies beyond our unaided power. In spiritual things we are apt to be remiss, and these are of first importance. It is here especially that the Holy Spirit comes to our aid.

Pray without Ceasing

One passage of the Bible tells us to "pray without ceasing," but in another passage we are told that, if the Lord wants us to have something, He will give it to us while we sleep. Please explain the connection between the two passages.

There is certainly no disagreement between these passages of Scripture. Jesus once told a parable to illustrate and to impress the fact "that men ought always to pray and not to faint," Luke 18:1–8. In Romans 12:12 the apostle exhorts, "continuing instant in prayer," and in I Thessalonians 5:17 he makes it still stronger by enjoining us to "pray without ceasing." All these passages tell us the same thing. They do not admonish us always to be engaged in prayer. That is impossible. How can we be in prayer while we are in unconscious sleep? How can we be in sincere prayer (and no other kind is acceptable) when, for instance, we are engaged in solving some difficult problem in mathematics? We are never to be negligent in prayer; we are always to be in a fit condition to approach God in prayer, no matter where we are or what we are doing. Moreover, there can be and there should be in my soul a hungering and a thirsting for God and His righteousness at all times, whether I am always thinking about this or not. This, too, is prayer, an unceasing longing to be with God and to do His bidding.

Through the prophet God promises, "And it shall come to pass that before they call, I will answer; and while they are yet speaking, I will hear," Isa. 65:24. Here the Lord is not telling His people that they need not pray or might as well be dilatory in prayer. His gracious promise is to encourage the very opposite. So ready is He to hear our prayers, so anxious to supply our every need and to gratify every helpful and rightful desire of His dear children, that He sometimes answers before they call, and they have their request granted before they have concluded their prayer.

But you have another passage in mind. It is this one found in Psalm 127:2: "It is vain for you to rise up early, to sit up late, to eat the bread of sorrows: for so He giveth His beloved sleep."

God is here not encouraging idleness or slothfulness. We are to be diligent and earnestly endeavor to do our full duty. But God does not want us to wring our hands in needless worry and distrust His providential care. We are implicitly to trust in His promises. Thus we shall have peace, and our sleep will be sweet and restful and undisturbed by needless, anxious worry.

Prayer in the Name of Jesus

We spoke of prayer in my Sunday school class last Sunday. I think I know what is meant by prayer in the name of Jesus, yet when I attempted to explain it I found that it is not as clear to my mind as it ought to be. I know you will gladly help me, and in doing so, perhaps, you will help many others.

In prayer we come before God with our requests. We, of course, hope to receive what we are asking for. On what grounds do we base our hopes? One expects to receive because he thinks it is coming to him, he is worthy of it, deserves it because of something he has done or suffered to merit it. Such a one comes in his own name. What he expects of God is not a gift but rather a just wage or reward which in his estimation is rightfully his.

Another admits, perhaps, that he deserves nothing. He realizes his guilt and unworthiness because of sin, but he expects God to close His eyes to sin and grant him his requests in spite of them. He pleads no atonement made in his behalf, he comes not to God through a mediator. He simply expects God in His sovereign power and grace to grant him pardon and every blessing though he deserves nothing. Such a one, too, comes in his own name.

A third one penitently comes to God pleading for mercy. He knows that he has broken God's holy law, and that law necessarily exacts penalty, for law without penalty would cease to be law. But to his great joy he has also learned that God in mercy has provided for him a Savior, who suffered the penalty of his trangressions and thus made atonement in his behalf. His trust, therefore, is in what this divine Benefactor has done for him. He pleads for mercy, but it is mercy through a Mediator, who has fully met the penalty of violated law in his behalf. This petitioner approaches the throne of God not in his own name, he trusts in nothing that he has done or ever hopes to do; he pleads the merits of his Savior and asks God to grant him forgiveness and every blessing for Jesus' sake, i. e., for the sake of what Jesus, his Redeemer and Savior, has done for him. That is praying in the name of Jesus.

Permit me to try again. This time by way of illustration.

A man goes to the bank with a check. It is a check bearing his own signature. He thinks that he has a deposit at the bank, but he is mistaken. The banker refuses to cash his check because it is worthless.

Another man goes to the bank. He knows that he has no deposit there. But he expects the banker to honor his check out of pure love and benevolence. He will go away a disappointed man.

A third man has a check with which he goes to the bank. He is a poor man, he has no money on deposit. He would not expect the banker to cash his own check. The check which he carries bears the signature of a wealthy depositor. As he has legally and honorably come into possession of that check, it is cashed without question.

Jesus gives you and me a checkbook. Each check bears His name. He bids us fill out these blanks as we have need and check against His account at the bank of heaven. This is prayer in Jesus' name.

The Golden Rule

Is there any gospel in the Golden Rule?

No, there is only law in the Golden Rule, perfect law. This do, perfectly do what the Golden Rule enjoins, and thou shalt live. But where is the man who can perfectly keep and in all things perfectly follow the Golden Rule? Such a man would not need a Savior, for he would be his own savior. Such a man would not need to pray: "Forgive us [me] our [my] trespasses," for he would have none to forgive. The Golden Rule is the straightedge to show us how crooked we are in order that we may see our need of pardon and flee to Christ, in and through whom it is offered.

Then when we have accepted Christ as our Redeemer and Savior, the Golden Rule gets to be the rule after which we in love and gratitude to Him try to regulate our life. We as His followers, who trust in Him and His redemption in our behalf, love Him and seriously want to do His will. His will is expressed in the commandments, and He says: "If ye love Me, keep My commandments." The Golden Rule is the sum of the second table of the law.

Every intelligent Christian will say: "I am saved not by my keeping of the Golden Rule because, alas, I do not and cannot keep it perfectly, try as I will; but I earnestly try to observe it because I am a twice-born man. My trying to keep the Golden Rule does not make me a Christian —that which makes me a Christian is my new birth from above—but I try to keep the Golden Rule because I AM a Christian."

Do you see the difference? The law can only condemn but never save a sinner. The law reveals sin, but it cannot relieve us of sin. But the great lawgiver can, and He in mercy offers us redemption and full pardon through Christ, the divine Savior. The Christian accepts Christ as his Savior, trusts in Him, and clings to Him. He cannot do otherwise as His grateful and devoted follower than to try as best he can to do His bidding. He will manifest many weaknesses. Every day he will penitently have to plead for new mercy and pardon, but every day he also asks for grace to grow more and more into the image of Him who is his perfect Master.

PART TWO

THE CHURCH

1. *About Its Origin, History, and Authority*

The Apostolic Church

Did the disciples have a church as we consider it today?

The followers of Jesus did not at once have church edifices in which to worship. When they could no longer worship in the Temple or synagogue because the Jews refused to accept Jesus as the Messiah they had their place of assembly in some home. (See for example, Acts 12:12; 18:4–7; 20:20; Romans 16:5.) Gradually as the number of believers increased in any certain place or locality, a home would no longer suffice for their place of general assembly. Then it was that special buildings were erected and dedicated to the purpose of public worship.

But by "church" you, no doubt, refer to the congregation. Certainly, from the very start there were organized bands or groups of believers. The old mother congregation was at Jerusalem. It was under the leadership of the apostles. In the course of time deacons, too, were elected (Acts 6). Soon we have little congregations springing up throughout Palestine, Syria, and Asia Minor. The whole book of Acts is largely an account of the founding and the development of these primitive congregations or churches. When Paul wrote a letter "unto the church of God which is at Corinth" he was, of course, sending a message to the group of Christian people, or congregation of believers, which was located in the city of Corinth.

Just what the order of service was when the early disciples assembled for worship we do not know. But we do know that these Christians of apostolic days had all the distinguishing features of Christian worship. There was reading of Scripture or the oral reciting of the Word of God.

There were preaching and teaching of the revealed Word of divine truth; there were prayer and singing, and the two sacraments, baptism and the Lord's Supper, were administered. All our worship and service of today centers around these same essential features.

We know "the faith which was once delivered unto the saints," and which we are exhorted earnestly to contend for (Jude 3). If the Evangelical Lutheran Church does hold and proclaim this faith, but does not contend earnestly for it, it has no right to exist.

Unity of the Faith

In Ephesians, chapter four, Paul exhorts us "to keep the unity of the Spirit in the bond of peace." And he also tells us that God gave us various leaders in the church "for the perfecting of the saints; for the work of the ministry, for the edifying of the body of Christ; till we all come in the unity of the faith," etc. Does this unity refer only to some churches or to all?

Of course, God wants the holy Christian Church to be one. And, indeed, the real church is one: one holy catholic (that is, universal) apostolic church. "Upon this rock I will build *My church*," Matthew 16:18. "Christ also loved the church, and gave Himself for it," Eph. 5:25. The church in its essence is one. "I believe in the holy Christian Church, the communion of saints," we confess in the Apostolic Creed.

Surely, you know what we mean by the church. We do not refer to a building (though we also call the edifice in which we regularly worship a church); we do not refer to a certain congregation or denomination; we refer to "the communion of saints," i.e., to the aggregate or sum-total of all true believers in Christ. All Christians taken together form one church. There always has been only one, and there always will be only one. Is this the Lutheran Church? No! it is "the communion of saints." All of God's people taken together form "the body of Christ," Eph. 4:12. I do not have to say: "I *believe* there is a Lutheran Church." I *know* that. That is a visible organization of people. But I have to say: "I believe there are true believers on earth." Well, whoever these true believers are, or wherever they are, they form the one holy Christian Church.

But God wants us also to be one outwardly, i.e., one in the unity of faith and practice. It is wrong that we are divided as we are. We ought to all teach the same truth, live the same truth. There should be no divisions among us. Who is responsible for these divisions? Those who teach contrary to God's Word. We are earnestly warned against false teachers and false teaching. We do not want outward union at any price. There must be unity in the truth. But as long as we are wicked, selfish, fallible people, there will doubtless be divisions among us. But we are earnestly and prayerfully to strive for unity. However, this outward disunity does not disrupt the unity of the real church, the invisible church, "the communion of saints."

The Apostolic Succession

My neighbor and I are good friends, but we cannot agree on religion. In our conversation last evening we got on the subject of the power and rights of the priests. My friend repeatedly quoted the passage: "He that heareth you, heareth Me; he that despiseth you, despiseth Me." He insisted that Jesus thus plainly says that he who hears and obeys the apostles whom He sends, hears and obeys Christ. And he who rejects and ignores the apostles thus treats Jesus, whom they represent and by whose authority they speak. From this he argued that, since the properly ordained priests of the holy Catholic Church which Christ founded are the successors of the apostles, therefore the priests of the Catholic Church speak and function as the representative spokesmen of Christ. Will you please give us your interpretation of the passage referred to above (Luke 10:16)?

Did you look up this passage and read it in its connection? Note that Jesus did not address these words to the twelve apostles. He was sending out seventy men to do some preliminary preaching in certain villages where He Himself expected later to follow (Luke 10:1). These men were, indeed, followers of Jesus, disciples in the wider sense of that term, but they were not apostles (see Matthew 10:2-4). Thus the fundamental premise of your friend's argument is already taken away from him. However, these men were real messengers of Jesus, and to give proof of this He provided for them wonderfully and enabled them to do supernatural things. These were their credentials.

These seventy men were sent out to do what? To proclaim the gospel; to assure the people that Jesus of Nazareth was the Savior of the world, the great Messiah promised from of old.

When Jesus sent them out with this message He said to them: "He that heareth you [when you deliver this message], heareth Me; he that despiseth you [in the proclaiming of this message], despiseth Me," because it is His message that is being rejected. When Jesus says: "He that heareth you, heareth Me," does that mean that, when two of these disciples were walking down the street . . . for He sent them out two and two . . . a person could hear the footfalls of Jesus by the clatter of the sandals on the messengers' feet? Of course not. Suppose these messengers would have perverted the message with which they had been entrusted and thus at least in part would have delivered their own devised message instead of that of the Master, would He still have owned them as His messengers and endorsed what they said?

Jesus wished to say: "He that hears and heeds you when by My authority and in My stead you deliver the message with which I have entrusted you, hears and heeds Me, for it is My message which he receives and heeds. And he who rejects you when in My stead you proclaim My message rejects Me, for he refuses to accept My message."

The messenger must deliver the message of the Master or he is no longer the Master's messenger. It is not on the man, the messenger, that the emphasis must be laid but on the message. That must be the true message of the Master. Then it matters little who the bearer of the message is; whether it is an apostle or an ordinary disciple, a man or a women, an adult or a child. When a person says to me: "He that believeth and is baptized shall be saved," it is true no matter who it is that brings me that assuring promise. It is as true as if I heard that gracious statement from Jesus' own sacred lips. But he who says to me: "He that believeth and is baptized shall be saved after he has made satisfactory atonement for his sins in purgatory," is speaking falsehood, no matter who the bearer of that message is, or by what title he is known to the world.

As to the one holy catholic (universal) church which Christ founded, that was not the Roman Catholic Church, nor was it the Lutheran Church, nor any of the visible church organizations. That was the one holy, catholic, i.e., universal, apostolic church, which is "the communion of saints," as the church has ever confessed in the Apostles' Creed. The real church has no pretenders, no wolves in sheep's clothing, no hypocrites in it; it is the aggregate or sum-total of all true believers in Christ. He alone knows, infallibly knows, who these blessed ones are.

The holy Christian (catholic) Church of which Jesus is both the foundation and the head is not an organization with a visible head but a fellowship of believers which St. Paul calls the body of the invisible Christ.

The Authority of the Church

A visiting Catholic priest recently told an audience in our city that the Catholic Church was the authoritative teacher of the teachings of Christ. He called "absurd" such modern slogans as, "Each man has a right to worship God as he sees fit," and, "A good American

is a tolerant American." Would you care to comment on these statements?

Keep in mind that the real church is "the communion of saints." All *true* believers in Christ are these "saints" and constitute this "communion." All pretenders, hypocrites are on the outside, no matter what their rank or title may be in some church organization. Christ entrusted His Word to His faithful disciples. They were the authoritative teachers of their day. And inasmuch as God inspired them to record this eternal truth, they are the authoritative teachers of all time. Whatever is not in accord with this inspired record of divine truth as found in the Scriptures is false, no matter what visible church organization or leader of some church organization may teach or claim.

It is true that the church is the only authoritative teacher of the teachings of Christ. But this church is "the communion of saints," not some church organization. Rome thinks of the church as an organization with a visible, human head, the pope of Rome. The church has a Head; it is the invisible Christ. "One is your Master, even Christ; and all ye are brethren," Matthew 23:8. Christ never made some certain individual His representative on earth.

Peter never claimed leadership over the rest of the disciples, and the other disciples never acknowledged him as their superior. Leo the Great (440–461) was the first who claimed that he, as the bishop of Rome, was by divine right the head of the whole church. Listen to Peter: "The elders which are among you I exhort, *who am also an elder* [that is all he claimed to be], and a witness of the sufferings of Christ, and also a partaker of the glory that shall be revealed: Feed the flock of God which is among you, taking the oversight thereof, not by constraint, but willingly; not for filthy lucre, but of a ready mind: neither *as being lords* over God's heritage, but being ensamples to the flock," I Peter 5:1–3.

Christ is still the sole Ruler of the church. He has poured out the divine Spirit upon His true followers and promised that He will guide them into all truth. But this promise is given to you and to me as disciples of His as well as to any other individual on earth. No human being has a monopoly on all wisdom. And no human being ever was or ever will be the exclusive, authoritative spokesman of the Lord Jesus. Christ indeed says, "He that heareth you, heareth Me." Who is this "you"? It is the one who delivers Christ's message. When the messenger faithfully delivers Christ's message, the one who hears that message hears Christ, and the one who rejects that message rejects Christ.

And now, what about the absurdity of the modern slogans: "Each man has a right to worship God as he sees fit," and, "A good American

55

is a tolerant American"? Error and falsehood must not be put on a level with truth. That is correct. Error and falsehood should always give way to truth. But what mortal has a right to dictate to you or to me as to what either of us must accept as truth? I am responsible to God for what I believe and whom I worship, but I am responsible to no one else, and neither are you. The right of faith and worship is an inalienable right of the individual. He is, indeed, accountable to his Maker but not to any mortal, no matter what his station or title. Deny the individual this, and you have religious persecution and tyranny, which is the worst of all tyranny. My neighbor shall have the right to believe and to worship God as he sees fit, but you and I, too, must and will demand that privilege.

Am I intolerant when I take this position? I am tolerant, and that is true, American, Christian democracy. This does not mean that it is a matter of indifference to me whether my neighbor believes truth or error. Duty to God and my neighbor demands that I try to enlighten him, bring him the gospel of Christ, and thus seriously endeavor by word and example to bring him pardon, peace, and salvation. But I shall never try to force him to accept my views.

If by persuasive love I fail to win him to my way of thinking I acknowledge my defeat, and he shall go his way unmolested to answer to his God. He shall have the right to try to convince me that I am in error, but he must not endeavor to coerce me by force, for that is tyranny of the deepest dye. But of such tyranny Rome is guilty and always has been and always will be wherever she has power to carry out her hellish doctrine on this point.

The Household of Faith

Who are the "household of faith"?

"As we have therefore opportunity, let us do good unto all men, especially unto them who are of the household of faith," Gal. 6:10. These words are plain, and you will certainly not find fault with them, for they are the Word of God. You are to deal your bread to the hungry and to clothe the naked (Isa. 58:7), but you will surely admit that your own hungry and naked children come first. If they are supplied, and you can assist your needy brother's children, do so. And if you can help that distant relative out of his difficulty, cheerfully do that also. But do not stop with him but reach out farther and ever still farther, as far as you can, as opportunities come to you.

But as a Christian you belong not only to a natural or bodily family but also to a spiritual household. The nearest of this spiritual household are those of your own congregation. If any of them are in need, you should, if possible, assist them, and you are under greater obligation to them than you are to outsiders. But as you have opportunity you are to extend a helping hand to that needy one in a sister congregation. Do your obligations stop there? Certainly not. As you have opportunity you are to assist others who are in need of your aid. And the follower of Christ in some other denomination is nearer to you than an unbeliever. But as opportunities present themselves you are to do good unto all men.

The Meaning of Indulgences

Will you, please, in a concise, understandable way give us something on the question: What are indulgences?

In the Roman catechism I find this definition: "An indulgence is a remission of the temporal punishment due to our sins, which the Church grants outside of the sacrament of penance." That is, to be eligible for an indulgence a person must be in a state of grace, i.e., he must recently have confessed his sins to a priest and received forgiveness. This priestly absolution, says Rome, takes away the guilt of sin and assures salvation until that person again commits a mortal sin.

But though the guilt of sin is remitted, a temporal punishment (that is, a punishment due in this present life) due to those forgiven sins remains. This punishment can be reduced or entirely cancelled by means of an indulgence. This indulgence is applicable to the person who earns it by doing what the church prescribes, or, at his option, it may be applied to the benefit of a soul presumably detained in purgatory.

"From what source do indulgences draw their power and efficacy?" To this question the Catholic catechism answers: "From the treasury of the abundant merit of Jesus Christ and of the saints." Thus, according to the teaching of Rome, there is a great treasury of unused merits accumulated by Christ, the Virgin Mary, and the other saints and martyrs. This treasury is at the disposal of the Roman Church. From this vast treasury the church has the right to draw at any time. These merits are credited to the benefit of the faithful who qualify by the prescribed works and prayers.

The idea of indulgences is based wholly on work-righteousness, the teaching that man can earn and merit pardon by his oft-repeated prayers and works of penance. It is absolutely contrary to the gospel of divine grace offered humanity by a gracious God because of the full atonement made in our behalf by our divine Redeemer. Indulgences are without foundation in the Word of God and were unknown to the early church. Indulgences, in the present sense of this word, appear for the first time in the 11th century, when Pope Urban II sent Christian knights and warriors on the First Crusade. He promised these soldiers full indulgence for their sins provided they otherwise remained true to the church. The first so-called holy year was solemnized in 1300. The pope of that day, Boniface VIII, offered generous indulgences to the faithful who took active part in the jubilee festivities of that year.

Most Romanists admit that the "sale" of indulgences in the days of Luther was an abuse of the "salutary" use of indulgences. Such a sale of indulgences for cold cash is said to be forbidden now. However, we read of very liberal offers made to those who make a pilgrimage to Rome. There are, no doubt, very tempting and very special offers of indulgences made to those who repeat certain prayers and do certain prescribed works of penance in this or that holy shrine or before some supposed sacred relic. Is this intended to make men and women more godly and Christlike or to bring shekels into the pope's treasury? Are we telling the untruth when we charge that Rome is still deeply interested in the "traffic of indulgences"?

There are two kinds of indulgences, plenary and partial. The former remit the whole debt of temporal punishment due to pardoned sin while the latter remit only a part of it. An indulgence of forty, sixty, or a hundred days is a remission of such a debt of temporal punishment as a person would discharge if he did penance for that length of time. Whether time is reckoned in purgatory the same as it is here on earth is questionable. Hence, I should advise always aiming at a plenary indulgence when coming to the aid of a dear one supposed to be suffering in the purgatorial flame.

The Meaning of an Interdict

What is an "interdict"?

An interdict is a severe penalty, imposed at times by the Roman Catholic Church. Interdicts are of various kinds. At times in years gone by a whole city, province, or kingdom was put under an interdict. Practically all church work was forbidden. The churches were closed; no services were held, no church bell dare be rung, no marriage be performed by any priest, no sacrament administered except it be perhaps baptism or Extreme Unction in cases of necessity; no Christian burial was permitted. An interdict may be directed against a congregation, in which case all these things are prohibited in that congregation. Or an interdict may be directed against an individual or a number of individuals. If anyone is under an interdict he is debarred from all services of the church, he is under the severest church discipline. A Roman Catholic is absolutely dependent on a priest, and it must be a priest who has received ordination from a bishop. A Roman Catholic knows of no way of pardon except through the sacraments of his church, and only a priest can administer a sacrament—except baptism in a case of necessity. Thus to be under an interdict is for the time being to be cut away from the church. And for a Roman Catholic that means to be cut away from God. For to him the church is not the "communion of saints," an invisible communion of all those who truly believe in Christ Jesus, but an external organization under the leadership of a visible head, the pope.

The Doctrine of the Ministry

May I ask you briefly to state the Lutheran doctrine concerning the Christian ministry.

We believe in the "universal priesthood." According to the Word of God all believers in Christ are priests or priestesses and in a private way have a right to perform priestly functions. The priesthood is no longer a select class within the church but is composed of all true Christians. And whatever rights and powers belong to the Christian priesthood belong equally to all believers. St. Peter says: "Ye also, as lively stones, are built up a spiritual house, an holy priesthood, to offer up spiritual sacrifices, acceptable to God by Jesus Christ."

This, however, does not say that every priest is a public minister of the church. We must not confound the Christian priesthood with the pastoral office. In our country the sovereignty is vested in the people, but this does not say that every citizen is a public officer. The pastor discharges certain public functions in the congregation, not because he belongs to a higher order of saints than does the ordinary Christian, but because his equals, recognizing the gifts with which a kind Providence has endowed him, and which render him competent for the work, have chosen him to officiate for them and publicly to administer the means of grace.

Pastors are not a superior order of Christians. "One is your Master, even Christ, and all ye are brethren." But for the sake of order and also for the sake of efficiency God has ordained that certain ones are to be chosen as pastors, shepherds, to feed and to watch over the flock, which Christ has purchased with His own blood. In other words, there is to be in the church a special pastoral office or ministerial calling, the duty of which is to oversee the work and publicly to administer the means of grace.

Who is to serve in this capacity? "No man taketh this honor unto himself, but he that is called of God, as was Aaron," says the holy writer.

During Old Testament time only a direct descendant of Aaron could become a priest. In the New Testament dispensation God still chooses His public servants and commissions them to go forth and proclaim His message. Jesus chose and prepared the twelve apostles. The same is true of their rightful successors in the pastoral office. Elders were ordained in every church. These "elders" were the pastors.

Jesus exhorts us to "pray the Lord of the harvest, that He will send forth laborers into His harvest." He still calls men into His service, commissioning them to do the work of the "ministry." But He no longer calls men directly and by name. The call is now given through the congregation. To the church has been entrusted the means of grace, and in the name and by the authority of God the church confers upon the individual the right publicly to administer these means in its midst.

If it is God who has called a minister to a certain field, it is He alone who has a right to determine when that relationship between shepherd and flock is to terminate. Therefore the call must be unlimited in time. The pastor is not the mere servant or hired man of the congregation. However, this does not say that the call is of such a character that it cannot be revoked or abrogated under any circumstances. Divine providence may clearly indicate that the relation between pastor and congregation should terminate. This is an intricate problem that we cannot go into here. The relation between pastor and congregation is intimate and of divine origin, and it should not be arbitrarily severed at any time by either party.

The Length of Pastorates

Why do Lutheran pastors remain in one congregation so many years?

Nothing in this world is perfect. Our method of placing pastors has its weaknesses. Mistakes are made. But if you know of a better method or a method that is more Biblical and more conducive to the welfare of the church and the growth of Christ's kingdom on earth you are wiser than the combined wisdom of the whole Lutheran Church. This is a subject that has been given serious, prayerful thought. The brightest as well as the most consecrated men in the church have studied this subject and discussed it from every point of view. But thus far we have found nothing that is more in keeping with God's Word and more conducive to the salvation of blood-bought souls.

Some of the denominations which have the custom of changing their pastors frequently are of late lengthening the period of time in which a pastor remains in the same parish. They are seemingly coming to the conclusion that these frequent changes are not always for the good of the church. No fixed time should be designated, and that is applicable to all cases. Each case must be considered on its own merits. A change in pastors is sometimes good for both pastor and congregation, and at other times a change would be detrimental to both pastor and parish.

You say, "Ten years is long enough." Suppose another member says eight years is long enough, and still another sets the limit at five years or even three. Which one of these opinions should be followed? Moreover, has the Lord God anything to say in these matters concerning His servants and the church of which He is both foundation and head? Is a shepherd to take to his heels as soon as he hears a couple of wolves howl? The LUTHERAN STANDARD brought the report of one of our older pastors being honored "after 40 years in one church." Is not that something to be happy about? He is still going strong, and so is that church.

I recall how one of our ministers told me twenty years ago that in his opinion it would be good, both for him and for his congregation, if he were to receive a call. That brother is still the honored and successful pastor of that same congregation.

One more word. You seem to be of the opinion that a minister has no "money" and no "life's blood" invested in the church which perhaps he, or at least one of his brother pastors, helped to build and to pay for, and where he has spent and been spent in pastoral service to souls. I do not know what is custom in the Middle West, but I do know that there is no appeal for funds that makes its round in my congregation or in any of the sister churches of this community where the pastor's name is not found. And it is usually near the top of the list.

The Position of a Pastor

Our church council claims that it just hires our pastor, and therefore he should have nothing to say pertaining to the operating of the church and its activities. Is this the correct attitude to take, or is the pastor to be considered the head of the church?

The word pastor means shepherd. Is the shepherd the hired man of the sheep in his flock? I wonder if your church officers ever read the printed "call" which your congregation sent to the man whom it, in the name of the triune God, requested to become its spiritual teacher and leader and in general to superintend and oversee the work of the church. It promised to receive him as a servant of God and to give him the honor, respect, and obedience due its chosen pastor.

In the patriarchal age the church was in the home. The father was the teacher and priest. Abraham was certainly not the hired servant of his household. At the time of Moses his brother Aaron was appointed high priest. His oldest son became his successor, and so it was to continue. Aaron's other sons and their descendants became priests.

In the New Testament era the time for priests is past. But we do need public ministers of the Word. Jesus Himself, we may say, was the first New Testament pastor. In Him the pastoral office has its crown and perfect model. What provision did He make for the continuing of the ministry of the Word? For it is through the proclaimed Word and the administered sacraments that the individual is brought and kept in personal and saving relation with God. Be it understood, then, that the New Testament ministry is the office of the Word as it was exercised by Christ Himself in His day.

The gospel minister, in an important sense, is a successor of Christ. "As My Father hath sent Me, even so send I you." Christ carries on His official work in the church through the gospel ministry. "Let a man so account of us, as of the ministers of Christ, and stewards of the mysteries of God," says St. Paul in I Corinthians 4:1. Again he affirms: "God was in Christ, reconciling the world unto Himself, not imputing their trespasses unto them; and hath committed unto us the word of reconciliation. Now then we are ambassadors for Christ, as though God did beseech you by us; we pray you in Christ's stead, be ye reconciled to God," II Corinthians 5:19, 20. "Take heed therefore unto yourselves, and to all the flock, over the which the Holy Ghost hath made you overseers, to feed the church of God which He hath purchased with His own blood," Acts 20:28.

How different we pastors would look upon our work and go about our daily tasks if we would ever keep in mind that we are the public representatives of the Lord Jesus, and with what greater respect the minister would be treated for his office's sake if all would remember that he is an "ambassador of Christ" and a "steward of the mysteries of God"!

The Office of the Keys

Please explain St. John 20:23: "Whose soever sins ye remit, they are remitted unto them; and whose soever sins ye retain, they are retained."

This is the basic Scripture passage for our doctrine of "The Office of the Keys." It must, of course, be interpreted in connection with parallel passages such as Matthew 16:19; Matthew 18:17–20; II Corinthians 2:10, etc.

This doctrine of the Office of the Keys is very puzzling to many of our people, and not a few think that we are aping the Catholics when we speak of "Confession and Absolution." I feel sure that I shall be giving you the information you desire if I explain our doctrine of the Office of the Keys. I shall do so under this caption: *The Roman Catholic and Lutheran Teaching on Confession and Absolution Briefly Compared.*

1. Rome insists that all mortal sins committed after baptism which one can remember must be confessed, i.e., enumerated with the necessary circumstances to a priest in order to obtain forgiveness.

The Lutheran Church teaches that, while we should humbly confess our sinfulness before God and man and admit our guilt when we have wronged another, such an enumeration of all sins is neither necessary nor possible.

2. Rome teaches that the power to forgive sins was given only to the apostles and their successors in office, the bishops and the priests; hence only the clergy have the right to pronounce absolution.

Lutherans teach that this power to forgive sins was given to the church, hence to every believer. We believe in the universal priesthood of all believers, and therefore this right to pronounce absolution in the name of God belongs to every believer, man or woman. In a public way, of course, only the rightly called or appointed minister should do so.

3. The Romanists claim that the priest pronounces absolution as a judicial sentence. That is, after hearing a detailed enumeration of a person's sins, the priest as the authorized judge of the Almighty has the right to impart or to withhold the forgiveness of that person's sins. This authority Rome claims the priest has by virtue of his apostolic ordination. But there are certain heinous crimes which an ordinary priest cannot forgive; these are reserved for the bishop or even in extreme cases for the pope.

Our church teaches that no one can forgive sins but God only. By virtue of the atonement made by Jesus for all humanity God is ready to forgive all. Any sinner who will permit the Holy Spirit through the Word and the sacraments to bring him to repentance and faith in Jesus receives full pardon. But how are the divine Word and the sacraments through which alone the Spirit of God operates upon the human heart brought to us? Only through some human being does God bring us this precious gospel. And this "good news" not only informs us of offered grace and pardon but imparts it to us if we accept Him of whom it tells, and through whom these gifts are offered. In this sense the confessor or anyone who proclaims the gospel forgives sins in that he brings the sinner God's signed and sealed letter of pardon.

4. Rome teaches that God never forgives sins except through the sacraments, seven in number. In exceptional cases a layman may administer baptism, but the other sacraments no one may administer except an

apostolically ordained clergyman. Hence, sins committed wilfully after baptism can be forgiven only through an apostolically ordained man.

We teach that God offers and imparts forgiveness in no other way than through His Word and the sacraments of baptism and the Lord's Supper. Every man, woman, or child who has this Word or knows this Word is authorized to pass it on. And wherever this Word goes, God is offering, and through it He is desirous of imparting, the forgiveness of sins.

5. Since Rome teaches that the sacraments confer grace on the recipients by the mere external act, it necessarily follows that the priest's absolution, given in good faith on his part, always confers grace.

Our church teaches that only the penitent believer receives pardon when absolution is spoken upon him. He who comes without faith brings only the greater guilt upon his soul for acting the hypocrite and thus slighting God's proffered mercy.

Who Forgives Sin

A friend of mine, a very religious man but of a different denomination, claims that we Lutherans believe that a minister can forgive sins, and that we go to him for forgiveness before we partake of the Holy Supper. He says that we teach that God forgives us through the pastor. Will you kindly straighten him out on this question and at the same time also clear up the matter in my mind? I am not an educated man, so please make it very plain. Thanks.

Your question has to do with the meaning of the gospel. The gospel is the good news that a gracious God for Jesus' sake, i.e., for the sake of His atonement in our behalf, is willing to forgive us and to reinstate each one of us as His dear child and heir. It is also God's letter of pardon that imparts and bestows full forgiveness on everyone who accepts it in trustful faith.

Permit an illustration. Let us assume that Jim Black is a prisoner in the penitentiary at Columbus, Ohio. The governor of the state, on the recommendation of the board of pardons, decides to grant him his freedom on July 4 of this year. A news item about this appears in an issue of the Columbus *Dispatch*. A copy of that issue gets into the hands of Jim Black. He receives this information with great delight, it is good news to him. But does that bring him pardon and freedom? Of course not. It tells him only what the governor intends to do. And if it should prove to be a false report, Jim Black gets out of it nothing but a bitter disappointment. Is this all the gospel is, the good news that the King of heaven declares Himself willing to pardon you and me as rebels against His authority? It is more, it is a letter of pardon to each one of us.

Permit me to continue my illustration. The governor writes a letter of pardon and signs and seals it as the chief executive of the state. By messenger he sends this document to the warden of the penitentiary. The warden asks Jim Black to come to his office. "Jim, I have good news for you," says the warden, and he reads to him the letter of pardon. "On the authority of this document, Jim, you may pack up your belongings and report here on the fourth day of July."

This is done, and on the appointed day the heavy iron door to the great outside opens, and Jim steps forth a free man. Who gave him his pardon? The governor did. Did the governor himself hunt up Jim Black and hand him his pardon? Did he unlock the door and invite Jim to step out a free man? No, the warden did that. The warden? Has he the right to pardon a guilty criminal and bid him cheerfully go forth? He has the right if he is properly authorized by the chief executive to do so.

Suppose the warden would have been sick on July 4 and the deputy warden would have handled the case. It would not have changed in the least the pardon duly coming to Jim Black. It would simply have been a different man that brought him the governor's letter of pardon. Now, suppose the deputy warden would have been out of town, and the sick warden would have entrusted this entire matter to his wife. Would that have made any difference? Not in the least.

Now, let us apply this. By nature we are all prisoners of sin and Satan, under the curse of the law of God which we have violated. But the Lord of mercy decreed our freedom. Not by simply closing His eyes to our sins—justice forbids that—but by having another take our place, suffer the penalty of our sins, and thus merit our release. This was done to the perfect satisfaction of all heaven. And therefore Christ's disciples are now sent as messengers into all the world to announce and at the same time also to bring and impart full pardon to every penitent, believing human being. We are to say to everybody: "Listen, I have good news for you. You may have perfect pardon for all your sins through your Substitute, our Lord Jesus Christ. I bring forgiveness and salvation to you. I offer it to you in the name and by the authority of the King of kings and the Lord of lords. Desire it, and you shall receive, accept it in confident faith, and it is yours." Dare we speak thus? Most certainly. Not only have we the right, but it is our most solemn duty to do so. As disciples of Jesus, men, women, and children, we are authorized to do this very thing.

God is a God of order, and, therefore, in a public, formal way no one is to pronounce and bestow forgiveness in the name of the triune God except the properly chosen servant of the Lord. But in private any disciple of Jesus has the right to announce and to pronounce pardon on the penitent. In fact, whenever and wherever the sweet gospel is being proclaimed, no matter who proclaims it, it is God's letter of pardon that is being proclaimed.

When in the confessional service you penitently confess your sins and hear the word of absolution, i.e., of pardon, pronounced upon you, receive it, depend upon it, and rejoice in the assurance of complete pardon, not because a man in a ministerial robe pronounced upon you the words of forgiveness, but because he brought you the letter of pardon of your merciful heavenly Father. Lay no stress whatever upon the man, who is merely the messenger. Lay all the stress upon the sweet gospel which is the power of God unto salvation, the letter of pardon, and he who in God-wrought faith receives what it offers, he has it.

Who pardons the guilty man? Only the infinite, merciful God can do that, against whom the offense has been committed. But this gracious divine Father has entrusted His gospel, His letter of pardon, to the church, which is the discipleship of Jesus. God uses some human messenger to bring His forgiveness to the penitent, believing sinner. Rome lays all the stress upon the messenger, it must be an apostolically ordained priest, says the papacy. We lay all the stress upon the Word of God which the pastor brings to us. It must be the gospel of our Lord Jesus Christ, for that alone is the power of God unto salvation to everyone that believeth.

Roman Catholic Saints

From the daily paper I learn that the Roman Catholic Church recently canonized another saint. This new saint died in 1645 in Quito, Ecuador. She is popularly known as the "Lily of Quito." She was beatified in 1853, we are told. Now I am inquisitive about several questions. In what way do beatification and canonization differ? Where does Rome get the authority to declare certain persons to be saints? What benefit is it to humanity to be ever adding to the number of saints?

Beatification in the Roman Catholic Church refers to an act by which a departed person is officially declared to be beatified or blessed. It is a step toward canonization or the raising of one to the honor and the dignity of a saint. As a rule, a person must be dead at least fifty years before he can be beatified. By that time such a good person will certainly be out of purgatory.

When a person is recommended for beatification, the pope institutes a formal court of investigation. There are lawyers and witnesses who solemnly testify to the qualifications and merits of this person, including miracles which he performed. And there are those who try to belittle these alleged merits and virtues and to cast doubt on the genuineness of the miracles ascribed to him. Finally the pope gives his decision. If it is favorable as it, no doubt, usually is, the reputed saint is solemnly beatified. This always takes place in the Vatican.

Later, if it can be proved that miracles have been performed by using the relics of this beatified person or through his intercession, that departed one may be a candidate for canonization. Again there is a solemn investigation of all alleged proofs of his merits. If the examination is satisfactory, that person is officially declared by the pope to be a saint. A day of the year, usually the anniversary of his birth or death, is dedicated to his honor and named after him. His name is inserted in the canon (hence canonization) or register of the saints. Churches and altars may be consecrated to him. His remains are carefully preserved, and the faithful are encouraged to invoke his intercession in prayer.

Beatification differs from canonization in this, that "whereas the cultus of a canonized saint belongs to the universal Church, and churches and altars can be freely erected in his or her honor . . . in the case of one of the Blessed it is otherwise. The honor and veneration which was authorized in their regard are limited and partial; and because the cultus of one of them is permitted to one country, or city, or order or branch of the order, it does not follow that it should be practiced elsewhere; and the attempt to extend it without special permission is condemned."

In 1170 Alexander III pronounced it an exclusive privilege of the papal chair to declare anyone to be a saint. Where did he get his authority for this? As the vice-regent of Christ on earth he claims he has full authority to do as he sees fit to do, so why ask such a needless question? When the Bishop of Rome speaks *ex cathedra,* i.e., as the head of the Church, he is supposed to be infallible.

Of what profit are these saints? The faithful doubtless consider them very helpful because of their intercession in their behalf. And the Church as a whole knows these saints to be very profitable because of the shekels they bring into the treasury. The relics of these saints are great drawing cards. Mother Cabrini was canonized in 1946. In a book by Mr. Paul Blanshard, *American Freedom and Catholic Power,* we read on page 222: "When Mother Cabrini was canonized in Rome, fifty thousand tickets for the ceremony were given out; but this was not enough to meet the demand, and eager Americans offered as much as $200 for a ticket." The shrine of Mother Cabrini in New York, we are told, draws thousands of visitors every day. They "file past a lifeless image of the famous saint in repose, many believing that they are viewing her miraculously preserved body—whereas the image is plastic and the shrine possesses only the bones."

By the way, have you read the book, *American Freedom and Catholic Power?* That book will answer your many questions about the Roman Catholic Church. See to it that your Sunday school library has at least one copy of that book and keep it circulating.

Roman Catholic Penance

Do the Roman Catholics by the expression "do penance" and the word "penance" mean practically the same as we do with the words "repent" and "repentance"?

They do not. There is a vast difference. When John the Baptist and Jesus repeatedly exhort: "Repent ye," it literally means, "Change ye your hearts and minds"; or, "Be sorry for the wickedness of your course, turn from it." It signifies a "right about, face!" As used in Scripture in respect to us, these words mean a change of our whole attitude toward sin and toward Christ; a turning away from sin and guilt to Christ and the pardon and newness of life which He proffers. This includes sorrow of heart because of the wickedness of the past, but the best Greek scholars inform us that the New Testament Greek word for repent and repentance means a complete change of mind.

We sometimes use the word *repentance* in a narrow sense to signify only contrition: "sorrow of heart to regret them and to abstain therefrom." But, as a rule, the word is used to signify both contrition and faith and thus means the entire conversion of man. It is "the change of heart when a man turns from sin unto Jesus Christ, his Savior."

The Catholic Bible—Douay Version—translates Matthew 3:1, 2 thus: "And in those days cometh John the Baptist preaching in the desert of Judea. And saying: Do penance; for the kingdom of heaven is at hand." A footnote explains "do penance" thus: "Which word, according to the use of the scriptures and the holy fathers, does not only signify repentance and amendment of life, but also punishing past sins by fasting, and such like penitential exercises." Webster's *New International Dictionary* defines penance as an "action performed to show penitence and as reparation or satisfaction for the sin, as the undergoing of some punishment, whether self-imposed or imposed by a superior; religious discipline undergone as a proof of penitence and as an amend for the sin."

Repentance to us necessarily includes sorrow of heart because of sin, but it primarily means a breaking with sin and a turning away from sin to Christ as our helper and rescuer from its guilt and damning power.

Penance for the Romanist includes sorrow and amendment of life, but it especially stresses punishment, self-imposed or imposed by a superior, thus to make satisfaction or reparation for sin.

Repentance, as used in the Bible and understood by us, excludes all self-merit and self-atonement by suffering. Penance, as used and understood by the Romanist, lays chief emphasis on the act of man, whereby, through these imposed penalties, he renders satisfaction and atonement, at least in part, for his sins. This is the seat of their pernicious error of work-righteousness.

The Roman Church also has a Sacrament of Penance, which is defined as "a Sacrament in which the sins we have committed after Baptism are forgiven." It consists of contrition for sin; confession to a priest; satisfaction, as some discipline or observance, imposed by the priest on the penitent; and absolution by the priest. We, indeed, have what we know as the "Office of the Keys," but we have no Sacrament of Penance.

2. About Different Communions and Practices

The Protestant Episcopal Church

Would you, please, contrast the difference between the Roman Catholic Church and the Protestant Episcopal Church?

Some of the main teachings of the Roman Catholic Church are the following:

Rome accepts the apocryphal books of the Old Testament as a part of the inspired Word of God. Tradition is of equal authority with the written Scriptures.

The pope, as the bishop of Rome, is Christ's vicar on earth. As such he is the absolute visible head of the church. Apart from him there can be no true church and no salvation.

The Church of Rome pronounces a curse upon the doctrine of justification by grace through faith in Christ alone. Jesus, it is claimed, did not fully and completely redeem man from all sin. In part man must by his good works merit his own pardon and salvation.

The saints and the angels and especially the Virgin Mary are to be invoked for their intercession with God. Mary was conceived and born immaculate, i.e., absolutely undefiled by sin. She is now *bodily* in heaven. The pope has officially proclaimed the dogma of the "assumption" of Mary's body into heaven.

The relics of the saints and martyrs are to be venerated, and by means of these many cures have been effected.

There are seven sacraments: Baptism, confirmation by a bishop, the Holy Eucharist (Lord's Supper), penance (which consists of contrition, auricular confession of all known sins to a priest, and satisfaction by works of penance, especially prayers, fasting, and alms), holy orders (ordination by a bishop), matrimony (marriage by a priest), and extreme unction. These sacraments confer some benefit even without faith on the part of the recipient.

Christian faith is not trust and confidence in the promises of God and the Savior but assent to what the Church of Rome teaches.

The mass is a real but unbloody sacrifice of the Lord Jesus for the remission of the sins both of the living and of the dead in purgatory.

In the Protestant Episcopal Church there are three tendencies: (1) "The High Church," which is very ritualistic and manifests a Romanizing tendency, harking back to Roman Catholicism; (2) "The Broad Church," which is quite liberal, rejecting some of the fundamental truths of the Christian religion; (3) "The Low Church," which tries to mediate between the other two extremes.

The Episcopal Church, as the name implies, lays great stress on the ancient episcopacy (government by bishops). The Episcopalian does not see how there can be a true church without an *episcopus*, i.e., a bishop. And it must be the ancient, successive episcopacy. The Episcopalian insists on "apostolic succession," which means that a bishop of today must have been ordained by another bishop, and this one still by another, and thus there must be an unbroken line or chain of the laying on of hands in ordination that can be traced back to the apostles. The Episcopalians, like the Greek and the Roman Catholics, hold that the clergy is a distinct order in the church, separate from the laity. Among the Episcopalians the bishops rule, yet not in an absolute way as among the Roman and the Greek Catholics.

The Protestant Episcopal Church is one of the church bodies which comprise the Reformed branch of the Christian Church and in general follows the teaching of John Calvin and his associate reformers. It believes in the baptism of children and does not insist on immersion. In this respect it differs from the various branches of the Baptist Church. In general, I think we may say that the official teaching of the Episcopal Church is evangelical, but in practice it is quite ritualistic, externalistic, and rationalistic.

The Greek Orthodox Church

Please tell us something about the Greek Orthodox Church; also something about the Russian Orthodox Church.

The Greek Orthodox and the Russian Orthodox Church are practically one and the same church. The official name is, "The Holy Oriental Orthodox Apostolic Church." The Eastern Church (Greek Catholic) separated from the Western Church (Roman Catholic) in 1054. The Greek-speaking churches of eastern Europe and western Asia would not accept the bishop of Rome as being greater than the bishop of Constantinople. This rivalry, together with some political causes, led to this historic separation.

Some of the errors which crept into the Roman Catholic Church since 1054 are not found in the Greek Church as, for instance, the withholding of the cup from the laity in Holy Communion, the sale of indulgences, etc.

In the Nicene Creed we confess that the Holy Ghost "proceedeth from the Father and the Son." The Greek Church rejects this and says that the Holy Ghost proceeds only from the Father. Like all Protestant churches, it denies that the pope of Rome is the vicar and vice-gerent of Christ. But the spiritual authority of the chief patriarch is little inferior to that of the pope. Like the papists, the Greek Church accepts tradition along with Scripture as divine authority and grants the right of interpretation only to the church. Saints and angels are invoked in prayer, and relics are to be venerated. The Greek Catholic Church also regards the celebration of the mass as an unbloody sacrifice of Jesus for human guilt. It has seven sacraments and believes in a purgatory. Man must largely merit salvation by works of penance. Baptism is administered by a threefold immersion. This church believes that bread and wine in the Holy Supper are changed into the body and the blood of Christ. Even small children are given Holy Communion. It insists on unleavened bread, and that the wine be mixed with water. Priests must be married, but only once. This marriage must take place before ordination.

The Lutheran Church before Luther

Where was the Lutheran Church before Luther?

Your question is not a new one. I have been repeatedly asked to answer it. A dear old lady of my first congregation came to me one day in great agitation because of this question. A neighbor lady had been worrying her with an argument which ran about like this: "Where was the Lutheran Church before Luther? Where was the Methodist Church before John Wesley? How can your church or any of the Protestant churches be the true church since all of them have arisen since the so-called Reformation of the sixteenth century? The Catholic Church dates back to Jesus Christ, its founder. Your church was founded by Martin Luther, the Methodist by John and Charles Wesley," etc., etc.

This argumentation is supposed to be unanswerable. It is continually being used by the Romanists, and they seem to think that it infallibly proves that the Roman Catholic Church is the one Holy Apostolic Church, outside of which there is no salvation.

What is our answer?

The word *church* does not always mean the same thing. Sometimes by "church" we mean a building, sometimes a congregation, at other times a denomination, etc. Now, what is meant by "the church" when Jesus says: "Upon this rock [not on Peter, but on the rock from which Peter derived his name—the Greek is *petra*, not *petros*] I will build My church," Matt. 16:18? Or when Paul affirms: "Christ also loved the church and gave Himself for it," Eph. 5:25? It means not one certain congregation or denomination, but it refers to the "communion of saints," i.e., the aggregate or sum-total of all true believers in Christ. In this sense there is but one church, composed of all true believers in Christ. "He that believeth and is baptized shall be saved" and hence belongs to the one holy catholic, that is, universal church, the *church invisible*, for we cannot look into man's heart and see his faith. All true Christians—God alone infallibly knows them—form "the church." All mere pretenders or false Christians are not a part of the church though they may hold membership in some church organization. All the true children of God of all the various Christian denominations form the one holy Christian Church, the only Church of Christ that ever existed or ever will exist, made up of all those who in living faith draw life from and cling to Christ, their Redeemer and Savior, as a branch to the vine.

The outward church organizations, congregations, and denominations include believers and pretenders; they differ in name and in purity of doctrine and practice. Some denominations gradually change, get worse or get better, farther away from the whole truth of the Bible or nearer to it. Sometimes the best part of an organization is compelled to cut loose from the rest because the latter permits errors to creep in and persists in clinging to them. The new division gets a different name, but it is a part of the old church in a purer form.

72

You ask: "Where was the Lutheran Church before Luther?" I answer by asking another question: "Where was your face this morning before it was washed?" It is the same church, as the same face, but washed.

The Roman Catholic Church

Will you, please, give an answer to those who say the Lutheran Church is so much like the Catholic Church and therefore they refuse to join us. In what way are we like the Catholics?

That which makes some people think that the Lutherans are like the Catholics is that our ministers wear a robe and sometimes wear other ecclesiastical vestments. As a rule, we have a high altar, and on the altar you will usually find a cross or a crucifix and candlesticks. On the church steeple, perhaps, you will find a cross; in the art-glass windows and in the fresco work you frequently find various church symbols. Even statuary is to be found in Lutheran churches. Moreover, as a rule, we have a liturgical order of service. We have versicles and responses, we have chants of praise; we have printed introits and collects, and usually we read the regular Epistle and Gospel of the day.

But may I remind you that all these things are nonessentials of Lutheranism. A congregation can be a true Lutheran church without a robed minister or a robed choir, without an altar, without a cross or candelabra of any kind. It can be a true Lutheran service though there be no set liturgy, no response, no chants. "To the true unity of the church, it is enough to agree concerning the doctrine of the gospel and the administration of the sacraments. Nor is it necessary that human traditions, rites, or ceremonies, instituted by men, should be everywhere alike" (Augsburg Confession).

In doctrine we are farther from the Roman Catholic Church than are any of the larger Protestant denominations. Practically all that we have in common with Rome is this, that both accept the Bible as the inspired Word of God. (Yet, remember, Rome accepts the apocryphal books as a part of the inspired Bible and claims that the "traditions of the fathers" also are a source and norm of faith.) The Roman Catholic and the Lutheran both believe in the Triune God, Father, Son, and Holy Ghost, both accept Jesus as the incarnate Son of God, and the sacrament of baptism as "the washing of regeneration." But apart from these few fundamentals Roman Catholicism and Lutheranism have practically nothing in common.

Permit me just to mention a few things Catholicism teaches:

Man must in part make satisfaction for sins committed after baptism.

Forgiveness of sins after baptism is to be had only through the sacrament of penance, which consists of contrition of the heart, confession of all known sins to a priest, and works of satisfaction rendered as imposed by the priest.

Christ is not man's only Mediator before God; the saints also have merit in God's sight and, if invoked, also intercede for us.

Not only to the Triune God is prayer to be made but also to the angels and to the saints, especially to the Virgin Mary.

The Virgin Mary was conceived and born immaculate, i. e., without the least taint of original sin.

Christian faith is not confidence and trust in the promises of the gospel but acceptance of what the Church of Rome teaches.

Rome believes in a purgatory and teaches that the sacrifice of the Mass and the almsdeeds and the prayers of the faithful will shorten the term of those confined to its flames.

There are seven sacraments says Rome—Baptism, the Lord's Supper, Confirmation, Marriage, Ordination, Penance, and Extreme Unction.

Rome teaches that the bread and the wine in the Lord's Supper are changed into the body and the blood of Christ; that the consecrated host, as the body of Christ, must be worshiped as Christ Himself; that the consecrated wine is not to be given to the laity; that in the Mass Christ is sacrificed by the priest in an unbloody manner for the sins of the living and the dead.

According to Catholic teaching the church is not the "communion of saints," i. e., the invisible communion of all true believers in Christ, but the visible fellowship of all who submit to the authority of the pope.

The church cannot exist without properly ordained bishops, and by this Rome means, there must be an uninterrupted and unbroken transmission of ministerial authority by the laying on of hands, back to the apostles (apostolic succession).

The pope is the visible head of the church, the vice-gerent of Christ and the infallible teacher of the true church.

The laws of the church must be observed as conscientiously as the commandments of God.

The clergy must not marry because celibacy is more pleasing to God than married life, etc., etc.

The Name "Evangelical"

Can you tell us why the word Evangelical is used in the name of every Lutheran Church? We know that the Lutheran Church is an

Evangelical Church, but there are other churches who claim to have the right to be so termed.

The disciples of Jesus were first called Christians at Antioch, and the name was probably applied to them in derision. Thus the followers of Dr. Martin Luther were derisively called "Lutherans." This was very distasteful to the great reformer. His wish was that the Church of the Reformation be known as the Evangelical Church, i. e., the gospel church, in contrast to the legalistic Church of Rome. However, the people, as a rule, continued to refer to the followers of Luther as the Lutherans. In time the official name got to be "Evangelical Lutheran." The name Lutheran had to be retained in order to differentiate between those who accept the Augsburg Confession and other Protestant bodies who reject it and yet are evangelical in their teachings.

The Name "Protestant"

Give the historical origin of the name "Protestant."

The year 1517 is usually designated as the year when the great religious movement known as the Reformation was started. It was on the evening of October 31 of that year that Luther nailed his memorable 95 theses to the door of the Castle church at Wittenberg. It was that bold act that stirred all Europe and led to a revolt against the tyranny and the falsehoods of the papal church. Luther was excommunicated in 1520. The next year he was summoned to appear before the emperor at the Diet at Worms. He was asked to recant, but refused to do so, being bound in conscience by the Word of God. Luther was now declared an outlaw, under ban and interdict, as it was called. However, he was to be unmolested until he again reached his home at Wittenberg since Emperor Charles V had promised him in writing safe conduct to and from the city of Worms where the diet was held.

It was on his journey home from Worms that his friends abducted him and kept him in hiding at the Wartburg Castle for almost a year. In the meantime the reformatory movement grew greatly in momentum. When Luther came forth from his retreat he had friends strong and numerous enough to protect him.

In 1526 another diet was called by Emperor Charles. This was held at Speyer. Here the Reformers gained a decided victory, for it was agreed that in matters pertaining to conscience each prince should have liberty to deal in his own province as seemed best to him. However, three years later at the Second Diet at Speyer this liberty was taken from the princes. All teaching and practice contrary to the Church of Rome were declared unlawful and forbidden until the pope and the emperor had called a general council to decide the matter. The Lutheran princes and estates now presented a formal, solemn protest against this decree. This took place on April 19, 1529. The princes of Saxony, Brandenburg, Hesse, and Anhalt, the dukes of Lueneburg, and the representatives of fourteen free and independent cities signed this protest. This was the origin of the name "Protestant." The term applied first to the adherents of Luther in Germany, but in time the name got to be applied generally to all Christian denominations that differ from the Church of Rome.

The Doctrine of Purgatory

The Catholic people base their theory of purgatory on Matthew 12:32 and Luke 12:59. Please explain these Bible passages.

Matthew 12:32 reads thus: "And whoever says a word against the Son of man will be forgiven; but whoever speaks against the Holy Spirit will not be forgiven, either in this age or in the age to come" (R.S.V.).

The Pharisees accused Jesus of being in league with Beelzebub, the prince of demons. This was nothing short of blasphemy against the Son of man, who is the eternal Son of God in human form. Verse thirty-two tells us what blasphemy is; it is to say "a word against the Son of man" or to speak "against the Holy Spirit."

There is pardon for the former sin under proper conditions. These conditions are not stated here but are clearly stated elsewhere. Only the truly penitent and believing can find pardon. These Pharisees were evidently on the verge of blaspheming the Holy Spirit and thus placing themselves beyond the possibility of ever being forgiven. He who blasphemes the Holy Spirit drives from him the One through whom alone man can come to repentance and faith in Jesus as his Savior. There comes a time when the Spirit of God ceases to strive with wilful men. If He has persistently resisted, the Spirit finally leaves man to his fate. This is why there is no pardon for blasphemy against the Holy Spirit, no pardon in time or in eternity. The person who blasphemes the Holy Ghost thereby, at that very moment, places himself beyond the reach of hope. "Whoever blasphemes against the Holy Spirit never has forgiveness, but is guilty of an eternal sin," Mark 3:29, R.S.V.

"I tell you, you will never get out till you have paid the very last copper," Luke 12:59. Man's first and chief concern in life should be the salvation of his soul. Jesus warns against needless anxieties (verse 16, etc.). Faithful discipleship is commended (verse 31, etc.). Keep yourself in readiness (verse 41, etc.). Watch the signs of the times and not only the prospect as to the weather (verse 54, etc.). With another illustration (verses 57–59) Jesus warns His hearers to seek release from the debt of guilt before they are brought before the supreme Judge. "Do the wise and sensible thing and make peace with your opponent before he brings you before the judge. As a guilty, penniless debtor the law will take its course, and you will be cast into prison, from which there will be no escape for you." This is the warning Jesus is giving in the concluding verses of this chapter. In this warning Jesus implies that there is a way of getting rid of the debt of sin. That way is not pointed out here, but again and again we are told that there is pardon full and complete through trustful faith in the "Lamb of God who taketh away the sin of the world." If pardon is not found before the guilty debtor is brought before the great Judge, there is no escape from the prison into which he will be cast. All payment there will be impossible.

Other portions of Scripture compel us thus to understand these two passages under consideration. Neither of them supports the idea of a purgatory or of another time of probation after death. "When the wicked man dieth, his expectation shall perish: and the hope of unjust men perisheth," Prov. 11:7. "Behold, now is the accepted time; behold, now is the day of salvation," II Cor. 6:2. In his book, *The Faith of Our Fathers,* the late Cardinal Gibbons admits that the doctrine of purgatory is only "insinuated in the New Testament." Thus Rome concedes that the two passages you refer to are poor authority for its doctrine of purgatory.

Christian Science

Will you, please, tell us something about the religion of the Christian Scientists? Many of our people, I fear, are falling for this strange cult.

Christian Science is a false religion which is neither Christian nor scientific. Its bible is *Science and Health, with a Key to the Scriptures,* by Mrs. Mary Baker G. Eddy. In practice it places this book above the inspired Word of God. The fundamental truths of Christianity this cult denies. Therefore it is a very dangerous and soul-destroying sect. It denies the Trinity, the deity of Jesus, the atoning character of His death, His resurrection, ascension, and bodily return to earth. Christian Scientists believe that at death all men enter into a better world. The mighty works of Jesus they claim were not supernatural but supremely natural. Sin and physical disease do not actually exist but are only delusions of the perverted mind. "The physical healing of Christian Science results now, as in Jesus' time, from the operation of divine Principle before which sin and disease lose their reality in human consciousness, and so disappear as naturally and as necessarily as darkness gives place to light, and sin to reformation." This is their claim. But the Psalmist said, "Blessed is he whose transgression is forgiven, whose sin is covered." And Jesus prayed: "Father, forgive them for they know not what they do," and taught us to pray: "Forgive us our trespasses, as we forgive those who trespass against us." Repeatedly Jesus said to the penitent and believing: "Go in peace, thy sins are forgiven thee." But Christian Science would have us believe that God does not forgive but annihilates sin.

Christian Science speaks a great deal about the love of God but knows nothing about His justice and His righteous indignation because of sin. The death of Christ was merely that of a noble Christian martyr, we are told. The Christian knows that his debts are canceled because Christ made full payment in his behalf. The Christian Scientists, like the modernists of our day, expect an indulgent God to cancel debt without just payment being made. The Christian knows that we have peace in our heart because the divine Prince of peace has made peace for us with God. "He is our peace," Ephesians 2:14. The Christian Scientist has a feeling of security which rests on a man-made foundation. Theirs is a peace from which there will be a terrible awakening, for it does not rest on the reconciliation made for us by the heaven-sent Peacemaker. "No man cometh unto the Father but by Me." And this "Me" is the Lamb of God which taketh away the sins of the world by the sacrifice of Himself.

The Cause of Sects

"If the papists would follow *their* Bible they would all be Protestants." If the Protestants follow *their* Bible, why are they not all Lutherans? Why so many sects?

It is sad that the church is divided into so many different factions. But, remember, it is only the visible church that is so rent into denominations of various shades of doctrinal teaching and faith. The real church is "the communion of saints" as we confess in the Apostles' Creed. That is, all true believers in Christ as man's only Redeemer and Savior form the one, holy, apostolic, catholic (universal) church. God alone infallibly knows who these people are, and how many there are. But no matter where they live or in what visible organization they hold membership, if they are truly believers in Christ Jesus, vitally united with Him like a branch in the vine, they are a part of His church and heirs of eternal glory. If they are in the wrong visible church organization, it is an error of the head and not of the heart. They want to follow God's Word, and do so to the best of their knowledge and understanding. This is certainly the sincere aim of every true Protestant.

However, to the Roman Catholic the church is not the "communion of saints," i.e., the aggregate of all true believers in Christ. The Roman Catholic thinks of the church as a visible organization, with a visible head, the bishop of Rome, known as the pope. He who does not submit to that man, says Rome, does not belong to Christ's church, he is on the way to perdition. To the Roman Catholic, Christian faith is not trust and confidence in Jesus Christ as man's only Redeemer and Savior. To him Christian faith is belief and trust in what the Roman Catholic Church teaches, whether it is in agreement with the Holy Scriptures or not.

Now, please, do not write to me and tell me I do not know what I am talking about. Before me lies the Catholic catechism by P. Jos. Deharbe, S.J. Question 15 reads: "Why must we believe Tradition as well as Holy Scripture?" Here is the answer given: "Because Catholic Tradition and Holy Scripture were alike revealed by God." The next question is: "What, then, must a Christian believe?" What answer is given? "A Christian must believe all that God has revealed and the Catholic Church teaches, whether it is contained in Holy Scripture or not." Thus the Catholic Church does not even claim that it finds all its teachings in the Bible. For example, St. Peter never claimed authority over the other apostles. He was only an "elder" on a par with the other elders (I Peter 5:1). He was not the chairman of the first conference of the apostolic church (Acts 15). Not until the Vatican Council in 1870 did the Catholic Church, by a small majority of the delegates present, decree that henceforth every member of the true and only Church of Christ on earth must confess and believe that the pope is infallible when he speaks as the head of the Church.

Thus I could go on and point out to you one important doctrine after the other which Rome does not even claim to find in the Holy Scriptures. Therefore, I reiterate the statement I have made before. If the Catholics would wholeheartedly follow *their* Bible they would all be Protestants. You will remember that at that time the emphasis was on the great difference between the Catholic and the Protestant Bible. That big difference I deny. I could accept the Catholic Bible and not have to change one important doctrine of my faith.

If all Protestants follow the Bible, why are not all Protestants Lutherans? According to my convictions all would be Lutherans if they truly, wholeheartedly accepted the Scriptures as their only norm and guide. My brother Protestant of another denomination would, of course, say: "It is my conviction that if everyone would fully and without preconceived bias accept the Scriptures, they would all be of my denomination." At any rate, we earnestly want to follow the revealed truth as found in the Scriptures, and we do not make the claim that in our church, i.e., in our denomination alone, salvation is to be found. We claim that no church can save you. It is Christ alone who saves. "I am the door: by Me if any man enter in, he shall be saved," John 10:9. "No man cometh unto the Father, but by Me," John 14:6.

If you can find Christ better and remain more faithful to Him in some certain group of people, that is where you belong. We cannot expect that infallible human beings are going to agree on all points in religion any more than in other things. However, truth is truth, and error is error. What you consider truth you cannot put on a level with what you are convinced is error. And that applies to me if I have convictions. In such important matters we should not merely have opinions but Spirit-wrought convictions. In the end the dear Lord knows them that are His, and He looketh upon the heart. We want and we insist on religious liberty. I want the right to teach and to believe as my conscience, enlightened by the Word of God, dictates to me. And I shall fight that you may have that same right.

Mohammedanism

I am bringing to you a question which was put to me by a fellow workman a few days ago. Your answer will, doubtless, be of interest to others as it will be to my friend and myself. What are some of the chief characteristics of the Mohammedan religion?

"There is no God but Allah, and Mohammed is his prophet." This is the fundamental doctrine of Mohammedanism. Mohammed was born in Mecca, Arabia, about the year 571 A.D. He married a wealthy widow. This gave him leisure for study and contemplation. The various tribes of his native country were steeped in paganism, with their numerous idols. Mohammed realized the folly of these man-made deities and came to the conviction that there is but one God, the Creator and Sustainer of all things. There were some Jews and some Christians in Mecca and its community, and it was, doubtless, from the Scriptures that he got the idea of one God and not many. He claimed to have had visions in which God or the angel Gabriel appeared to him, and that God repeatedly spoke to him in dreams. For several years no one believed him except his wife and a few near relatives and servants. Opposition against him became so bitter that his life was threatened. He fled from Mecca to Medina in the year 622 A.D. This event is known as the Hegira, and from it the Mohammedans reckon time to this day.

The inhabitants of Medina received his doctrines with great enthusiasm and in a short time began the "holy war" for the spread of Islam. Moral persuasion and an appeal to reason and conscience made few converts, but when force began to be used, and it was either suffering and very often death or Mohammedanism, converts flocked to the crescent, the standard of the new religion. By the time of Mohammed's death in 632 A.D. the whole of the Arabian Peninsula was under his sway. Under the successors of Mohammed, the Caliphs, one country after the other fell into their hands. Christianity seemed doomed. Finally, in the providence of God, Charles Martel gained a brilliant victory over the Mohammedan army at Tours in Spain. This put a stop to its progress westward. Yet for several centuries the Mohammedan power continued to be a menace to Christendom.

The Mohammedan religion is composed of pagan, Jewish, and Christian elements. Moses, Elijah, Jesus, and others were eminent prophets of God and are greatly to be revered, but, according to Islam, Mohammed is the greatest and the last of God's prophets. Although Mohammedanism cannot compare with true Christianity in purity, nobility, and loftiness it enforces a higher morality than do the old pagan religions. It abhors all worship of images. The soul of man is immortal according to its creed. Eternal bliss awaits the faithful; eternal misery the unbeliever. No atonement is necessary, for by his own good deeds, especially by prayers, fasting, alms, self-abnegation, etc., man can gain paradise, where the richest sensual pleasures are enjoyed. Mohammedans are fatalists. They believe that God has predetermined, not only man's destiny, but every important act and event in his life. This makes them bold soldiers, especially since they believe that he who falls in the defense or propagation of their religion is certain of salvation.

One of the deepest shadows in the Mohammedan religion is the degradation in which it places woman. She is not put on a level with man but is only his servant. Mohammed permitted polygamy and practiced it himself.

Pious Mohammedans are very punctual in the saying of their prayers. When they engage in the act of prayer they always face toward Mecca. Fasting is quite prevalent among them. The use of liquor is forbidden. Their day of rest is Friday, which, as a rule, is quite generally observed.

The sacred book of Mohammedanism is the Koran. It is a collection of disconnected writings by Mohammed, borrowed largely from the Hebrew Scriptures but not published until after his death. It contains some lofty precepts. It enjoins justice, honesty, truthfulness, charity, forbearance, humility, etc.

Like all false religions, Mohammedanism knows of no Savior. Salvation for it is not a gift of divine grace offered man without money and without price because of an atonement made in his behalf by the divine Redeemer. It is pure work-righteousness, salvation by law. Of sweet gospel "good tidings of great joy" it knows nothing.

3. About Festivals, Observances, Worship, and Membership

The Festival of the Ascension

Why do most Lutherans not observe Ascension Day?

It is true that Ascension Day is no longer observed among us as it was in years gone by. When I was a child, we always had church on second Christmas Day, also on Easter Monday and the day after Pentecost. Epiphany, too, was observed and Candlemas, etc. Does this mean that we have been giving way to the spirit of the world? It would seem so, but this conclusion does not necessarily follow. In those days we had time to hold our Lenten services on Friday mornings, and we would have a full confessional service on Saturday afternoon previous to the Sunday of Holy Communion. In those days we usually took a whole day off for a wedding. No one begrudged giving a half a day for a funeral and furnishing a carriage, the best he owned, together with one or two horses and a driver. But does this necessarily mean that the Lutheran people of today are less spiritual and Christlike than were those of thirty, forty, and more years ago? I hesitate to answer, for there is doubtless room here for controversy.

Let us remember that God has not bound us of New Testament time to the observance of any set days or seasons. Even the fixing of Sunday as our day of worship is not because of any direct command of God. Christmas was not observed until in the fourth century. The time for the Easter festival was not definitely set until in the year 325 A. D. The apostles centered all their preaching around the empty grave. "With great power gave the apostles witness of the resurrection of the Lord Jesus." But the church year or the custom of having set days and specified seasons for the special observance of certain events in the life of Christ was of gradual development. These customs have changed from century to century in the past and will, no doubt, continue to do so in the future.

Your letter betrays to me that you lay undue emphasis upon the outward observance of a certain specific day. If the Lord had specified a certain day for the commemoration of some specific event, it would be different.

Membership in the Church

Can a person be a Christian without being a church member?

By "church" you, of course, mean some church organization. The word "church" has various meanings. It can refer to a building. Or it may mean a congregation. You are a member of Trinity Lutheran Church of ...., ... If you say, "You belong to the Lutheran Church," it is a denomination that is referred to.

When in the Creed we confess, "I believe in the holy Christian Church," we mean "the communion of saints" as the creed specifically states. That is, we refer to the fellowship of all true believers in Christ as their personal Savior. In this sense there is only one church, the aggregate of all who stand in grace with God as His pardoned children and heirs of eternal glory. There are hypocrites in all the various church organizations of all denominations, but there are no hypocrites in the communion of saints, the real church. We can count the members of any church organization or of all of them taken together. But who knows how many wolves in sheep's clothing we are thus counting as sheep? We can deceive others, and we can be self-deceived, but we cannot deceive Him who knows all. He alone can truthfully affirm, "I know My sheep." A person may be a leader, even the very head, of a church organization and still not be a member of the holy catholic (universal) church, the communion of saints. There is no salvation apart from the real church, the communion of all the saints, for there is no salvation apart from Christ. But all those who by a trustful faith are vitally united with the God-sent Savior as a branch in the vine make up the one holy catholic (universal) church.

There is a possibility of a person's being a Christian and yet never having been connected with a visible church organization, a Christian congregation. But such a case would certainly be a rare exception, for how can an intelligent, properly informed disciple of Jesus be on intimate terms with Him and not want to be intimately associated with the rest of His disciples? A person cannot be brought to faith and sustained in true faith without some use of the Word of God as the means or channel of God's grace. True, that is possible without a formal connection with some church organization. But if all would do this, the church would soon cease to exist, for all preaching and teaching of the gospel would soon come to an end. Hence, though it is possible to be a Christian without belonging to an organized Christian church, such a case would be abnormal and exceptional.

Preparation for Church Membership

Why must non-Lutheran adults go through so much "red tape" before joining the Lutheran Church?

That is a good question, my young friend, because it is so commonly heard in connection with our church. Let us talk the whole matter over in an informal manner.

First, there is that expression you have used—"red tape." There are two kinds of "red tape," the real and the imaginary. The former kind exists within an organization which, in its effort to be systematic to the slightest detail, overdoes the thing and becomes a bureaucracy, where system, instead of being an aid to its work, becomes a hindrance. The ensuing jumble is picturesquely called "red tape" and has a right to be severely criticized and should be eliminated by reason either of ignorance, misinformation, or misunderstanding. Being a child of faulty thinking, it, too, must be eliminated, not by a change in organization (since it does not exist there), but in a change of thinking, in a dissemination of right information. The "red tape" which you speak of in connection with the process by which non-Lutheran adults unite with a Lutheran congregation belongs to this latter class. It is purely imaginary.

The Lutheran Church has always been a staunch advocate of religious education, and this "joining process" is just one form of religious education. Some pastors call it "confirmation class," some "adult instruction," others "church membership class." I prefer the name "adult study and round-table discussion group" because I feel that name describes its character best. At the meetings of such a group, time is given for real study of the vital facts of the Christian faith as revealed in God's Word and taught by the Lutheran Church. A very informal, round-table discussion follows in which every member of the group may bring forward his questions, his doubts, his fears, his perplexities, his misunderstandings. The meetings are open to Lutherans who desire to review the faith, to people who merely want to become better acquainted with the

Lutheran Church, and, of course, to those who wish to unite with the church.

Now you ask: "Why all this, particularly for those who are Christians, coming from other Christian churches, before they can join the Lutheran Church? It may be nice for those who care for it, but why make it necessary?"

In the first place, I think that a Lutheran pastor has no right to ask a non-Lutheran to join his church without first giving him the opportunity of knowing exactly what the Lutheran Church is—what it preaches, teaches, and practices, and what uniting with the church means. A minister, who in his desire to swell the membership rolls of his church rapidly, avoids the work and the time that are required in giving people this opportunity of "knowing before joining" is absolutely unfair both to the church and to its new members. Just as unfair as the insurance salesman who asks his prospective client to "sign on the dotted line" without giving him occasion to study the policy and to ask questions concerning it.

In the second place, uniting with a church is not a casual, everyday occurrence in a Christian's life. It is one of life's high points. Before God the new member makes a definite profession of faith. He is given glorious spiritual privileges by the church, and he assumes certain definite obligations toward the church. I am sure that a man would not want to go into something as important as this blindly. It is most logical to assume that he would care to join a church only on an intelligent basis.

Therein lie the fundamental reasons for a definite education in preparation for church membership. The whole matter, therefore, resolves itself to this, that the method of uniting with the Lutheran Church, instead of being a procedure of obnoxious compulsion, is in reality a glorious privilege. You see now that it is a process, which, when rightly understood, is not even akin to anything that can really be termed "red tape," but rather the only logical and fair way for non-Lutherans to enter the Lutheran Church. It closes the back door of a church through which so many noninformed and casual members slip away soon after they have joined. It prevents later misunderstandings and doubts. It makes for spiritually intelligent church members and worshipers. It fosters real loyalty and consecration to the church and the kingdom. It has also been the means of beginning some very beautiful and lasting friendships among people who have attended the study group together. Its best advertisers are the very ones who have entered the church in this, the intelligent, the fair way. If you or your friends are in doubt about the whole matter, the best advice that I can give is Jesus' continual invitation to those who in His day hesitated—"Come and see."

Why Belong to Church?

A member of no church says she is about as good as the best in the church and much better than many of them. She sees no reason why she should belong to the church. How can you meet her argument?

The apostle Paul says: "With me it is a very small thing that I should be judged of you, or of man's judgment. . . . He that judgeth me is the Lord," I Cor. 4:3, 4.

Reputation and esteem among men is not to be wholly disregarded. Paul does not say that it is nothing to him what the people may think of him, but he does affirm that it is a small matter to him to be judged of men. It is well to have "a good report of them which are without." The church member who professes to be a child of God should "let his light so shine before men that they may see his good works." The exhortation of Paul to Titus is applicable to every Christian: "In all things showing thyself a pattern of good works." It is to be deplored that many church people are so careless as to their conduct, and that the best of us still manifest so many weaknesses. Our sins give "great occasion to the enemies of the Lord to blaspheme," to make light of and even sneer at our religion. The churchman, therefore, ought to "walk circumspectly before men" and endeavor to abstain even from all appearance of evil.

But on the other hand, "who art thou that judgest another man's servant? To his own master he standeth or falleth," Romans 14:4. In judging another man's servant one is meddling in that which does not belong to him. On the judgment of his own master he will stand or fall. It ill becomes your neighbor to judge the Lord's servants. That is over-reaching her authority. God sees not as man sees. He judgeth according to truth, and His verdict is, therefore, unerring. "The Lord knoweth them that are His." It is well for the Christian that his fate does not depend on the judgment of men. He is sometimes considered and treated as the very filth of the earth. The proud, self-righteous Pharisees considered themselves far in advance in holiness of the Prophet of Galilee. For was not He a breaker of the Sabbath, a wine-bibber and gluttonous fellow, and even in league with Beelzebub? In meekness and holy awe and yet in all confidence let every Christian say: "He that judges me is the Lord."

But there is something even more serious. Those who stand aloof from the church because they think their chance of salvation is as good as that of the church people are trusting in self, in their own goodness. They expect to be able to stand before the Lord and to be acceptable to Him because of their own worthiness. In other words, they expect to be their own saviors. Every Christian knows that he has no merit of his own. His hope is not in what he has done or ever can do. His hope is in his Redeemer and Savior, to whom he has entrusted himself, and through whom he has found grace and pardon and reconciliation with God. The one is trying to be saved through the law—an impossible way. "All that the law can do is to make men conscious of sin," Romans 3:20 (Goodspeed translation). The other is finding salvation in the gospel— the only possible way, for it "is the power of God [the letter of pardon] to every one that believeth," Romans 1:16. "I am the way, the truth, and the life," affirms Jesus, "no man [that also includes your neighbor] cometh to the Father but by Me," John 14:6.

On Going to Church

Why is it that people who belong to no church are sometimes more loving, kind, and generous than people who take great interest in church work? My best neighbors, as a rule, are nonchurchgoing people.

There may be several reasons for this. You know that a friend must show himself friendly. Your letter would indicate to me that you think little of the church, perhaps are not even a member. You are, therefore, apt to be somewhat prejudiced against church people and have your more intimate friends among those of your own class. Naturally those with whom you are most intimate and chummy will, as a rule, be the first to come to your aid when you are in need. "Birds of a feather flock together." This, however, does not excuse the Christian from being kind, loving, and neighborly, and if he is a true follower of Christ he will be a good neighbor.

You naturally and rightfully expect more from a person who professes to be a Christian than from one who makes no such profession. The faults of the former loom larger than do the same faults in the latter. A small speck on a white garment is more noticeable than is a much larger blemish on a darker garment. The Christian should keep this in mind and do everything from the viewpoint of his professed standing with the Savior. But, doubtless, here we have a reason why to some people it appears that nonchurch people are sometimes more loving, kind, and generous than members of the church.

A member of the church may be generously supporting the home church, the various institutions of the church, the work of missions, etc., but if he is not as liberal in community projects as some others he is reported as being close-fisted. How easily we can thus wrong each other and condemn someone unheard, that is, report something as true when we are not at all certain about it!

However, with sorrow we are willing to admit that some church people are Christians in name only, and others are very weak Christians. It is true, alas, that some church people act like worldlings and even worse than worldlings. Their morality is beneath that of many people who make no claim of being Christians. Their home life and their everyday conduct are a disgrace, which reflects greatly on the church to which they belong. They are a hindrance to the church and a stumbling block to those who are without. Woe to them if they repent not and prove their repentance by walking in newness of life! The hypocrite shall receive the greater damnation.

Permit me to add that the more one realizes his own many, many faults, the more charitable he is in criticizing others.

Frequent Communions

Reading the history of the early church, we notice that Communion was celebrated at every service. Why is it now that three or four times a year is considered sufficient or even too often by some?

The Lord does not tell us how often we are to commune. This is left to our own enlightened conscience and feeling of need. The early church did not only commune every Sunday but met frequently during the week for worship and "breaking of bread from house to house." In connection with the Lord's Supper there was also a common meal, called the *agape* or love feast. No one was permitted to be present except the faithful. Before communing they greeted each other with the fraternal kiss. In Kurtz's *Church History* we read: "In the African and Eastern Churches John 6:53 was interpreted as applying to the Communion of children, who (of course, after baptism) were admitted to this ordinance. . . . At the close of public worship the deacons carried the consecrated elements to the sick and to the prisoners of the congregation. In some places, part of the consecrated bread was carried home and partaken in the family at morning prayers, in order thus to set apart for God a new day."

The early believers "had all things in common; and sold their possessions and goods, and parted them to all, as every man had need." But this soon proved to be impracticable and utterly impossible among sinful men. The *agape* soon led to abuses as is evident from St. Paul's sharp rebuke found in I Cor. 11. Thus we see that the early church cannot be followed in all things. Here, too, the admonition is in place: "Prove all things, hold fast that which is good."

The Lord's Supper is certainly not to be neglected. Our Lord thought it helpful and needful for His disciples to institute it. Shall we not think it helpful and needful to observe it? But, on the other hand, we believe that the Lord's Supper can be made too common. It is to be something exceptional, out of the ordinary, a high feast that we partake of only occasionally and only after prayerful preparation, penitent heart searchings, and a special study of the deep meaning of it all. There is no benefit from the mere outward act of eating and drinking.

"As often as ye eat of this bread, and drink of this cup, ye do show the Lord's death." Ye do set forth and proclaim anew, ye do forcibly remind yourselves and others again of His death; the just laying down His life for the unjust, that He might bring us to God. Will this not cheer and comfort and draw us closer to Him? Christ here deals individually with each one of His followers. Given for YOU, shed for YOU, for the remission of YOUR sins. In a special way Christ here wants to seal and to pledge to us all the blessings and benefits which are ours through His death in our behalf. To His glory and to their comfort and blessing and as a testimony to the world Christ's followers are thus again and again to set forth the Lord's death "till He come." But how often this is to be done Jesus does not prescribe, this He leaves to our love and devotion to Him and to our own feeling of need.

The Use of Hands at Communion

Would it not be better for our pastors to give the Communion wafers into the hands of the communicants for them to put into their own mouth instead of the pastor doing this at our Communion services?

I think that we are all agreed that this is a matter concerning which the Word of God gives us no specific directions. We are told that "Jesus took bread and blessed it and brake it, and gave it to the disciples, and said, Take, eat; this is My body." In what way Jesus gave the bread to them, whether into the hand or directly into the mouth of each disciple, we cannot say with certainty. Nor is it a matter of vital importance.

The Passover Supper was a family festival. The father was the officiating priest, so to speak. We have reason to believe that he dealt very intimately with all who made up his household on this festive and solemn occasion. He explained the meaning of the holy supper, he spoke the words of blessing and thanksgiving; he broke the unleavened bread and handed portions of it to each one. Did the father not dip some of his bread into the vessel containing the *chasoret* or salad, made up of various bitter herbs and fruits, before he handed it to the recipient?

If this is true, he certainly handed this "sop" directly into the mouth and not into the hand of the recipient.

In answer to John's question concerning the identity of the betrayer Jesus answered: "He it is, to whom I shall give a sop, when I have dipped it. And when He had dipped the sop He gave it to Judas Iscariot." Did Jesus give it into his hand or into his mouth? This, indeed, occurred, not at the exact moment of the instituting of the Holy Supper, but a bit earlier. But it does indicate to us that Jesus dealt most intimately with His disciples on that occasion. Yet we cannot definitely state how or in what manner it was that Jesus gave to His disciples the consecrated bread at the time He instituted the Holy Supper.

You are of the opinion that it would be "more natural and more sanitary if the pastor placed the Communion wafer into the hand of the communicant, for him to put it into his mouth himself." That, no doubt, would be more natural under ordinary circumstances. But the Lord's Supper is something quite exceptional. Our present method is certainly more impressive and indicates greater intimacy, sacredness, and dignified solemnity. I cannot see how the method you propose could possibly be more sanitary, for each wafer would then pass through two hands instead of one.

You are wondering if our custom did not grow out of the Roman Catholic transubstantiation idea. To the Romanist it is not merely sacred bread but the very body of Christ that is here touched, handled, and conveyed, something too sacred for ordinary, sinful hands. There is, indeed, a sacramental union between the bread and the body of Christ during the sacramental act, but the latter is present only in an intangible, supernatural manner and can thus not be touched and contaminated. Yet the Lord's Supper is something most sacred and holy, and it must be so treated and safeguarded in every way possible. The officiating pastor's hand is that of a sinful person, but he is the chosen servant of the church to do this work. His hand, although sinful, is the official hand of the church and should be regarded as the officiating hand of the Master.

I am still of the conviction that our method is the more beautiful, impressive, dignified, and solemn one, and that it tends to safeguard the sacredness of the holy sacrament.

The Use of Wine in Communion

Why do Lutherans use intoxicating wine in Communion?

We use wine, real fermented wine, in the Holy Supper because that was beyond question what our Savior used when He instituted the

Sacrament. The use of fermented wine in Holy Communion has been the established usage of the entire Christian Church throughout the centuries. The use of grape juice by some is of recent date and is advocated only by those who have become extremists on the liquor question. When a person advocates the use of grape juice instead of fermented wine because wine is an intoxicating drink he is finding fault with the Master, and that is no small offense.

The Roman Catholic Communion

What is the status of the Catholic layman since he does not receive the wine in the Lord's Supper? Does he receive the whole sacrament or only half of it or nothing?

The Roman Catholic Church withholds the cup from the communicants. The claim is made that, since body and blood are virtually united, when you receive the one you also receive the other. Thus when you receive the body you also receive the blood. Our dear Lord seemingly did not know that there is a natural union or concomitance between the body and the blood. He tells us that with the bread His body is imparted and together with the wine His shed blood is conveyed to the recipient. If the sacramental union between body and blood is identical with the natural union, the Lord did a needless thing in passing around the cup as well as the bread. Yet He distinctly enjoined, "Drink ye all of it," and St. Mark tells us, "And they all drank of it."

It will, perhaps, be of interest to know that the cup is denied not only to the laity but to the clergy also when they come as communicants. Only the celebrating priest partakes of the cup. When a priest receives Holy Communion privately, even on his deathbed, he receives not the cup but only the bread. On Holy Thursday, when the bishop of each diocese usually celebrates, the communing priests do not receive the cup.

How strange all this sounds to us who believe that Christ is still the ruling and reigning Head of the church! Rome admits that all the disciples drank of the cup. They did this, says Rome, because they were the special representatives of Christ and not mere lay members of the church. St. Paul and the early church must have known of no such distinction when they celebrated Holy Communion together. "Whosoever shall eat this bread and drink this cup." "But let a man examine himself and so let him eat of that bread and drink of that cup." "As often as ye eat this bread and drink this cup." Such general terms as "whosoever," "a man," "as often as ye," certainly include all without distinction.

Rome further admits that for centuries it was the common practice of the church to administer Holy Communion under both kinds, that is, to give the cup as well as the bread to each communicant. The late Cardinal Gibbons, in his book, *Faith of Our Fathers,* says that the time may come when the Church will see fit to return the cup to the people.

Come to think of it, I have not yet answered your question. Nor do I intend to give you a categorical answer. The status of the Catholic layman in respect to Holy Communion, which he receives in mutilated form, I shall leave to Him who judges the heart. Rome surely does not have the Lord's Supper which He instituted on the evening before His death. But as to the standing of the individual with his God, that we leave to Him who knows all things, and who judges righteously.

Consubstantiation

Does the Lutheran Church believe in consubstantiation?

Many people are under the impression that we teach consubstantiation, but this is not true. To consubstantiate means, "to regard as, or make to be united in one common substance, . . . to be united in substance." Consubstantiation therefore means, "the actual substantial presence and combination of the body of Christ with the bread and wine of the sacrament of the Lord's Supper, as distinguished from transubstantiation" (*Webster's International Dictionary*).

The Roman Catholic Church teaches transubstantiation. This means that, when the priest speaks the words of consecration, the bread and the wine are substantially changed into the body and the blood of Christ and consequently cease to exist as bread and wine though they appear to be and continue to have all the attributes of bread and wine. Consubstantiation, on the contrary, means that after consecration bread and wine continue to exist in their original form but are now substantially joined with the body and the blood of Christ.

We believe there is, indeed, a *sacramental union* between the consecrated bread and wine and the body and the blood of Christ, which is a very different thing from that of a *substantial* union. We teach that the bread and the wine are present in the natural way, but that the body and the blood are present in a supernatural way. Bread and wine have not been united with body and blood into a third substance different from both. The bread and the wine are swallowed and digested. The body and the blood are present only when the earthly elements are received by the communicant, and no longer. To believe that the body and the blood are received in the same manner as the bread and the wine, is known among us as the "Capernaitic error." Thus the people of Capernaum seem to have understood Jesus (John 6:52).

The Address, "Father"

How do you explain Matthew 23:9, which reads: "And call no man your father upon the earth: for one is your Father, which is in heaven"? In our family there were five children (one brother a Lutheran minister). Each and every one of us, when we addressed the head of the family, always said father.

You certainly did right in always respectfully addressing your parents as father and mother. "Honor thy father and mother." God calls our parents father and mother, and we can do no better than in due respect to address them by these dear terms.

A Scripture passage must always be studied in its connection and in the light of the rest of God's Word. If we do this with Matthew 23:9, it presents no special difficulty. Jesus was warning against the scribes and Pharisees. He accuses them of being proud and vain hypocrites who pretend to be very pious when in reality they are not. They love to be seen of men, desire their honor, and crave high-sounding titles. Moreover, they lord it over the people as though they had all authority and possessed all wisdom though they ignore God's Word and pass by the Great Teacher and Savior whom God has sent them.

In these words under consideration Christ does not forbid us to give our leaders certain official titles, much less does He want to tell us not to address the man who begot us as father. "Thy father and I have sought thee sorrowing," said Mary to her son Jesus (Luke 2:48). Abraham is respectfully referred to as "Father Abraham." We in reverence sometimes say "Father Luther" and thus also at times address aged men whom we love and revere. This is perfectly in place, and it is an evidence of good training.

Necessity compels us to have certain official names for our various leaders. Paul says: "He [Christ] gave some, apostles; and some, prophets; and some, evangelists; and some, pastors and teachers," Eph. 4:11. Here we have official names and titles. It is not these titles but the *love* of these honors and titles that Jesus brands as an offense unto Him. Seeking titles for titles' sake, self-exaltation—this is the sin Jesus refers to, and He warns that in due time these proud hypocrites shall be humbled.

What Jesus here forbids is that any teacher or pastor make himself too important, look down upon the people as beneath him, and assume an authority which sets aside our true Father, Rabbi, and Master who is in heaven. Such haughty and high-handed procedure destroys that equality which puts us all on a level under Christ as "brethren." Note that Jesus does not say: "Ye are all pupils." One may be rightfully teacher and the other pupil, but as believers in Christ they are alike children of God, and thus in the essential thing they are on a level. And he is greatest among us who in all humility most faithfully serves God and his brethren.

Why Do We Observe Lent?

Why do we Lutherans keep Lent?

We do not observe Lent because of any direct command of God. We observe no holiday because God has commanded us to do so. The Old Testament people of God were expressly enjoined to keep the Passover, the Feast of Tabernacles, and other festival days and seasons. But you will look in vain for a divine command concerning any sacred day or season in New Testament time. Why do Christians then keep Christmas, Good Friday, Easter, Pentecost, and other festivals? Why do we have an Advent season, the season of Lent, etc.? We do so in love and gratitude to our Savior and thus the better to consider and to commemorate His great deeds for our salvation.

When the apostles became convinced of the fact that Jesus had truly arisen from the grave they went forth and with great fervor and boldness preached this everywhere. "Ye killed the Prince of life," Peter told the Jews on the day of Pentecost, "whom God hath raised from the dead; whereof we are witnesses." "This is the stone which was set at nought of you builders, which is become the head of the corner. Neither is there salvation in any other: for there is none other name under heaven given among men, whereby we must be saved." "With great power gave the apostles witness of the resurrection of the Lord Jesus."

The church rests on the great truth of the resurrection. "If Christ be not raised, your faith is vain; ye are yet in your sins. Then they also which are fallen asleep in Christ are perished." All the preaching of the apostles centered around the death and the resurrection of Christ. Easter was, therefore, observed from the start. In a sense we commemorate the resurrection of Jesus every Sunday. His death was an atoning sacrifice for human guilt. He died because of our sins, "the just for the unjust, that He might bring us to God." The sufferings and the death of our Savior are of such supreme importance that the early church set aside a certain season before Easter for their special consideration and study. Gradually this season became a fixed period of forty days. And thus it has now continued for centuries.

We have no set rules or laws concerning the observance of Lent. It is a beautiful custom among many of us, however, to abstain more or less from parties and other gaieties and to deny ourselves luxuries and bodily pleasures; not because of any command of God or our church; not with the idea of thus gaining merit with God, but out of love and gratitude to our Savior, who bled and died that we might live. We give special time to study, prayer, and meditation, in private, in the family, and in the house of God. And the whole object is to honor our God and Savior, to deepen our repentance because of sin, and to strengthen our faith in Jesus as our Redeemer and Savior from sin. Devotion to our God constrains us to bring special offerings for the extension of His kingdom and for works of mercy and benevolence.

How Is Lent Determined?

How are the 40 days of Lent determined?

The custom of having a forty-day fast before Easter arose quite early in the church. However, there are forty-six days from Ash Wednesday to Easter because the six Sundays are not counted. They are strictly speaking not a part of Lent. Sunday is a day of holy joy and gladness. Sunday commemorates the resurrection of our Lord and is, therefore, a feast day rather than day of mourning and fasting.

The Proper Observance of Lent

What is a proper observance of Lent?

Our reason for observing Lent is not because God commands us to do so. It is a beautiful, old church custom, that is all. But it is a helpful and salutary custom if observed in the right manner. Its true observance, however, does not consist mainly in external things just as Christianity in general consists not in outward ceremonies. "The kingdom of God is not meat and drink," i.e., what you eat and drink, or what you pass by and leave uneaten and undrunk. Neither the one nor the other makes you a child of God, "but righteousness and peace and joy in the Holy Ghost, for he that in these things serveth Christ is acceptable to God and approved of men," Romans 14:17, 18. God wants a hungering and thirsting after righteousness, not a slavish abstinence for a few weeks from certain meats and drinks and innocent sports without a turning from sin.

The proper observance of Lent is not a matter of set rules, least of all a matter of merit. On the contrary, it consists in making the sufferings and the death of Christ a subject of special study; wholehearted turning unto God in deep repentance and love, prayer and meditation; seeking comfort and peace in the blood-bought redemption of our soul,

95

and pouring out our heart in thanksgiving to Him, who out of love unspeakable was willing to pay the price of our redemption. How easy it would be to abstain from certain worldly things for six weeks, only to gain new relish for them after a rest of forty days! God wants sincere repentance and not outward show and pretense. True spiritual worship He will have or He will have none.

Note well, however, that there is a God-acceptable fast. Read the 58th chapter of Isaiah, which describes the true fast. It is to be truly sober and temperate in all things, pure in thought, word, and deed; honest in all our dealings; kind, loving, unselfish, forgiving, patient, humble, etc., and that all out of love and gratitude to Him who first loved us.

Fasting—it is to give time and talent, loving service, and hard-earned money, and that to the point of self-denial, in the work of the Master. It is to subdue the flesh and to be led by the Spirit of God, for then only are we truly sons and daughters of God.

Come aside then, friend, drop distracting cares and pleasures, and, like Mary of Bethany, let us sit at Jesus' feet and hear what He has to tell us during this sacred season. Come, let us look upon the Master in His abject humiliation as He bears the accursed load of our guilt. Learn anew what a hideous, horrible thing is sin. Nowhere is it so plainly shown as at the foot of the cross.

Doubting soul, draw nigh; here thou canst read thy title clear. See thy Surety makes full payment for thy debt. Will eternal justice demand payment twice for the same offense? Sing and shout for joy, for thou art free. "Christ hath redeemed us from the curse of the law, being made a curse for us." Come, learn more fully the conditions on which Christ bids thee lay thy claims.

Maundy Thursday

What is the origin and the meaning of the name "Maundy Thursday"?

In connection with the ceremony of "feet washing" in the medieval church the priest would begin by saying: *Mandatum novum do vobis,* that is, "A new commandment I give unto you." This ceremony took place on the Thursday before Good Friday. Someone would be sent out on the street to gather up and bring into the church a group of beggars. Some church dignitary would get down on his knees and wash their feet. Each beggar would then be handed a little basket, called a "maund," containing a gift. These terms "maund" and "Maundy Thursday" are derived from the Latin word *mandatum,* the first word of the Latin sentence quoted above. As a rule, we now speak of the Thursday preceding Good Friday as "Holy Thursday."

Repetitious Prayer

When a person prays to God for something to take place within a week, should he repeat this prayer each day and each night, or should he pray it just once and have faith that it will come true?

If a person sincerely desires some blessing, and he wants it badly, very badly, he will certainly plead for it, and he will do so again and again. Does not the touching example of Jesus in Gethsemane come to your mind? Three times within an hour Jesus pleads on His knees with His heavenly Father, using practically the same words each time. (See Matthew 26:36–44). Why should we not do likewise?

When your pastor or anyone else says that "we should not repeat our prayer," the warning intended undoubtedly is this: Do not merely say words; do not listlessly and thoughtlessly repeat the words of some prayer and then think that you have prayed. If your heart and soul was not in that petition, you did not pray at all. You were merely taking God's holy name on your lips in vain and thus sinning against the Second Commandment. We are not merely to repeat the Lord's Prayer, we are to pray or to plead the petitions of the prayer that Jesus taught us. And thus all praying must come from the heart, or it is all sham and pretense.

Jesus indeed says: "When ye pray, use not vain repetitions, as the heathen do: for they think that they shall be heard for their much speaking," Matthew 6:7. The mere thoughtless repetition of words is what is here warned against. But humble, sincere, heartfelt prayer may and should be repeated again and again. God sometimes delays His answer in order to test us and to drive us to more earnest prayer.

Please bear in mind also that when praying for temporal things, for things that pertain to the body and this life, we are to pray conditionally as did Jesus in Gethsemane, "Not My will, Father, but Thy will be done." If it please Thee, Father, because it is for my soul's welfare, grant me this or that. But if my request is not in accord with Thy will, because Thou seest that it would not be for my eternal good, not my will, dear Father, but Thy will be done.

Kneeling in Prayer

Why do other Churches such as the Catholic, Episcopalian, and, in some instances, the Methodist, have their congregations kneel during prayers and certain chants while it does not seem customary in the Lutheran Church? Did not our Lord kneel in prayer? Do we account ourselves better than the publican in the Temple? Are we too proud, like the Pharisee at prayer in the Temple?

I say the above because in the Lutheran church of which I am a member we kneel in humble prayer before and during worship, at prayers, and during Holy Communion; yet those who are members of other churches of our synod dub us as being "too Catholic."

In Gethsemane Jesus "kneeled down and prayed." To my knowledge that is the only time it is expressly mentioned that Jesus knelt while in prayer. We are repeatedly told that "Jesus lifted up His eyes" in prayer, but otherwise we do not know what posture He would assume while communing with His Father in heaven.

You seem to be of the opinion that the publican in the Temple knelt in prayer. You are mistaken, for we are expressly told, "The publican standing afar off, would not lift up so much as his eyes unto heaven." He, indeed, took a humble position, but he did not kneel, for the ordinary custom among the Jews was to stand in prayer.

We unworthy sinners have all reason to appear before our holy God in deepest humility and reverence, even with fear and trembling, and it well becomes us often to prostrate ourselves in the dust before Him. Yet I believe in public worship we should reverently arise, bow our heads, and fold our hands. Dr. Joseph Stump, in *Bible Teachings*, says: "In the public services on the Lord's Day we stand during prayer, because it is the day of the Lord's resurrection and a day of joy."

I recall a private interview with one of my sainted professors, in which we discussed this subject. His explanation has always fully satisfied me as to the correctness of our position. Here it is. As willful sinners against our Lord and Maker we deserve naught but punishment. But we are redeemed sinners, and through the atoning blood of our Redeemer and Savior we have full reconciliation with our Father in heaven and are reinstated as sons and daughters. Through faith in Christ we again have the rights of children, and He gives us the spirit of adoption and bids us come before Him and call Him Father and in the name of Jesus boldly and confidently ask for everything we need. We come, and He certainly wants us to come, not as a cringing slave, but as an affectionate, grateful, and obedient child. That is why ordinarily in our public worship on the joyful Lord's Day we do not kneel but only respectfully stand while in prayer or while His Word is being read to us.

For this reason, too, my sainted teacher thought it most appropriate not to receive the Lord's Supper on our knees. We kneel in deep humility and with contrite hearts and broken spirits while we confess our sins unto Him and plead for mercy. But when in absolution we hear His voice as from the upper sanctuary say unto us: "Be of good cheer, thy sins are forgiven thee," we arise. And when we further hear Him say: "Lift up your hearts," there is ample reason for the custom that prevails among us, namely, that we ordinarily do not kneel for prayer. We joyfully answer: "We lift them up unto the Lord." When all is in readiness for the feast of joy and reconciliation, we appear respectfully as invited, honored guests. The merciful Savior who forgives all our sins and gives us a seal and a pledge of it in the Holy Supper, does not want us so to deport ourselves as though we doubted His loving-kindness and our complete forgiveness. It is to emphasize and to symbolize this that the custom prevails among us not to receive the Holy Supper on our knees.

Pardon me if I yet relate the illustration which my teacher used in this connection. When the Prodigal Son returned he, no doubt, confessed his sins before his father on his knees. But the father lovingly raised him up and embraced him and bade him say no more about it. New garments were put upon him, the garments not of a hired servant but of a son; the fatted calf was ordered killed, work was suspended and a holiday declared. When all was in readiness and the happy household gathered around the feast, would the father have looked upon it with favor if the pardoned and reinstated son would have partaken of it on his knees while the rest joyfully sat or reclined at the table? Such conduct on the part of the son, though ever so well meant, would have been a reflection on the goodness of the father. He had been fully and completely forgiven, and his status and standing with the father was that of a child.

Prayer Meetings

Why do we Lutherans not have prayer services sometime during the week?

We Lutherans, as a rule, never did go in strong for the so-called midweek prayer meetings. We certainly do not want to belittle the need and the efficacy of earnest, believing prayer. But we do not only want to speak to God, we also want Him to speak to us. And this latter part, we fear, was usually neglected, or at least given minor attention, at prayer meetings. While prayer and the giving of personal testimony were emphasized, the study of God's Word was usually considered as of minor importance.

A weekly service for the study of the Word of God under the leadership of the pastor together with prayer and praise would certainly be helpful. Such a service could be held on Sunday evenings or on some evening of the week. At our Luther League meetings as well as at the meetings of other organizations of the church we certainly try to have a period of real worship that includes study of some Bible truth or important topic concerning Christian life and work. Thus at least some of us have special gatherings for prayer and study in addition to our regular Sunday morning worship.

Street Preaching

In our town a group of Christians of another denomination have of late been having street preaching. They usually have it on Saturday evening when the stores are open, and more people than usual are on the streets. They have fine musicians and good singing, and the pastor has a brief sermon. We discussed this in our Sunday school class. Will you, please, give us your opinion of street preaching?

It is certainly not wrong to proclaim the sweet gospel on the street corner or wherever we have a chance to do so. Jesus was willing to preach and to teach wherever He found listeners. When you think of great sermons, the Sermon on the Mount at once comes to your mind or Jesus' sermon from Peter's boat to the people sitting on the seashore. Where did John the Baptist do all his preaching? We do not know that he even once preached in Temple or synagogue. Jonah brought the wicked city of Nineveh to repentance and thus by God's grace saved the city by street preaching.

We are glad that we have beautiful and attractive church buildings, but no matter how inviting we make them, there are some people whom we cannot get to come to church. Cannot, perhaps, some of these be won if we take the gospel to them wherever they may be? I think there should be more open-air preaching where people are prone to congregate: in the city parks, especially on a beautiful Sunday evening; at the factories while the workmen are resting over the noon hour, if permission is given. Of course, all should be done with becoming dignity, reverence, and respect. Our missionaries in foreign lands build churches and use them as soon as it is possible for them to do so, but they would not think of giving up their street preaching or their teaching individuals whenever or wherever possible. Why should not we follow the same plan? We do not like the method that some emotional people use, but we should do well to emulate their zeal and go out seeking the lost and straying sheep. "Go out into the highways and hedges, and compel them to come in, that my house may be filled," Luke 14:23. Beyond a doubt we lack real missionary zeal.

By the way, do we make sufficient use of the printed page? How many suitable gospel tracts do *you* hand out in a year? Would it not be well for each one of us to form the habit of carrying some concise, well-written tracts on our person so that we have a gospel message to hand to a friend or stranger as the opportunity presents itself? Kindly ask him to give it due attention at his leisure and then in thought pray God not to permit His Word to return unto Him void. Do you ever think of putting a tract in the letters you write?

Preaching by Women

If it is quite fitting and proper for a woman to give her time, energy, money, and even her life for the sake of the gospel, why should she not be permitted to preach from the pulpit? I think it is very unfair because I would like to be a minister of the gospel. I do not see why we should let St. Paul make all the rules for the Christian Church. I think he is very inconsistent, for he says: "There is neither Jew nor Greek, there is neither bond nor free, there is neither male nor female: for ye are all one in Jesus Christ." And then he says that women are to keep silent in church.

Please do not think that we are permitting the man Paul to make all the rules in the Christian Church, for in his epistles he writes by inspiration, and thus it is God who is speaking to us through His apostle. "Paul an apostle—not from men nor through man, but through Jesus Christ and God the Father, who raised Him from the dead," Galatians 1:1, R.S.V. "All Scripture is given by inspiration of God," II Timothy 3:16.

I cannot help it that God saw fit to make you a woman and not a man. I am sorry if you are dissatisfied with your lot as "a helpmeet," instead of some man being your helpmeet. When Jesus sent out His apostles as His first public "ambassadors" (II Corinthians 5:20) they were all men; when He sent out "other seventy," as St. Luke tells us in the tenth chapter of his Gospel, there was no Mary among them though some Marys of that day were very devoted followers of the Master, and their work was deeply appreciated and very helpful.

The apostle gave orders to Titus that he "ordain elders in every city." He was to exercise care in the choice of these leaders in the several churches. "If any be blameless, the husband of one wife," etc., Titus 1:

5–7. Whenever you are "the husband of one wife, vigilant, sober, of good behavior," etc., you have some of the requisites of "a bishop" (I Tim. 3:1, 2).

Revival Meetings

Why is it that the Lutheran Church does not have revival meetings, prayer meetings, and "Youth for Christ" rallies?

To revive a church is to re-awaken a dead church. At any rate, this is what the word revival means. You can revive only a thing that at one time had life, was permitted to languish and die, and is then again restored to life. How much better to keep a church vigorously alive at all times! This is what we should seriously, prayerfully aim to do.

Why do we object to the so-called revival method? It rests on a false conception of the work of the Holy Spirit. We know that by nature man is "dead in trespasses and sins." He therefore "must be born again." Only the Spirit of God can give man this needful rebirth. He does so only through the means of grace, the Word and the sacraments. Where the Word of God is being proclaimed, read, or meditated upon, the divine Spirit is at work, inviting and urging men to accept and to depend upon Christ Jesus as their only Savior. The Spirit is trying further to enlighten, sanctify, strengthen, and preserve each individual in union with Jesus Christ in the one true faith. The revival method seems to rest on the idea that the Holy Spirit is not effectively present in the regular and ordinary services Sunday after Sunday. For conversion there must be something extraordinary. Does the Holy Spirit come to us only at certain intervals? Jesus promised that the Comforter, even the Spirit of truth, was to *abide* with us (John 14:18). Because of the weaknesses and the faults of even the best of us "times of refreshing" are helpful and even needful. We should then individually and collectively give ourselves more earnestly to prayer, to the fervent use of Word and Sacrament, and spend more time and put forth more effort by precept and example to win souls for Christ and the church. Such a "revival," if you want to call it by this name, is always in place. But this is not a shouting, exciting, high-pressure method, playing on the emotions of people until some of them are in a state of frenzy.

Because the revival system is more or less indifferent to sound doctrine and to careful, proper instruction and depends mainly on stirring up the emotions, the revivalist pays little attention to teaching. He stresses soul-rending appeals and exhortations. He tells startling experiences and touching stories which are intended to make the tenderhearted weep and the hardhearted tremble. The audience is urged to sing emotional songs with stirring music, and to sing them over and over while the evangelist is shouting to the unconverted to surrender and to come forward, and the brethren are urged to go and speak to some unconverted person. All is intended to stir up the emotions, to affect the nervous system, and bring about strange sensations. Then when the feelings are aroused to the highest pitch, and excitement reigns, frantic appeals are made to come and kneel at the "mourners' bench." This is supposed to be the true and only way of real conversion. This is "getting religion," the "old-fashioned religion," and he who has not come to Christ and into the church in this way has, in their estimation, reason to doubt that he is a reborn man. Truly, we cannot conceive of the meek and lowly Jesus or His disciples conducting a modern revival service. "Let all things be done decently and in order," exhorts St. Paul.

We believe we have a better method, and that is carefully, prayerfully to instruct the person whom we are endeavoring to lead to Christ and to bring into the church. This should, of course, be done, not in a cold, professional way, but in the spirit of the Master, by a truly consecrated servant of His. We should remember that we are dealing with blood-bought souls, and that we teach and influence more by what we are and do than by what we say. We must insist on true conversion and stress the fact that a reborn man walks in newness of life. He loves the habitation of God's house and the place where His honor dwelleth. He diligently makes use of the means of grace to nourish and to strengthen his faith. He takes an active part in the work of the church, earnestly endeavors to walk in the footsteps of the Master, and to grow in Christian virtues.

We too, alas, have those who prove to be unfaithful and make shipwreck of their faith. But we are convinced that we have not as many "backsliders" as have those who depend on the modern revival method. We are willing to admit that the shouting revivalist will be able to win some for Christ whom we seemingly cannot touch. God, in His goodness, can and does overrule our weaknesses and many shortcomings and in spite of them enables us by His grace to do at least some effective work in the upbuilding of His kingdom. But, surely, we should endeavor to use the wisest and the most efficient method, the method of Christ and the apostles, and that method we are convinced we have. If God could only move us all to use our method with greater diligence, zeal, and consecration, what progress we should have to report!

As to prayer meetings, they have never been very popular among Lutherans. You are wondering why. If they are properly conducted such meetings would doubtless be of great benefit. The greater part of such gatherings should be devoted to Bible study. Prayer should not be monologue but dialogue. We must permit God to speak to us, and not only we to Him. To listen to Him and to sit at His feet are of first importance. The Word of God is the channel of divine grace and of all spiritual blessings. We ask for these blessings in prayer, and we return thanks and praise His holy name in grateful prayer. Fervent prayer and the diligent, devout study of God's Word must go together, properly proportioned. In the usual so-called prayer meeting this is not done. There is too much emphasis on what man does and not enough on what the Lord must do. This, in my opinion, is the main reason why the prayer meeting was never looked upon with great favor among us.

Have you ever attended any of our youth Bible camps? Have you ever attended any of the state or international Luther League conventions? Have you any firsthand knowledge as to what is done at our youth and leadership training schools, our church workers' institutes, etc.? You would be agreeably surprised, and you would know that we have youth for Christ rallies of our own.

On Welcoming Visitors

Several persons have complained to me at various times about the unwelcome attitude Lutherans seem to show toward strangers who visit their services. Is there something to this? If so, why is it?

Of many of our people, I fear, this accusation is true, but I do not think that it is as pronounced as in years gone by. Most of our parents or grandparents came from the old country. There they were accustomed to state churches, i.e., the state supported the church, and every one in a certain community was reckoned as a member of that parish. They were not accustomed to the competition which here exists between the various denominations. The language question, no doubt, also played a part in this apparent coldness and aloofness of our people in the affairs of religion. We are also very adverse to proselytism, i.e., to attempt to win people from some other church. Therefore we do not want to leave the impression that we are trying to lure them away from their own church. Then, too, our attitude toward the church is different from that of many people. To us it is a sacred place, the house of God, set aside and dedicated for holy purposes only. All unnecessary and promiscuous talking and visiting in the Lord's house we consider as out of place.

This, however, is not to say that we are to be cold and indifferent toward visitors at our services. We should greet them with a friendly handshake, welcome them at the door, and usher them to a good seat. They should also be supplied with a hymnal and thus encouraged to enter heartily into the worship. At the close of the service at least several of the members should express appreciation of their presence and ask them to come again. Every congregation should have at least several friendly and tactful ushers, one of whom is always at the door to welcome and to be of assistance to strangers and visitors. It should be done with grace and warmth but also with becoming dignity.

The Sunday Offering

Does I Cor. 16:1, 2 justify the present-day Sunday morning offering?

The Christians in Jerusalem and, perhaps, in other parts of Palestine were in deep financial distress. This was, no doubt, caused by persecution and famine. Paul was very anxious that the Christian brethren of Asia Minor and Europe come to their rescue. In the verses referred to above he tells the Corinthians that he had already given instructions to the churches of Galatia as to how to proceed with the raising of these funds. This important matter must have been brought to the attention of the Corinthian Christians before this epistle was sent to them. They knew of the offering to be raised as well as of the method which Paul had given to the Galatian churches for the raising of the money. The apostle asks the Corinthian congregation to follow the same method. This method is now stated: "Upon the first day of the week let every one of you lay by him in store, as God hath prospered him, that there be no gatherings when I come." Each member is to lay aside Sunday after Sunday a gift for this purpose. The size of the gift is to be in proportion to his ability to give, "as God has prospered him." These weekly gifts, it would seem, were not brought along to church and deposited in the church treasury each Sunday, but each member was to keep this growing fund in his own possession until the time of Paul's arrival in their midst. Then all the saved-up funds of each individual would be put together. A properly elected and approved committee should then take their "liberality" to Jerusalem. Or if it seemed more suitable to them that Paul, too, should go to Jerusalem, this approved committee of the congregation should accompany him.

From these apostolic instructions we may rightfully draw the following inferences: 1. Each one is to give: "Let every one." 2. He is to give regularly: "Upon the first day of the week." 3. He is to give according to his ability to give: "As God hath prospered him." In other words, our giving is to be *individually, systematically,* and *proportionately.*

Every thing belongs to God. We ourselves belong to Him. We shall have to give an account to Him as to how we use our time and our talents. We are accountable to God as to how we make our money, and as to how we use it. We are His stewards. In fact, all of life is a stewardship. God wants us to realize and acknowledge our stewardship. When God asks us to give, it is not because He is in need—foolish the thought—it is for our good, for the exercise of our faith. It is to keep us from becoming self-centered. It is God's antidote for human selfishness. It is God's way of honoring us and making us fellow workmen with Him in the upbuilding of His kingdom. Therefore He asks us to give cheerfully and liberally and assures us that it is more blessed to give than to receive. Love cannot help but give. To love is to be Godlike. "God so loved . . . that He gave."

To give to God of our time, our efforts, or our earthly means is a service, an act of worship. We worship Him "with hearts and hands and voices" as we sing in one of our hymns. "Bring an offering and come into His courts," Psalm 96:8. "Bring an offering and come before Him: worship the Lord in the beauty of holiness," I Chron. 16:29. "Jesus sat over against the treasury, and beheld how the people cast money into the treasury," Mark 12:41. God's Word lays down certain fundamental principles as to giving. It is to be a freewill offering prompted by love, our loving attitude and relationship to God. Each loving and consecrated child of God will certainly want to give, and do so regularly and liberally. But whether he drops his gift into the offering plate each Sunday, or deposits it in a treasury chest when he enters or leaves the house of God, or whether he lays it by regularly to be handed in as needed, this is left to circumstances. But "let all things be done decently and in order." Each one will cheerfully want to conform to the rules and customs of his church as long as these are not directly contrary to the express will of God.

On the Covering of Women's Heads

Should women appear in church with uncovered heads?

In apostolic times it was the common usage that women appear in the public assemblies and join in public worship, veiled. They not only wore some kind of head covering, but their faces, too, were veiled. Now if we interpret St. Paul (I Cor. 11) as laying down a rule which is to obtain for all nations and in all ages we shall have to insist that women appear in church, not only with some kind of covering on their heads, but also with their faces veiled. Moreover, we shall then not dare permit male graduates or men of some academic degree to appear before the altar and take part in a divine service with a covering on their heads.

We believe that St. Paul is giving this rule for the Christians of his time only because modest and decent women in that age always appeared in public veiled. The apostle is simply laying down the general principle that in the house of God all things "be done decently and in order," and that this also includes proper regard for good and approved social customs of the day and country in which we live.

In Oriental countries women do not appear in public uncovered. In Paul's day only women of loose morals would do so. Paul warns the Christian women of Corinth not to appear in the public assemblies of the congregation uncovered lest this bring them under suspicion. That which was a disgrace in Corinth because of the custom of that time is not necessarily a disgrace in our day and country. Yet it is a time-honored custom among us for women to appear in church with their heads covered. We must not give offense, hence it is best if we depart not from this custom.

It is not a sin for a woman to be in Sunday school or the church service without a head covering, but under present prevailing customs I believe that, as a rule, it would be inexpedient.

I would advise you to respect the time-honored custom of your mother and of our church in general. But happy is the man that does not make that a matter of conscience which is not forbidden.

The Use of Musical Instruments

My milkman thinks it is wrong to use musical instruments in connection with Christian worship. He claims that the New Testament says nothing about musical instruments. How would you answer him?

We read nothing about radio, television, or motion pictures in the Word of God, so, I suppose, these newfangled things are taboo when it comes to using them in the work of the church. What strange ideas some people have when it comes to Bible interpretation! Permit me in this connection to point out a fundamental principle on which we differ from many Bible interpreters. We hold to the principle, "All that is not forbidden in the Bible is a matter of Christian liberty." Others say, "All that is not commanded is forbidden." Keeping this in mind, you can see why with a good conscience we can permit ourselves many liberties which many other well-meaning Christian people must deny themselves. They feel themselves hedged in by many restrictions of which we know nothing. I believe we may say, they think of themselves as servants while we know ourselves as children. They still serve under the law and are constrained by law; we are under grace and are motivated by gratitude and love (Romans 6:14; Galatians 5:18).

It is not altogether true when the claim is made that we read nothing about musical instruments in the New Testament. In I Corinthians 14:7 St. Paul mentions *pipe* and *harp,* and in the next verse he tells us something about the *trumpet.* 'Tis true, they are not mentioned as being used in worship, but St. John was given a vision of the blessed in heaven in which he "heard the voice of harpers harping with their harps," Revelation 14:2. Was their worship not spiritual because they used harps in connection with it?

The "Sweet Singer of Israel," King David, was a skilled harpist, and he and others surely used this instrument extensively in worship. "Praise the Lord with harp; sing unto Him with the psaltery and an instrument of ten strings," Psalm 33:2. "Upon the harp will I praise Thee, O God, my God," Psalm 43:4. "Praise Him with the sound of the trumpet: praise Him with the psaltery and harp. Praise Him with the timbrel and dance: praise Him with stringed instruments and organs," Psalm 150:3, 4. Why should such worship be acceptable to God in Old Testament time and in heaven but not on earth in our day? Sweet music is soothing and quieting, it is inspiring and edifying. When the evil spirit of melancholy came upon King Saul, he would send for David, who played for him on his harp. "So Saul was refreshed and was well, and the evil spirit departed from him," I Samuel 16:23. Many a soul has been drawn heavenward by angelic music. Music has played an important part in the service of God from time immemorial.

Since music was used in the worship of God in all ages and is commended again and again throughout the Old Testament, Christ and the apostles would certainly have directly forbidden it in connection with worship were it displeasing to God.

The Apostles' Creed

Who wrote the Apostles' Creed?

The Roman Catholic Church teaches that the Apostles' Creed was written by the apostles, and that each one composed a certain portion of it. This claim is not sustained by history. The exact wording of the creed as we have it today, no doubt, was of gradual formation. In all probability some brief, simple formula of faith existed from the beginning. But the exact form as we have it today cannot be traced back farther than the fifth or possibly the fourth century.

Thus we do not know who wrote this confession of faith known to us as the Apostles' Creed. It was obviously not written by one man, nor by a group of men assembled for that purpose. The wording of the creed as we have it today was in all probability compiled from the various brief statements of faith in use among the apostles and early Christians.

The Apostles' Creed is so called, not because it was written by the apostles, but because "it is a summary of the articles of Christian faith as taught by the apostles."

The Nicene Creed

When and where and by whom was the Nicene Creed written, and why is it only occasionally used in our services? Also would like to be informed as to the Athanasian Creed.

Early in the fourth century Arius, a presbyter of Alexandria, gained quite a following for his erroneous views concerning Christ. He taught that the Son did not exist from all eternity, but that before the commencement of time He was created out of nothing by the will of the Father in order that the world might be called into existence through Him. Since the Son was the most perfect image of the Father and had carried into execution the divine purpose of creation, Arius did not object to referring to the Son as God, but not in the full and proper sense of that term.

To settle this controversy Emperor Constantine summoned a General Council at Nicea in Bithynia, Asia Minor, in 325 A.D. Mainly through the enthusiastic eloquence of the youthful Deacon Athanasius and the influence of the emperor the error of Arius was condemned, and he was deposed from office and excommunicated. It was this council that adopted the Nicene Creed. However, this brought about no peace. For many years the Arian controversy vexed the church. The wording of the original confession of faith as adopted at Nicea in 325 was considerably changed in later years. It was at the Council at Chalcedon in 451 that the Nicene Creed in its present form (with the exception of one word) was accepted as the orthodox teaching of the Christian Church.

The Lutheran Church regards the Nicene Creed as fundamental for its theology. But as a part of the liturgical service it is used, as a rule, only when the Holy Communion is celebrated and on certain special and high festival days.

During the post-Nicene era (the fourth to the seventh century) there were many bitter controversies concerning the doctrine of the Trinity. In time a confession of faith was formulated which was gradually accepted as a brief but comprehensive statement of the orthodox faith of the church on this subject. This confession of faith is known to us as the Athanasian Creed. While this creed has its name from Athanasius, the bishop of Alexandria, who is sometimes called the "Father of Orthodoxy," it seems certain that he was not the author of it. Just who the writer was or when it was written is not known. Our church accepts this creed as the third of the general creeds of the Christian Church but has never used it for liturgical purposes except perhaps on Trinity Sunday.

The Assumption of Mary

We have been informed that the pope recently has officially proclaimed the assumption of Mary as a dogma of the Roman Catholic Church. Now if it is a historic fact that Mary was bodily taken to heaven a few days after her death, why did not the infallible popes of bygone days know about this? If the assumption of Mary is a historic fact, it has been true all through the centuries since it took place about 1,900 years ago. Has some ancient relic or historic document recently been found that has brought to light this marvellous event? It seems strange to me that so important an event in the life of the mother of our Savior should have taken place, and that neither sacred nor profane history of the early centuries should tell us a thing about it. What brought this alleged historic fact recently to light?

To my knowledge there has been no ancient relic or historic document recently discovered which would in any way cast new light on the history of Mary, the mother of Jesus. Rome needs nothing like that in order to discover a new "truth," which in time is officially declared a dogma of the Roman Catholic Church, and which must be accepted as truth by the faithful on pain of excommunication.

The church historian John Henry Kurtz says: "The worship of Mary arose at a period subsequent to that of the martyrs, and chiefly in connection with the Nestorian controversy. [This controversy raged in the fifth century.] . . . But through the victory of the doctrine that Mary was the mother of God, in the Nestorian controversy, Mariolatry became again more general in the Church." He then tells us of certain feasts that were instituted and celebrated in honor of certain events in the life of Mary. Among them was the feast "of the Ascension of Mary." This feast later came to be known as "The Assumption of Mary." It was introduced at the close of the sixth century and has since been celebrated on August 15. This assumption of Mary into heaven "was founded on a legend—first broached by Gregory of Tours, (ob. 595)—to the effect that immediately on her decease, angels had raised the 'Mother of God' and carried her to heaven."

Of a later period the same historian says: "Another ceremonial in connection with the growing reverence paid to the Virgin was the feast

110

of the Immaculate Conception, on the 8th of December, which was introduced in the twelfth century. . . . St. Bernard protested equally against this doctrine and festival, and Bonaventura and Thomas Aquinas were also opposed to it. From the time of Duns Scotus the Franciscans, however, again contended for this doctrine, which only induced the Dominicans to oppose it all the more energetically. Still the festival, at least, was pretty generally observed during the thirteenth century; and in 1389 Clement VII sanctioned it as one of the regular feasts of the Church."

The idea of the immaculate conception of Mary grew in favor throughout the Church of Rome. Finally the time came when the pope felt safe in declaring the immaculate conception of Mary as a sanctioned dogma of the Roman Catholic Church. This official declaration was made on December 8, 1854. Thus since that date the faithful must believe that Mary was conceived and born without the slightest taint of sin. Now Rome is ready to go a step farther. After November 1, 1950, anyone who denies that Mary was raised and her body carried to heaven a few days after her death has an official curse pronounced upon him by the Church of Rome.

I hope that I have given you some idea how "never-changing Rome" does change and adds one strange doctrine after the other to that growing list of which the apostles and the early church knew nothing.

Death of Mary

Do we know anything definite about the latter years and the death of the Virgin Mary?

We do not. The last definite information we have of the mother of Jesus is found in Acts 1:14, where we read: "These all continued with one accord in prayer and supplication, with the women, and Mary the mother of Jesus, and with His brethren." This refers to the day on which Jesus ascended into heaven. Mary was with the apostles and others as they were assembled in the "upper room" in Jerusalem after witnessing the glorious home-going of the Master from Mt. Olivet.

From the cross the dying Jesus commended His mother to the care of His beloved apostle John. "And from that hour that disciple took her unto his own home." John must have continued to make Jerusalem his headquarters for some time after the outpouring of the Holy Spirit on Pentecost because St. Paul meets him there several years later (Galatians 2:9). Of the various churches founded by the great St. Paul and his helpers none was of greater importance than the church at Ephesus. After the days of Paul, John seems to have become the pastor of this church. If Mary was still living when John took up his abode at Ephesus, he, of course, took Mary with him to that city. The following I quote from *The Popular and Critical Bible Encyclopedia:*

"The traditions concerning the death of Mary differ materially from each other. There is a letter of the General Council of Ephesus in the fifth century, which states that she lived at Ephesus with St. John, and there died and was buried. Another epistle of the same age says she died at Jerusalem, and was buried in Gethsemane. The legend tells that three days after her interment, when the grave was opened (that Thomas the apostle might pay reverence to her remains), her body was not to be found, 'but only an exceeding fragrance,' whereupon it was concluded that it had been taken up to heaven. The translation of Enoch and Elijah, and the ascension of the Lord Jesus Christ, took place while they were *alive,* and the facts are recorded by the inspiration of God; but when the *dead* body of Mary was conveyed through the earth, and removed thence there were *no witnesses,* and no revelation was ever made of the extraordinary and novel incident, which certainly has no parallel in Scripture. This miraculous event is appropriately called 'the Assumption.'"

However, the Church of Rome must accept this legend as true as the translation of Mary is annually commemorated on the fifteenth day of August. We are not surprised at this since Rome believes and teaches many things about Mary which are not only without any authority in Scripture and authentic history but are directly opposed to both Scripture and dependable history.

The Ave Maria

Will you, please, give us the derivation of the familiar prayer used so frequently by our Catholic neighbors, known as "Ave Maria" or "Hail Mary"?

This prayer is also known as "The Angelical Salutation." It consists of three parts: 1) The salutation of the angel Gabriel to Mary: "Hail [Mary], full of grace, the Lord is with thee, blessed art thou among women." (Thus the Catholic Bible translates Luke 1:28.) 2) The words of Elizabeth to Mary: "And blessed is the fruit of thy womb," that is, Jesus. 3) An addition made by the church, "Holy Mary, Mother of God, pray for us sinners now and at the hour of our death. Amen."

The Roman Catholic catechism divides the prayer into two parts: "A prayer of praise" and "a prayer of petition." The prayer of praise is composed of "the words of the Archangel Gabriel" and "the words of St. Elizabeth." "The prayer of petition is composed of the words added by the Church." To the question: "Why were those words added by the

Church?" the answer is given: "These words were added by the Church, to implore the intercession of the Blessed Virgin in all our necessities, and to obtain through her the special grace of a happy death."

"Call upon Me in the day of trouble," is the injunction of our heavenly Father in Psalm 50:15. "As for me, I will call upon God; and the Lord shall hear me," Psalm 55:16. "O Thou that hearest prayer, unto Thee shall all flesh come," Psalm 65:2. "There is one God and *one mediator* between God and men, the *man Christ Jesus*," I Timothy 2:5. Why does the *model prayer* ("After this manner therefore pray ye," Matthew 6:9) not contain at least a word or two of praise and petition to Mary if that is so important? What an oversight on the part of Jesus!

"The whole Ave Maria, as it now stands, is ordered in the breviary of Pius V (1568) to be used daily before each canonical hour and after compline, i.e., the last of the seven canonical hours" (*The Popular and Critical Bible Encyclopedia*).

Other Children of Mary

Did the virgin Mary have other children born to her after the birth of Jesus? I had always thought that Jesus was her only child, but recently my attention was drawn to Mark 6:3 in proof that Jesus had brothers and sisters. What is your answer to this?

We read repeatedly of "His (Jesus') brethren" and "His sisters." See, for instance, Matthew 12:46–50; 13:55, 56; Mark 3:31–35; 6:3; John 2:12; 7:1–10; Acts 1:13, 14; Galatians 1:19. Who were these "brethren"? It cannot be definitely proven who they were. Three suppositions have been advanced. 1. Some hold that they were the children of Joseph by a former marriage. If this is true, Joseph was a widower with at least six children when he became the husband of Mary. 2. Others hold that they were the children of Joseph and Mary born to them after the birth of Mary's supernatural child, Jesus. 3. Still others believe that they were the orphaned children of a brother or sister of either Joseph or Mary, and that the holy couple opened their home to them and reared them to maturity. If this is correct, they were in reality cousins of Jesus but were referred to as brothers and sisters as they were reared, at least in part, in the same family circle.

The first of these three suppositions seems the least likely to me though it is the position taken by the Greek Catholic Church. The Roman Catholic Church insists on the third supposition. It could not well do otherwise since it lays so much stress on "Mary, ever Virgin." I believe that present-day Protestant commentators incline more and more to the view that these brothers and sisters were the children of Joseph and Mary, conceived and born in the regular course of nature after the birth of Mary's supernatural child, Jesus.

We have no reason whatever to believe that Joseph and Mary did not live together naturally as husband and wife after the birth of Jesus, Mary's "first-born" son (Luke 2:7). Why refer to Him as the "first-born" if there were no other children born to her? Matthew tells us: "When Joseph woke from sleep he did as the angel of the Lord commanded him; he took his wife, but knew her not until she had borne a son," Matthew 1:24, 25. RSV. This implies that Joseph lived with Mary, his lawful wife, in the usual and natural way after the birth of Jesus. If we accept this view as correct, what is there to prevent Joseph and Mary having had children born to them in the natural way, the same as other couples? By taking this view we are not forced to interpret "brother" and "sister" as in reality meaning "cousin." That Jesus had brothers and sisters who were the children of Mary is doubtless the one explanation which an unforced explanation of the language requires.

But if Mary had other sons and daughters, how can we account for it that Jesus commended His widowed mother to the care of St. John? My answer would be: A true spiritual son was nearer to Jesus and more dependable than a blood relative who was an unbeliever. At that time these "brethren" did not believe in Jesus as the Messiah (John 7:5). On the contrary, they thought Jesus was quite beside Himself in His claims, and that He was endangering His safety. Study carefully Mark 3:20, 21; Matthew 12:46, 50; Luke 8:19–21. We are happy to learn that these brethren later came to faith in Jesus as the world's Redeemer.

Prayer to Mary

Does prayer to Mary constitute worship?

It certainly does. Roman Catholics, indeed, deny this. They claim that they venerate Mary, but that they always remember that she is a creature and, therefore, do not worship her. The homage paid to saints and angels they call by the Greek word *douleia*, i. e., "service." To the worship paid to the Triune God they assign the name *latreia*, also meaning "service." For the veneration due the Virgin they appropriate the newly coined word *hyperdouleia*, implying a service above the service called *douleia*. This distinction between *douleia* and *latreia* is absolutely groundless, for the two words are used interchangeably in the Greek New Testament as well as in the Greek translation of the Old Testament. And such a word as *hyperdouleia* Scripture does not know.

He who prays to Mary deifies her. The invocation of Mary necessarily implies her omniscience and her omnipresence. How can Mary hear the millions of prayers addressed to her throughout the world, in hundreds of different languages, and in thought as well as in word, without being all-knowing and everywhere present? Or shall we believe that God Himself, hearing the prayer addressed to Mary, communicates a knowledge of it to her and then receives back from her the prayer of the human petitioner?

He who prays is giving to her the honor, the homage, and the service that belong to God alone. And the same is true of the invocation of any of the saints. "Doubtless Thou art our Father, though Abraham is ignorant of us, and Israel acknowledges us not; Thou, O Lord, art our Father, our Redeemer; Thy name is from everlasting," Isa. 63:16. This passage plainly tells us that the departed are ignorant of the doings of the living on earth. Abraham knew nothing about his descendants in Isaiah's day, and neither did Israel, i.e., Jacob. They were at rest and no more worried with the affairs of this world. And the same is true of Mary and of all the blessed. We come to God with our troubles, our prayers, and our praises. He is our Father, our Redeemer; His name is from everlasting, He abideth forever.

The Virgin Mary

If Mary the Virgin was born in sin, how could she give birth to a Son who was sinless (granted that His Father was God)? Wouldn't that make Him sinful or at least partly sinful? For is not original sin handed down?

A neighbor of the Roman Catholic faith once said to me, "If the Virgin Mary gave birth to an immaculate Child she must have been immaculate herself." If this were true, then also the mother of the Virgin must have been immaculate, for how could Mary's mother give birth to a sinless daughter without being absolutely untainted by sin herself? Do you see what trouble we get into when we believe that the Virgin Mary was immaculate?

Mary, of course, had a human father as well as a human mother. She was conceived according to the natural laws of human nature, the same as all the rest of us. With David and with all of humanity she, too, had to admit, "Behold, I was shapen in iniquity, and in sin did my mother conceive me," Psalm 51:5. "As by one man [Adam] sin entered into the world and death by sin, and so death passed upon all men," Romans 5:12.

Sin does, indeed, pass from parent to child. It is "handed down" as you express it. But the transfer appears to be through natural conception. "In sin did my mother *conceive* me," Psalm 51:5. The personality of

Jesus did not come from Mary. The divine Son did not assume a human personality but only a human nature. It is His deity that imparts His personality. And while the second person of the Trinity assumed human nature in the body of the virgin and thus became our Brother, it was the perfect, untainted humanity that Adam and Eve had before the fall.

We cannot understand or explain this mystery. But we do know that the "Word," as John repeatedly calls the second person of the Trinity, "was made flesh, and dwelt among us" (see John 1:1–3, 14). The only-begotten Son of God assumed human nature. He became "incarnate by the Holy Ghost of the Virgin Mary, and was made man" (Nicene Creed).

The Virgin Birth

What is the Virgin Birth, and why is it important?

Jesus had a human mother but not a human father. He was born in the natural way, but His conception was supernatural. According to the laws of nature a woman must have the aid of a man in order to become a mother. She must have a father for her children or she remains childless. God created us male and female, and it takes one of each sex to produce a human child.

However, the conception of Jesus, the divine Child, was wholly supernatural. When the angel Gabriel brought to Mary the startling announcement that she was soon to become a mother, she could not understand how that could possibly be. "How shall this be, seeing I know not a man?" The angel assured her that "with God nothing shall be impossible." "The Holy Ghost shall come upon thee, and the power of the Highest shall overshadow thee: therefore also that holy thing which shall be born of thee, shall be called the Son of God," Luke 1:35.

Joseph was not the father of Jesus. He was indeed espoused (engaged) to Mary of Nazareth, but "before they came together, she was found with child," Matthew 1:18. Joseph was grieved beyond measure. He believed that Mary had been unfaithful to him, and he was about to break the engagement. He intended to do this in as quiet and private a way as possible since he did not want to make a public scandal of the affair. While he was pondering these sad thoughts and making his plans, "the angel of the Lord appeared unto him in a dream, saying, Joseph, thou son of David, fear not to take unto thee Mary thy wife: for that which is conceived in her is of the Holy Ghost," Matthew 1:20.

Jesus had no human father. Mary was still a virgin when she became a mother. It was a miraculous conception, wholly above and beyond the laws of nature. This is what we mean by the "virgin birth."

116

The virgin birth is a cardinal doctrine of the Christian religion. How dare we deny the clear statements of Scripture? To uphold the honesty of Scripture we must accept the miraculous conception of Jesus.

The virgin birth is of highest value for the proper understanding of the unique and sinless personality of Jesus of Nazareth. "Behold, I was shapen in iniquity, and in sin did my mother conceive me," Psalm 51:5, confesses David, and that is true of you and me and all mankind. But it is not true of Jesus. He was "without sin," One "who did no sin, neither was guile found in His mouth." "Ye know that He was manifested to take away our sins; and in Him is no sin," I John 3:5. How can we explain the sinlessness of the Christ if we believe that He was conceived and born in the natural course of nature?

The virgin birth of Jesus is necessary to explain this supernatural person. If He was truly "conceived by the Holy Ghost, born of the Virgin Mary," as we confess in the Apostles' Creed, a supernatural element must have entered into His person. If He was the very Son of God in human flesh, there must have been a miracle, the most stupendous miracle in the universe, in His origin. Without a miracle such a person as Jesus could not have been. The marvelous virgin birth of Jesus corresponds with His marvelous life, His wondrous works, His amazing resurrection and ascension. Accept the one, and the rest naturally follows; deny the one, and how can we rightfully accept the other?

The virgin birth of Jesus is needful for the fulfillment of promise and prophecy. It was the "seed of the *woman*" that was to crush the old serpent's head. Why was the promised Redeemer called the seed of the woman? We should rather expect that the man be emphasized instead of the woman. The world's Redeemer was to have a human mother but not a human father. The virgin birth made this possible and was the fulfillment of this promise.

"The Lord Himself will give you a sign: behold, a virgin shall conceive and bear a son, and shall call His name Immanuel," Isaiah 7:14. Thus predicted Isaiah. The inspired St. Matthew tells us that this prophecy was fulfilled in the miraculous conception and birth of the Virgin Mary's Son.

Furthermore, the honor of Mary requires the virgin birth of her child Jesus. She was great with child before she was married. If Jesus had a human father, who was His father? Joseph? Then the account of Joseph's grief and disappointment, as given by St. Matthew, is naught but a fable. Or if some other man was the father of Mary's Son, then (I say it with all reverence) He was an illegitimate child, and Mary was an adulteress.

Moreover, if Jesus was the natural offspring of Joseph and Mary, then

He is no more the Son of God than any other child. Then He was human and only human. In the end, this is why many deny the virgin birth. They deny the deity of Jesus. If Jesus is not "God manifest in the flesh," then is our preaching vain, we are still in our sins, and they who have fallen asleep in Jesus have perished.

Baptism of Infants

Please give Biblical grounds for infant baptism. Where in the Bible does it say that a babe should be baptized? I believe baptism is for believers only (Mark 16:16). Kindly explain why the Lutheran Church baptizes infants whereas the Word of God says, "Repent and be baptized."

Many good, well-meaning people believe that we were baptized in the wrong way if we were not immersed. They also insist that we were baptized at the wrong time if we were baptized in infancy. Now let us examine our grounds for baptizing infants.

1. Christ's command to baptize "all nations" includes infants. "Go therefore and make disciples of all nations, baptizing them" Matthew 28:19, R.S.V. The disciples were commissioned to Christianize the world, to "make disciples of all nations." How is this to be done? "Baptizing them [the nations, whose populations consist of old and young, men, women, and children] in the name of the Father and of the Son and of the Holy Spirit; teaching them to observe all that I have commanded you." In this divine commission we have but one imperative verb in the Greek, *matheteusate*, correctly translated "make disciples." Two participles, *baptizontes* and *didaskontes*, tell us how this is to be done: "baptizing them" . . . "teaching them." Do you know of a "nation" that has no children or that does not accept its children, even infants, as a part of the nation?

2. Children are born in sin (Psalm 51:5; Romans 5:12) and must be regenerated. They are born spiritually dead (Ephesians 2:1), outside of the flock of the Good Shepherd. All of us "were by nature the children of wrath, even as others," Ephesians 2:3. "Truly, truly, I say to you, unless one is born of water and the Spirit, he cannot enter the kingdom of God. That which is born of the flesh is flesh, and that which is born of the Spirit is spirit," John 3:5, 6, R.S.V. We know of no way of giving an infant the new birth except by "water and the Spirit." We believe this refers to baptism. Paul calls baptism "the washing of regeneration and renewal of the Holy Spirit," Titus 3:5.

3. Christ commanded that little children should be brought to Him. We obey this command by baptizing them, giving them "the washing

of regeneration," and then teaching them of God and the Savior as early as it is possible to do so. Why did the disciples try to keep the mothers from bringing their "infants" (Luke 18:15) to Jesus? They thought these little ones were too young to get any benefit from the touch and the blessing of Jesus. Let them grow up, thought the disciples. Then they will have at least some understanding of their need of a divine Savior. Jesus thought otherwise. He was moved to indignation and said to His disciples: "Let the children come to Me, do not hinder them; for to such belongs the kingdom of God," Mark 10:14, R.S.V. If the kingdom of God belongs to the children as well as to the adults, why should they be denied the sacrament by which we enter God's kingdom? "Jesus did not baptize these children," do we hear you say? The New Testament sacrament of baptism was not formally instituted until the day when shortly before His ascension Jesus commissioned His disciples to go into all the world and make disciples of all nations. The little boys of that group of children had doubtless been circumcised at the age of eight days. They, together with their little sisters, stood in covenant relation with God according to the Old Testament dispensation.

4. As children were received into covenant relation with God during Old Testament times by the rite of circumcision, which was a type of baptism (Col. 2:11, 12), so now during the New Testament dispensation God desires that they be brought into covenant relation with Him by the sacrament of baptism. There is in this world such a thing as the kingdom of God, the kingdom of grace. God made provision for the reception of babes into the kingdom of grace during the Old Testament dispensation by the rite of circumcision (Gen. 17:12–14). Is it possible that He has made no provision for the receiving of these little folks into covenant relation with Him during the New Testament dispensation? If this were true, the new dispensation would be poorer than was the old dispensation. That cannot be. Baptism is the rite of entrance into the kingdom of grace. It is the sacrament of regeneration, for it imparts that higher life, even spiritual life, which is eternal life begun.

5. The promise of God's grace belongs to the children. "For the promise is unto you and to your children," Acts 2:39. When did God ever enter into covenant relation with parents without including their little ones? We noted above that during Old Testament time infants stood in the same relation to the kingdom and covenant of God as their parents, and the sign and token of this relation was the same, viz., circumcision. This outward sign of the covenant relation with God was given to children as early as the eighth day after their birth. If baptism has not taken the place of circumcision, what has? Baptism is a step forward, for it is intended for all without exception, male and female.

The exact time for this rite is not commanded, but it is certainly God's will that this very important matter be attended to early, very early in life.

6. Children have the capacity for faith. "Whoso shall offend one of *these little ones which believe in Me*, it were better for him that a millstone were hanged about his neck, and that he were drowned in the depth of the sea," Matthew 18:6. We do not mean that a little child can have a full, conscious faith made up of knowledge, assent, and confidence, but God can bring a child into a saved relationship to Him, and this blessed state and standing with God the Bible designates faith. The essence of Christian faith is trust. Who will say that the Creator is unable to instill in even the smallest child a trust in Him which is beyond human understanding? At any rate, the child and not the adult is the model subject for the kingdom of God. "Verily I say unto you, Whosoever shall not receive the kingdom of God as a little child, he shall not enter therein." If a little child is the model subject for the kingdom of God, why should it not also be the model subject for the sacrament which is the God-given rite of entrance into this kingdom?

Objectors to infant baptism say that baptism is for believers only, implying that when we baptize a little child we are baptizing a little unbeliever. But Jesus holds up that child as the model. "Truly, I say to you, unless you turn and become like children, you will never enter the kingdom of heaven. Whosoever humbles himself like this child, he is the greatest in the kingdom of heaven," Matthew 18:3, 4, R.S.V. And yet some want to tell us that a child cannot be reckoned as a believer because he has not yet grown up. We teach that baptism kindles spiritual life in the infant. If a child cannot be brought into a state of faith he is lost, for "he that believeth not shall be damned." These children are either among the saved or among the lost. There are only two groups of people traveling toward eternity, the pardoned and the unpardoned, those who stand in a saved relation to God and those who do not. Where are you going to put the children? Ignore them as nonentities, as not being a part of the lost whom Jesus came to seek and to save? We know that our baptized little folks are in a state of grace with God, for the very nature of a sacrament is such that it bestows and imparts grace where there is no wilful resistance. A little child does not play the hypocrite as, alas, the adult so often does.

"He that believeth and is baptized shall be saved." Do not these words state that we are to be believe first and then be baptized? I do not so understand them. He that believeth and *is* baptized, is a baptized one, he shall be saved. But he that believeth not, or disbelieveth, he is lost, whether he is baptized or unbaptized. Baptism may be administered before or after full, conscious faith. In the case of an adult it should come after, in the case of a child before. Other passages of Scripture compel me thus to understand the words of St. Mark.

Moreover, the words of commission as given by St. Mark: "Go ye into all the world and preach the gospel to every creature," and the commission as given by St. Matthew: "Go and make disciples of all nations," refer to one and the same work: Christianize the world. Bring the gospel and, if possible, impart the gracious gifts of the gospel to *every creature,* including the smallest babe. How are you going to bring the gifts of the gospel to the little child except through the sacrament which is primarily intended for him, for it is the "washing of regeneration and renewal of the Holy Spirit"?

7. The apostles baptized entire families, assuredly then also children. The apostles surely understood the meaning and the scope of the divine commission. Then practice under this command must be taken as a clear and final explanation of what the Savior meant when He sent them forth to Christianize the world. If they baptized children, we must certainly conclude that children should be baptized. The question then arises, Did the apostles baptize children? St. Paul baptized Lydia "and her household," Acts 16:14, 15. In that same city, Philippi of Macedonia, the same apostle baptized the jailer, "he and all his." The Revised Standard Version gives it thus: "And he [the jailer] was baptized at once, with all his family," Acts 16:33. In I Corinthians 1:16 we read: "And I [Paul, the writer of the letter] baptized also the household of Stephanas." Cornelius of Caesarea was a "devout man and one that feared God *with all his house,*" Acts 10:2. St. Peter was directed to visit Cornelius who had assembled "his kinsmen and near friends." While Peter was preaching to them, "the Holy Ghost fell on all them which heard the word." These people were baptized before that service ended. Have we not reason to believe that with Cornelius the members of his pious family were also baptized since we are expressly told that an apostle baptized the families of Lydia, of the jailer at Philippi, and of Stephanas?

When we go to the history of the early church, what do we find? Tertullian, who died in 230 A.D., was the first of the church fathers who opposed infant baptism. The very fact that he opposed it proves that it must have been the general practice of the day. Why did he oppose the baptizing of children? Not because he considered it contrary to the divine commission, but because he feared gross sins committed after baptism could not be forgiven. Many very serious people of Tertullian's day were so worried about the forgiveness of sins committed after baptism that they delayed being baptized until late in life or even until they thought death stared them in the face. The early church fathers, as they are called, including Polycarp (a pupil of St. John),

121

Hermas, Justin Martyr, Irenaeus, etc., all sanctioned and practiced infant baptism.

8. Baptism is not law but gospel. What do I mean? So many people think of baptism as primarily something that man does in obedience to a divine precept. He thus desires to manifest submission to God's will and indicate to the world that he wants to be a disciple of the Lord Jesus. In other words, many good people lay the emphasis on what man does when he is baptized and not on what a gracious God offers to do. They stress man's submissive act and not God's gracious promise. In baptism a man personally and consciously takes a decided stand on the Lord's side. This is the chief thing in the opinion of many. This is a vital mistake. No wonder that those who hold this view cannot understand how a little child can be a proper subject for baptism! "Can a babe personally and consciously take such a step?" they ask. "Does an infant desire baptism and confess faith in the Savior?"

Baptism is not primarily law but gospel. The gracious heavenly Father, for Jesus' sake, desires to bestow and impart an infinite gift upon the recipient of baptism, even forgiveness of sin and reinstatement as a child of God and an heir of eternal glory. Can a child be the fortunate recipient of a gracious gift without the child's being aware of this blessed fact? Certainly he can. Thank God, that is what takes place in "the washing of regeneration." What baptism signifies is not so much our conscious yielding to God, but it is a token of His infinite grace which is being bestowed upon us. Baptism is the sign of what God does rather than what we do. This imparting of divine grace always takes place in baptism if the baptized one does not wilfully resist and thus reject the proffered gift. A little child never thus resists. That is why the child is the model and not the naturally proud, independent, and self-sufficient adult.

9. The adult baptisms recorded in the New Testament are no argument against the divine sanction of infant baptism. We repeatedly find in Scripture such statements as these: "Repent, and be baptized every one of you in the name of Jesus Christ for the remission of sins." "And now why tarriest thou? arise and be baptized, and wash away thy sins." "What doth hinder me to be baptized? . . . If thou believest with all thine heart, thou mayest." On these and similar Biblical instances of adult baptisms the opponents of infant baptism lean heavily. They confidently believe that they are Scriptural proof for an exclusive adult baptism. They are certainly mistaken. Has it ever occurred to you that every one of these recorded baptisms was administered to a convert from either Judaism or heathendom? Of course, an unbaptized adult should repent and confess his sins before he is baptized. What Chris-

tian minister would demand less? But where in Scripture do you find that an adult born of Christian parents was baptized? To my knowledge neither Scripture nor the history of the first 150 years of the Christian era contains a single recorded baptism of an adult born to Christian parents. These descendants of believing ancestors must have been baptized in childhood.

"It is not the will of your Father which is in heaven, that one of these little ones should perish." It is the will of the heavenly Father that not one of these little ones be denied "the washing of regeneration." "Let the children come to Me, do not hinder them; for to such belongs the kingdom of God. Truly, I say to you, whoever does not receive the kingdom of God like a child shall not enter it," Mark 10:14, 15, R.S.V.

Baptism by Immersion

A friend of mine insists that Christ was immersed because of the fact that He was baptized in a river. How would you answer him?

If anyone could answer this question positively, one way or the other, it would contribute much toward settling the vexed question as to the mode of baptism. But that is just what no one is able to do. Some Greek scholars insist that from the Bible text it cannot even be positively known whether Jesus was in the water or at the edge of the water. While the old King James Version says: "And Jesus, when He was baptized, went up straightway out of the water," the American Revised Version translates: "And Jesus, when He was baptized, went up straightway from the water," Matt. 3:16.

The Greek term from which our word baptize is derived has various meanings, including sprinkling, pouring, and immersing. It is a word which has in itself no specific reference to mode. That it is thus used in the New Testament is evident. Read Mark 7:3, 4 and you will find the word wash or washing used three times. In the original Greek it is always the same term, "baptize." It refers to a ceremonial washing which was performed in various ways, wetting, sprinkling, dipping, etc. In Hebrews 9:10 the writer speaks of "divers washings," literally, "divers baptisms"; and in verse thirteen of the same chapter he tells us how some of these levitical baptisms or ceremonial purifications were performed, viz., by "sprinkling the unclean." Thus the term from which our English word baptize is derived was repeatedly used to signify a religious purifying, without regard to mode.

We are, indeed, glad that in our day this unhappy controversy about the mode of baptism is fast subsiding.

The Mode of Baptism

(1) I am not fully convinced that the Lutheran mode of baptism by sprinkling is correct. I believe that through baptism we are to represent the burial and resurrection of Jesus Christ. Romans 6: 1-5; Colossians 2:12. (2) I am told that immersion was used until the year 1311 when the pope changed to sprinkling for convenience' sake. If this is true, and if it is also true that the Greek word "baptizo" means to dip under entirely; the Greek word "rantizo" to sprinkle with, and the Greek word "cleo" to pour water upon an object, then can we say that Colossians 2:8-10 has reference to such things?

1. St. Paul is not speaking about the *mode* of baptism in Romans 6:1-11. He is referring to the *effect* of baptism. Emphatically and repeatedly the apostle had stated that salvation is by grace through faith and not by human effort. Salvation is a gift of God and not a just wage that is due to man because he has earned it. If this is true, shall we continue to sin so that the grace of God will be all the greater in nevertheless saving us though we continue in sin indifferently? "By no means. How can we who died to sin still live in it? Do you not know that all of us who have been baptized into Christ Jesus were baptized into His death? We are buried therefore with Him by baptism into death, so that as Christ was raised from the dead by the glory of the Father, we too might walk in newness of life. For if we have been united with Him in a death like His, we shall certainly we united with Him in a resurrection like His. We know that our old self was crucified with Him so that the sinful body might be destroyed, and we might no longer be enslaved by sin" (R.S.V.).

In baptism the "old man" is to die, and as that person goes forth from baptism he is to be "a new creature," "a new man." Here is a man by the name of Saul. He is not a Christian, but by the grace of God and the efforts of Christian friends he is brought to faith in Jesus as his personal Redeemer and Savior. Since he has become a Christian he wants a new name. He chooses the name Paul. It is Saul who comes to be baptized, but it is Paul who leaves after the baptism has taken place. What has become of Saul? He is dead, he died when he was baptized. 'Tis true, he is the same human being, but his attitude toward and his standing with God have changed. He is no more a stranger and a foreigner "but a fellow citizen with the saints, and of the household of God," Eph. 2:19. His attitude toward the world has changed. He has had a "fall out" with the wicked world. He and the world part company. He is, indeed, still in the world, but he is no longer of the world.

His attitude toward sin has changed. He now realizes that sin is his curse. He, therefore, diligently asks God for Jesus' sake to wash him of its stains and free him of its power. When he is tempted to sin he says: "Saul might have done that, but not Paul; Paul is a child of God, he walks in newness of life." That is what baptism is to mean to you and to me. We must now live and conduct ourselves as children of God. It is this that the apostle is emphasizing in Romans 6:1-11 and also in Colossians 2:8-15.

I do not believe that Paul is even alluding to the mode of baptism in the passages under consideration, much less emphasizing the mode of administering the sacrament. The body of Jesus was not lowered into a grave dug vertically into the earth. His body was carried horizontally into a tomb hewn into the side of a hill. Immersion does not represent or picture a burial of that kind. People who insist on immersion, as a rule, also love to point to the word "planted" in verse five as an allusion to their mode of baptism. To their dismay, no doubt, the new translation does not use the word planted. It renders verse five thus: "For if we have been united with him in a death like His, we shall certainly be united with Him in a resurrection like His." There is nothing here that even in a remote way symbolizes immersion. He died for us, He took our place; He undertook to answer to eternal justice in our behalf. We were united with Him, and when He by death paid the penalty of our transgressions, we died with Him. As newborn men and women we also arose with Him, and we are still "united with Him" as a living branch in the ever-living Vine. How can we, then, live in sin indifferently? "We know that our old self was crucified with Him so that the sinful body might be destroyed, and we might no longer be enslaved to sin," verse 6, R.S.V.

2. The word "sprinkling" is abhorred by some Christian people. Yet that word is found about sixty times in the Bible. The atoning blood of our Redeemer is called "the blood of sprinkling, that speaketh better things than that of Abel," Hebrews 12:24. "When Moses had spoken every precept to all the people according to the law, he took the blood of calves and of goats, with water, and scarlet wool and hyssop, and sprinkled both the book and all the people. . . . Moreover he sprinkled with blood both the tabernacle, and all the vessels of the ministry. And almost all things are by the law purged with blood; and without shedding of blood is no remission," Hebrews 9:19-22. Isaiah predicts that He (Christ) "shall sprinkle many nations," Isa. 52:15. "I will sprinkle clean water upon you, and ye shall be clean; from all your filthiness, and from all your idols will I cleanse you," Ezek. 26:25. The Holy Ghost is always spoken of as being "poured out," "shed forth," "shed on us," etc. See Acts 2:17, 18; Titus 3:6. "The Holy Ghost fell

on all them which heard the word," Acts 10:44. This visible pouring out and shedding forth of the Holy Spirit are called a "baptism" (Acts 2:5). No immersion here.

In what way were Saul of Tarsus baptized, Cornelius and his household, the jailor at Philippi and his family? Read the accounts as found in Acts chapter 9, 10, and 16 and see if you can find anything that even hints at immersion. Sprinkling and pouring as well as immersion were used from the very beginning. In the early church immersion was, as a rule, an immersion of only the head and not of the entire body. It is true that in time sprinkling or pouring more and more became the usual mode of administering baptism.

As it is used by the New Testament writers the Greek word *baptizein* does not mean only and always to immerse. As proof of this note the following: "And when they [Pharisees and Jews] come from the market, except they wash they eat not. And many other things there be which they have received to hold, as the washing of cups, brazen vessels and of tables," Mark 7:4. In the Greek the words "wash" and "washing" are a form of the word *baptizein*. Did the Jews immerse themselves before eating, did they immerse their tables (the Greek, *klinon*, literally means beds or couches)? A certain Pharisee invited Jesus to dine with him. "And when the Pharisee saw it, he marvelled that He [Jesus] had not first washed [Greek, *baptized*] before dinner," Luke 11:38. "Meats and drinks and divers washings, and carnal ordinances," Hebrews 9:10. "Divers washings," in the Greek, baptisms. Various Old Testament ordinances were performed by the sprinkling or pouring out of water or blood. What ordinance can you refer to that was administered by immersion?

PART THREE

THE CHRISTIAN LIFE, ATTITUDES, CONVICTIONS

The New Birth

Please explain John 3:3, "Except a man be born again, he cannot see the kingdom of God." How is this rebirth brought about: through baptism and faith? In I John 5:1 we read: "Whosoever believeth that Jesus is the Christ is born of God." Thus it seems possible to have the rebirth without and apart from baptism. A brief explanation will be deeply appreciated.

The new birth is absolutely necessary. The birth from your mother made you a living creature, but this natural life leaves you still spiritually dead, "dead in trespasses and sins," Eph. 2:1. Therefore you must be born again. This higher life, namely, spiritual life, can be given you only by the divine Spirit.

When Nicodemus asks for further explanation, Jesus tells him how this new birth is ordinarily imparted. It is not by being born a second time from one's mother. She is only a sinful human being, and the child born of her can be only like herself—a sinful creature. Like begets like. "That which is born of the flesh is flesh." Mother cannot give that higher life. Therefore to be a child of God one must be born of God. He alone can impart spiritual life. "That which is born of the Spirit is spirit." Spirit in contrast to mere living, sinful human flesh.

Now, this rebirth is usually imparted through water and the Spirit. The Spirit of God is the active, regenerating agent, and He works through the divinely appointed medium, namely, water. However, we must not think that water applied in the name of the Father, and of the Son, and of the Holy Ghost, works as by magic. A new and a blessed relation to God is offered, a new and higher life, spiritual life, is implanted, provided God's gracious work is not wilfully resisted. A little child does not wilfully resist, it is passive and receptive and hence always receives though it is unaware of this fact. This receiving, even on the part of a sleeping child, the Bible designates "faith." Without faith man rejects what God graciously offers. Hence without faith baptism profits nothing. "He that believeth not is damned" even though he has been baptized. Baptized persons may make shipwreck of their faith.

In the case of an adult the Spirit of God can effect the new birth by and through the Word alone. He who is brought to true repentance and faith in Jesus as his divine Redeemer and Savior is a reborn man. "Whosoever believeth that Jesus is the Christ is born of God." However, he will not ignore baptism. How can he who is a disciple of Jesus reject or neglect the sacrament which the Master positively enjoins? He will gladly and eagerly as a seal and strengthening of his faith receive the additional grace of baptism.

Knowledge of Conversion

I have a friend who believes that every truly converted man ought to know the exact time he was converted. He frequently speaks of the day when he was "saved." He thinks every Christian ought to be able to do this. What is your opinion?

There are, doubtless, those who can designate the very day on which they accepted Christ as their personal Savior. The jailer of Philippi could do this, also the woman of Samaria whom Jesus met at Jacob's well; likewise Zacchaeus. Perhaps also Paul. Yet in his case one wonders whether it was the day on which he beheld the vision or three days later when after intense thought and prayer he was baptized. On which day did he really surrender and yield himself as a penitent sinner fully to Christ?

John Wesley claimed that he knew the exact minute when he was converted. There are many others who make this claim, including your friend. Personally, I should not dispute their claim. They, however, are certainly mistaken when they think every truly converted person ought to be able to do this. Do you think that John the Baptist knew the exact day when he became a true believer in Jesus as his Redeemer and Savior?

How about the Virgin Mary? I believe Mary was in covenant relation with God from early childhood. Surely, many of us who were baptized as infants believe this concerning ourselves. In spite of our many weaknesses and failures we do not remember the time we did not trust in the Lord Jesus as our dear Savior, daily speak to Him in prayer, and aim to live as His followers. Who will dare to state that we are still in an unconverted state because we cannot point out an exact time when we turned to Christ?

In the case of some adults conversion is quite sudden. Something has brought a man to a realization of the terribleness of sin. He hears of the love of God and the grace that is proffered through the atoning blood of the divine Redeemer. He yields himself to the urgings of the Holy Spirit and accepts Christ as his personal Savior. The change is decisive and vivid and has come upon that person very suddenly. Such a person will readily recall and can definitely designate the day, perhaps even the hour, when, by the grace of God, he gave himself to Christ and became His devoted follower.

With others the process that leads to conversion is slow and gradual. Gradually they begin to see and to feel the guilt of sin. More and more, as they hear and ponder the sweet gospel, they cease wilfully resisting the divine grace that is offered. But just when it was that they actually yielded themselves to Christ and began to trust in Him as their Savior they are unable to say.

When we regard conversion as a process we mean that contrition and faith may come gradually to one by the working of the divine Spirit. On the other hand, when we think of conversion as a turning from sin and self unto Christ, a transition from a state of unbelief to one of faith, of spiritual death to spiritual life, it is instantaneous. There is a moment when a person is brought from unbelief to faith. When that moment arrived, God alone knows. The important thing is not whether you and I can recall the exact time of our conversion, but whether we now stand in grace with our Maker.

Religion and Morality

Distinguish between religion and morality.

Religion and morality are not the same. Religion refers to a person's faith in a deity and his attitude toward and his relationship with that acknowledged deity.

Morality pertains to man's natural sense of what is right, and what is wrong; it has to do with questions of conduct, proper or improper, virtue or vice.

A man may be very religious in this that he regularly mumbles his prayers and punctually performs his supposed religious duties and yet at the same time be a very immoral man. It is because he has a false or a sham religion. No man can have the true religion in the sense that he stands in the right relationship with his Maker and still be an immoral man. On the other hand, an infidel who disclaims faith in any deity may be what we regard as a good, moral man. That is, he is honest, truthful, kind, generous, chaste, and unselfish in his conduct.

Cowardice

A fellow workman claims that it is cowardly to be a Christian. He says: "People become Christians simply because they are afraid of being damned. That I call cowardice." Can you give me ammunition with which to meet such statements?

I have my home insured against both fire and windstorm. Is it cowardly to fear that either of these destructive forces might someday destroy my property? I carry insurance protection against accident and sickness. Is it cowardice on my part in good days to make provision for such a possible emergency? All prudent men are agreed that it is a fool's risk not to have one's property insured. But what is loss of property, or health or limb, or even of life itself, in comparison with irretrievable loss, the loss of one's soul? But suppose man has no soul, and death ends all, what then? Then the Christian is still as well off as the unbeliever. If there be no life beyond the grave, has the unbeliever any advantage over the Christian; did he get any more solid, satisfying joy, comfort, peace, and happiness out of his life than did the Christian? Did he put any more of these blessings into this world than did the follower of Jesus?

But suppose death does not end all, and the claims of Christianity are true, what then? Then the momentous verdict stands: "He that believeth not shall be damned." The Christian risks nothing and has everything to gain, the non-Christian risks everything and thereby gains nothing. Is not that man a fool who risks all when there is no possibility of any gain by doing so? That is why the Bible calls the unbeliever a fool. "The fool hath said in his heart, There is no God," Ps. 14:1. If there were no more than a mere possibility of future punishment, would it not be the part of prudence to try to escape it? But our evidence is such that it leads us not only to conclude that there is a possibility of future retribution, but it amply proves that it must be so. I do not know what a fool might call it, but ordinary intelligence and good common sense teach that it is prudent and wise to make provision for one's future welfare.

Let us look at this question from another point of view. Were the Christian martyrs cowards when they defied the fires and readily suffered excruciating tortures and death rather than renounce their faith in Christ? It took a hero to be a child of God in the days of persecution.

It takes a hero openly to be a Christian in Russia today. And it takes normal courage to be a devout follower of Christ in America or anywhere else. Lack of moral courage keeps many out of the kingdom of God. It takes moral backbone to stand up for Jesus in the midst of a promiscuous crowd. Many, many fear to own His cause and blush to speak His name because of lack of courage to do so. There are foes for the Christian to face. He must often stem a flood of ridicule and abuse.

> Is this vile world a friend to grace,
>   To help me on to God?
> Sure I must fight, if I would reign:
>   Increase my courage, Lord!
> I'll bear the toil, endure the pain,
>   Supported by Thy Word.

The true Christian is not only "the highest style of man," as Alexander Pope terms him, but he is also a moral hero.

Saint and Sinner

Can a person be a saint and at the same time a sinner? Will you, please, help my neighbor (a very devout woman of another denomination) and me to get into the clear on this subject?

Yes, one can be both a sinner and a saint at the same time—if you understand these terms "saint" and "sinner" properly.

There are saints on earth, and there are saints in heaven. Paul calls himself "the least of the saints," Ephesians 3:8, and writes "Salute . . . all the saints that are with them," Romans 16:15. In these and in other passages Christians here on earth are called saints. However, there are also saints in heaven, and they are free from every taint of sin. I cannot be a sinner and a perfect saint in heaven, but I can be a sinner and a member of the "communion of saints" here on earth.

Furthermore, there is a difference in the way in which the word "sinner" is used. By "sinner" we sometimes mean a wilful sinner, one who lives carelessly and indifferently in sin. Of course, such an unrepentant sinner cannot at the same time be one of God's saints—a forgiven child of God. But even those who are saints here on earth are sinners. "There is not a just man upon earth, that doeth good and sinneth not," Ecclesiastes 7:20. "If we say that we have no sin, we deceive ourselves, and the truth is not in us," I John 1:8. Note that the apostle includes himself in this last passage. Every day even the most saintly among us needs to pray, "Forgive *us* [me and others] our trespasses." For Christ's sake God does forgive the sins of penitent sinners and clothes them with the righteousness of Christ. Thus, although they are sinners they are at the same time saints—holy not in themselves but holy because they are joined by faith to Christ. "There is no condemnation to them which are in Christ Jesus, who walk not after the flesh, but after the Spirit," Rom. 8:1.

Christian Fiction

Is there such a thing as *Christian* fiction? My dictionary explains fiction as something that is not true, an untruth. In plain English these books would be Christian lies. Are lies ever Christian?

You certainly did not read all that your dictionary had to say about "fiction." I have only a small *Webster's Popular American Dictionary* before me. It defines fiction as "the act of feigning or inventing; that which is feigned or invented." Shall I stop here and say that fiction is an untruth, in plain English, a lie? Has the word "fiction" no other meaning? My little dictionary continues: "A literary production of the imagination in prose form, as a novel, romance, etc.; a legal assumption for the purpose of convenience, the furtherance of justice, etc."

Did you ever hear of a fable? Of course, a fable is a fabricated story of the imagination. But from time immemorial it has been used to make clear and to impress some important moral or religious truth. As the first definition of the word fable my dictionary gives: "A short fictitious narrative intended to convey some moral."

Jesus made extensive use of parables. What is a parable? I quote from my little dictionary: "An allegorical method of conveying instruction by means of a fable or short fictitious narrative." Need I say more?

When Is a Nation Christian

Is the United States a Christian nation?

There is a sense in which it may truthfully be said that the United States is a Christian country. The founders of our nation were largely devout Christians. They sincerely aimed to found this nation on Christian principles. In spite of many weaknesses and shortcomings we certainly aim to have fair and just laws which promote the happiness and the welfare of all our people. And in general I think we may state that our rulers desire to govern according to Christian principles. Christianity is the prevailing religion of our country and as a leaven has more or less permeated every section of the land. It largely influences all that is

132

here said and done. In this sense we may call the United States a Christian nation.

We are certainly a Christian nation when compared with Russia where infidelity is rampant, and all religion is not only discouraged but, as a rule, rudely suppressed. We are a Christian nation when compared with Turkey or Arabia where the Mohammedan religion prevails; or when compared with countries where most of the inhabitants are pagans or cling to Hinduism, Shintoism, or to some other false faith.

But while our nation is founded on Christian principles, and the professed Christians of the land outnumber the adherents of all other religions combined, let us not forget the sad fact that the majority of our people do not even profess any definite religious faith. We know that only a comparatively small minority of our nation are true followers of Christ. So in this sense we are not a Christian nation. Moreover, also keep in mind that the constitution of our land guarantees religious liberty. The government is to show preference to no religion. Before the law every religious faith is on a par. Every inhabitant of this country has the right to think of the deity, to teach about Him, to worship and to serve Him or neglect to do so, as he sees fit. Just so he does not interfere with the rights of others. In this sense the United States is not a Christian nation.

The Sin of Slander

Discuss: "Speak not evil one of another."

When the apostle exhorts: "Speak not evil one of another," he refers to slander, to the raising of false and defamatory reports. That injunction can also be translated: "Stop talking against each other," or, "Quit running each other down." Slander is the fruit of envy, jealousy, and malice. If that sad mother warns her friends and neighbors against that drunkard who so cruelly failed her in the hour of extreme need, will her motive for doing so be spite, hatefulness, and revenge, or will it be an act of kindness, sympathy, and love toward those who may some-day be in like dire need of help? A good deed can be produced only by a good motive, and an evil motive will never produce anything but an evil deed. Thus you can decide as to whether a deed is good or evil. What is the motive back of it?

When Jesus says, "Judge not, that ye be not judged," He is not contradicting what He says elsewhere: "Judge not according to appearance, but judge righteous judgment," John 7:24. "Do not ye judge them that are within?" that is, within the congregation, asks Paul of the Christians at Corinth. "Therefore put away from among yourselves that wicked person" (see I Corinthians, chapter 5). The impenitent sinner who willfully continues in sin must be excluded from the church. He is no longer a brother or a sister in the faith. "Let him be unto thee as an heathen man and a publican," Matthew 18:15–17. There could be no church discipline, there could not even be any warning, reproof, or exhortation, if we were never to judge between truth and error, right and wrong. In verse six of the portion of Scripture before us, Jesus exhorts: "Give not that which is holy unto the dogs, neither cast ye your pearls before swine." By dogs and swine are meant those who know the gospel, but who wilfully persist in living in vice and moral filth. The disciples of Jesus must judge as to who these "dogs" and "swine" are.

The "mote" in the one man's eye obviously denotes a small fault while the "beam" in the other man's eye denotes a correspondingly greater fault. But Jesus is not here speaking merely of faults or sins in general, some small, others great, but of moral perception and understanding, slightly defective in the one man, grossly defective in the other. He who is devoid of all truly moral judgment must not pretend to aid another who, perhaps, at times is slightly wrong in his judgments. The scribes and the Pharisees "trusted in themselves that they were righteous, and despised others." These are the people whose moral perception is so defective that they are like a man with a beam in his eye. Yet they are the ones who are like a man with a mote in his eye.

Legal Oaths

Jesus in His Sermon on the Mount definitely says: "Swear not at all," Matthew 5:34. By what right, then, dare we teach that legal oaths, such as the government requires, are permissible?

In interpreting Scripture we must always keep in mind that a passage must be studied and interpreted in connection with its context, that is, Scripture interprets Scripture. Other portions of God's Word which treat of the same subject must be considered as they will doubtless throw light on the passage under consideration.

Now, what do we find in connection with the words of Jesus, "Swear not at all"? In accordance with the preceding verse He had said: "Ye have heard that it hath been said by them of old time, Thou shalt not forswear thyself, but shalt perform unto the Lord thine oaths." Jesus wished to say, "Your teachers have told you that Moses of old forbids false oaths, and when you have taken an oath you must be sure to fulfil it." Jesus is not finding fault with what Moses wrote, for that would be disagreeing with what the Holy Spirit had written by the hand of Moses. However, He does not agree with the interpretation the teachers of His day put upon these words, and the way in which they were usually accepted by the people of that generation. They, indeed, understood Moses as prohibiting all perjury, that is, all false oaths, but that he gave general permission otherwise to use all kinds of oaths. Moreover, they were of the opinion that an oath in which the name of God is not directly named is not as binding as is one in which God's name is mentioned.

Jesus tells His audience that this interpretation of the law of Moses is false. Why does the law forbid perjury, why does it enjoin man to keep his sworn statements? Because in his wickedness man is inclined to lie even when he is under oath. Now, do Jesus' words give permission to the promiscuous use of all manner of oaths? They do not. On the contrary, they really say: "Swear not at all in this unnecessary, promiscuous way. Tell the truth, the unvarnished truth, and no oath is necessary." A child of God is truthful, he walks ever as in the presence of God. When he speaks he knows that God hears every word he says. Therefore he speaks the truth. Why should he then add an oath to his statements? If a person will not tell the truth out of fear and love to God he is apt to tell the untruth even though he swears to his statements.

However, Jesus is here not forbidding the legal oath. The government has to do with all kinds of people, and in order to bring all pressure possible upon a man to tell the truth so that justice may prevail, the government has a right to demand an oath under certain circumstances. That this is correct we can see from such statements as these: "Thou shalt fear the Lord thy God, and serve Him, and shalt swear by His name," Deut. 6:13. "For men verily swear by the greater; and an oath for confirmation is to them an end of all strife," Heb. 6:16. Jesus permitted Himself to be put under oath, for when the high priest said to Him, when He was on trial the night before His death: "I adjure Thee by the living God, that Thou tell us whether Thou be the Christ, the Son of God," He was certainly asking Jesus to swear to His testimony. And, thanks be to God, our Savior, in the face of death and in the most emphatic manner possible, clearly and distinctly declared Himself to be the Christ, the Son of the living God.

Capital Punishment

What must the Christian believe as to capital punishment?

There can be no doubt as to where the Lutheran Church stands on the subject of capital punishment. In Article 15 of the Augsburg Confession we affirm "that Christians may lawfully bear civil office, sit in judgment, determine matters of the imperial laws and other laws in present force, decree punishment according to law, engage in just wars, act as soldiers," etc. To "decree punishment according to law" includes also punishment by death. The original German text reads: *"Uebeltaeter mit dem Schwert strafen,"* i.e., "punish evildoers with the sword." In explanation of these words the late Dr. Loy says: "If his [the Christian officer's] loyalty to the government requires of him to decree capital punishment according to the laws of the land, he only shows himself to be a faithful Christian by refusing to let the pity which he feels for the criminal or for his family that may be innocent, hinder him in the discharge of the duties of his office which, according to the divine ordinance, has the welfare of the whole community in view. And for this the Christian should be all the more prepared and faithful because of the general law of the Lord: 'Whosoever sheddeth man's blood, by man shall his blood be shed,' Gen. 9:6."

Government is ordained of God; it is to be the avenger of God to execute wrath upon them that do evil. The government is to be "a terror" to those who persist in being a menace to the common good, and the representative of the law "beareth not the sword in vain," Romans 13:1–7. The sword has always been a symbol of death. If the proper official of the government is not to bear the sword in vain, Paul certainly means that he is to use it and, if need be, to use it with effect. For he is the representative avenger of God.

Law without adequate penalty ceases to be law and degenerates into mere advice, which may be disregarded without fear. For wilful, premeditated murder in sound mind there seems to be but one adequate penalty. It is the one that God not only sanctions, but Himself prescribes. He who wilfully takes human life shall be compelled to forfeit his own life in penalty for the one which in cold blood he has taken.

Mercy to hardened criminals is cruelty to society. There is a sickly sentimentality that holds up its hands in horror at the thought of executing a criminal. This is not at all in agreement with the inspired apostle, who says that the government is not to bear the sword in vain, and that it is ordained of Him "for the punishment of evildoers," I Peter 2:14. Society must be protected, life and limb must be safeguarded, and this false pity for a vile culprit that would jeopardize the peace and security of society in general is the very opposite of the decree of the God of love who says: "The soul that sinneth it shall die," and the plain statement of our merciful Savior who affirms that "all they that take the sword shall perish with the sword," Matthew 26:52. I am well aware of the fact that there are those who quote this passage in defense of their argument against capital punishment, but they certainly misinterpret and misapply Christ's words when they do this. Jesus orders Peter to put up his sword, but He does not order the officers to do so. Peter was resisting the "powers that be." He was making it appear as though the Master and His disciples were in opposition to the rightful authorities. If Jesus and His followers were being wronged, they must not resist the officers but take recourse to the court that was open to them.

Gambling

Is a Christian ever justified to wager money upon the outcome of a horse race?

Gambling, as defined by the dictionary, means to play for money, to stake money or any other thing of value, to be lost or won, upon an uncertain event; to hazard something upon a chance, to wager. Gambling is commonly referred to as a vice, for it is demoralizing. For this reason it has been denounced and warned against by the better class of people in all ages and among all nations.

What, then, is wrong with gambling? No doubt, all will admit that dueling is murder. It is certainly so regarded by all Christian people. Now just as dueling is murder, so gambling is stealing. The duelist does not sneak up on his victim and shoot him down or stab him to the heart unawares. He has agreed with his opponent that he is willing to run the risk of being killed by him if he will give him an equal chance to try to kill him. Can it be possible that any intelligent Christian will consider this anything short of murder?

The gambler does not forcibly break into another man's house and rob him of his property, neither does he sneakingly pick his pocket. (Though, I dare say, most gamblers are tricksters and cheaters and will take advantage of their victims if they think there is a possibility of doing so without being caught.) The gambler has agreed with his opponent that he is willing to run the risk of being fleeced by him if he will give him an equal chance to try to fleece him. The only difference, therefore, between gambling and stealing is this. In gambling the man knows that there is danger of his losing his property, and he is willing to hazard this risk if he is given an equal chance to try to win the other man's property. In neither case is an attempt made to produce property as is the case when one does some honest, constructive work.

By honest toil we make money or, at least, we attempt to create value. We do something constructive; we create and increase property. By stealing or gambling we simply acquire the property which the sweat of someone else's face has produced. The gambler, like the thief, wants to secure his living without honest toil. The Lord expects us, if at all possible, to earn our daily bread. We are to be producers. The thief or the gambler or the professional beggar makes no effort to produce, he is simply trying to get into his possession, and thus to have his living, on what someone else has produced. "If any will not work," says St. Paul, "neither shall he eat." Paul does not say, he that *cannot* work, neither shall he eat. The thief does not want work, neither does the professional gambler. They should go hungry.

The practice of trying to get something for nothing is not elevating, not ennobling. It is degrading. Every time you try to get something for nothing (like playing a slot machine or some gambling device or winning a bet); every time you seek to win money or property without putting forth equivalent effort of a kind which, in some way, furthers the general good you are letting yourself down; you prove yourself to be a shirk, who is trying to evade honest toil. And such actions always degrade and demoralize.

Note this, too, that in gambling your gain and pleasure are obtained, and can be obtained, only at the cost of loss and pain to another. It is different when you obtain something by honest purchase, trade, or toil. For in that case the person from whom you obtain it also receives directly or indirectly an equivalent gain, pleasure, and satisfaction.

The end does not justify the means. It is as wrong for the poor to gamble as for the rich. And in my estimation he can least afford to do so because ten to one if not fifty to one he will come out of the deal poorer than he went into it. And least of all dare the church resort to such questionable things and put her stamp of approval upon them. "To obey is better than sacrifice."

The Use of Money

May I not do as I please with my own money, which I have honestly earned?

Can you say of the money that is in your possession that it is absolutely "my own"? "The earth is the Lord's, and the fullness thereof." That includes also the money and other valuables which you for the time being possess. No, you do not own them. "The silver is Mine, and the gold is Mine, saith the Lord of Hosts." "Every beast of the forest is Mine, and the cattle upon a thousand hills." God is the owner, and what we have is simply entrusted to us for a while. We are God's stewards, and someday He will say to us: "Give an account of thy stewardship."

Your question clearly indicates that you feel that we as children of God cannot do as we please in the securing of money. It must be "honestly earned." So loyalty and devotion to Him, whose we are, and whom we serve, will not permit us to do with talents or wealth just as our selfish old nature might dictate. We are His with all that we have and are.

Tithing

In our Sunday school class we discussed the question: "Should we Christians tithe?" Some argued that tithing is a law of the Lord which all are under obligation to obey. It was decided to ask for your explanation.

Israel of old was commanded to give a tenth of all increase unto the Lord. There can be no doubt about that. See, for instance, Lev. 27:30–32; Num. 18:20–32; Deut. 14:22. All of God's people were strictly enjoined to bring in their tithe to the Lord's treasury. Now the question is, "Does that still apply to us?" The whole tribe of Levi received no land when Palestine was divided among the remaining tribes of Israel. From Levi came all the priests and their helpers, the Levites. They received their support largely from the tithe because they labored in spiritual things for the good of all Israel.

However, tithing seems to antedate Judaism. A tenth was paid by Abraham to Melchizedek (Gen. 14:20). Jacob vowed to give a tenth to the Lord if He would watch over him and someday bring him safely back to his native land (Gen. 28:16–22).

Tithing was and, doubtless, still is richly blessed of God. See Proverbs 3:9, 10; Malachi 3:8–10. Tithing is no longer commanded, but must we not say that it is commended to us and doubtless expected of us? Personally I am inclined to think so.

God is still the owner of all things. We are His stewards. A portion of that which He owns is entrusted to us, and He regularly expects His rental. What proportion rightly belongs to Him? In the Old Testament He demanded one tenth. Now He leaves that to our own feeling of love and gratitude to Him and to our interest in the welfare of humanity and the upbuilding of His kingdom. But He certainly expects no less of us than He did of His people in days of old.

St. Paul enunciates the New Testament principle of proportionate giving when he says: "Upon the first day of the week, let every one of you lay by him in store as God hath prospered him," I Cor. 16:2. This sounds very much like what Moses said to Israel: "Every man shall give as he is able, according to the blessing of the Lord thy God, which He hath given thee," Deut. 16:17.

Giving now, as in Old Testament time, is to be proportionate giving, as we have been prospered. The only question is, "What proportion does God now demand?" He makes no definite demand. Not from compulsion but from choice He expects us cheerfully and promptly to bring His portion to the Lord's treasury. Does He expect less now than He did from Israel? We have reason to believe that He expects more because of the many additional blessings which we enjoy.

I am convinced that God will richly bless the one who cheerfully and gratefully gives at least one tenth of his income to the Lord. With no compulsion, however, except the love of Christ constraining him.

Conscience

If a person follows his conscience, will he always do right?

Conscience is that function of the soul which commends us when we do that which we believe to be right, and which reproves us when we do that which we believe to be wrong. We sometimes say that conscience is the voice of God implanted in the human heart. This is not altogether true. My neighbor's conscience may condemn him if he eats meat on Friday. My conscience does not reprove me in the least if I make meat a part of my diet on Friday. Are my conscience and that of my neighbor both the voice of God? That would mean that God contradicts Himself. Conscience functions according to the knowledge and the convictions of the individual. If a person's knowledge and his convictions are in accord with eternal truth, conscience is a good and dependable guide, but if man is in error as to his faith and his convictions, conscience will be equally in error and wholly a false guide.

If a person follows his conscience he will always do right according to his convictions. But if his convictions are false, conscience will be equally false and will lead into error. Still a person must always obey his conscience. If he heeds not the voice of his conscience he is wilfully doing that which he believes to be sin. To him, therefore, it is sin. Never encourage anyone to act contrary to his conscience, for you thus encourage him to sin. If, for instance, you are convinced that your neighbor is in error when he has conscientious scruples about eating meat on Friday, enlighten him but tell him to follow his conscience until he sees clearly that he has been binding himself where a merciful Father has given him liberty. Then his scruples about eating meat on the sixth day of the week will be gone.

Sunday Baseball

Our pastor occasionally attends the Sunday afternoon baseball games of the local team. To me this seems out of place, and I know of others, both in and outside of our congregation, who feel about it as I do. I would like to have your opinion.

Our church is not legalistic but evangelical. We have no Book of Discipline in which we set up human laws and ordinances to bind the conscience of our people. In those things where the Word of God gives us specific directions we feel in duty bound to obey, but where the divine Word gives us liberty, we insist upon liberty. Our Lord's Day is not the Sabbath of old. Definite rules were laid down by God as to the proper keeping of the Sabbath, but He has given us no such specific directions as to the proper observance of the Lord's Day. In Old Testament time we may say God dealt with the people as with children, He deals with us of New Testament time as with grownup men and women. If we but have the right attitude toward Him and His Word, all these details as to our daily conduct will take care of themselves.

I have met people who would not even permit their children to play a quiet game of croquet in their own back yard "on the Sabbath" as they prefer to call Sunday. We are convinced that this is laying emphasis upon the wrong thing. Such people are still under the yoke of bondage and do not yet understand and enjoy that spirit of liberty which is ours in Christ Jesus, our Savior. If we be but truly devoted to Him and our supreme desire ever to serve and honor Him and to lead our family and others to Him, there will be no need of all manner of legalistic restraints, we shall then freely and spontaneously desire and choose that which is proper and right.

But I have not yet answered your question. "All things are lawful for me," says St. Paul, "but all things are not expedient." I doubt the expediency of a minister's mingling with a promiscuous, yelling crowd on the Lord's Day and "rooting" with them at some boisterous game of sport. According to your letter it is an offense to you and to others of your community. I am free to confess that I feel about it much as you do. "Be not conformed to this world," exhorts the apostle. This is one of the greatest weaknesses of the church, too much worldliness in it. People see this, and they conclude that there is no difference between the church and the world. And alas, Christian reader, only too often I fear we give them just grounds to draw this conclusion. If a brother be grieved at our conduct, we are not walking charitably. It is good that we do nothing whereby a brother is offended or that gives him an occasion to fall. By insisting upon our liberty, let us beware lest we thereby destroy him for whom Christ died. I am paraphrasing the advice of Paul.

The Third Commandment requires that we keep holy the Lord's Day, and it is hallowed when devoted to that purpose for which it has been set aside—the contemplation of God and the things that pertain to our soul's good. The wearied body and mind are to find the needed rest which is conducive to health, happiness, and efficiency. But God wants us to rest also in order that we may have time and leisure to devote to the higher things of life, the worship of our Creator, the study of His Word, communion with Him, and edifying fellowship with each other. And anything that detracts from this and sets it aside as a matter of indifference or of secondary importance and encourages others to draw this conclusion is certainly out of place.

To come to the point, I would say, it is not possible for us to lay down definite rules and say: "This is forbidden, and that is permissible; this is sin, and that is no sin." But anything that detracts from the sacredness of the Lord's Day, contributes to the neglect of God's Word and sacred contemplation, or tends to dissipate the good impressions which we may have received in the hour of worship should be avoided. And this is true not only of ministers but of all Christian people.

If the conduct of your pastor is an offense to you, go and speak to him about it in a brotherly way, and, no doubt, it will be corrected.

Prayer for Little Things

Is it wrong to pray to God for little things?

We should take everything to the Lord in prayer. As little children run to father or mother with all their cares, troubles, and sorrows and also with their joys and happy surprises and experiences, so Christians go to their heavenly Father with everything. Nothing is too trifling, nothing too great. The true Christian has the child attitude toward God. Through faith in Christ Jesus he has become intimate with God. He walks with Him, and he talks with Him, and there is nothing that he hesitates to speak to Him about in prayer.

But in things pertaining to this life and the body we pray conditionally. That is, since we do not know what is best for us, we are submissive to the Lord's wisdom and judgment and with Jesus add to our petition: "Nevertheless, not my will, but Thine be done." Our Catechism says: "All that is really necessary unto salvation we should ask for unconditionally; but all else under the condition: if it please God."

PART FOUR

HOME, FAMILY, MARRIAGE

The Equality of Man

In a recent meeting of our missionary society the discussion led to Lincoln's saying: "All men are created equal." Our pastor pronounced that saying a lie. Have we been taught a lie when all these years in school we were repeatedly reminded of the truthful saying of Lincoln: "All men are created equal"?

"God is no respecter of persons," Acts 10:34. See also Romans 2:11, 12; Eph. 6:9; Col. 3:25. God is partial to no one because he is white or black, Jew or Gentile. God will deal with absolute justice toward every individual. There is nothing in Scripture more clearly taught than this: Before God we are all on an equal footing. We are all by nature equally "dead in trespasses and sins." But God equally loves all and has made provision for all, irrespective of race or color, to be saved. And He will deal justly with every human being. That is certainly what Lincoln meant, and I believe it is so understood when we use this saying of the great Emancipator as an adage.

On the other hand, it is true that one seems to have a great advantage over another as he comes into this world. One is a weakling physically from his birth, the other comes to this world with a strong body in perfect health. The one is mentally weak, a handicap he can never fully overcome, the other has wonderful latent talent. Some are born into a Christian family while others are born and reared in ungodly or even pagan surroundings.

This is no doubt what your pastor had in mind. If so, his contention is true, and neither Lincoln nor you nor anyone else can venture to deny it. However, God takes all this into account when He deals with man. To whom much is given from him the more will be expected. Greater privilege brings greater responsibility. Therefore it still remains true: "There is no respect of persons with God."

143

Martin Luther

Why did Martin Luther leave the Catholic Church?

I suppose someone told you Luther left the Roman Church because he wanted to get married. This is the answer usually given by those who either deliberately want to deceive the uninformed or are themselves ignorant of history.

Because Luther could not find comfort and peace he suddenly gave up his college career and became an Augustinian monk. But in the monastery, too, in spite of all effort, he could find no real assurance of pardon. He was seeking it in the wrong way. He became a monk in 1505. Finally Dr. Staupitz, his superior, told him to cease his frantic efforts to find peace by menial works of penance and trust in God's mercy as offered through the atoning blood of Christ Jesus. He also advised him to give more time and attention to the study of God's Word. Luther did this, and the result was that his eyes were opened. He saw that in many respects the church was no longer teaching and following the inspired Word of God. His confidence in the holiness of the high dignitaries of the church was greatly shaken when he visited Rome in 1511.

He was called as a professor of the University of Wittenberg. In 1512 he was given the title Doctor of Divinity. All the more he felt that he must now by God's aid master the Scriptures and teach them in their truth and purity. It was on the evening of the 31st of October, 1517, that he nailed the memorable Ninety-five Theses to the church door at Wittenberg. This was the real start of the Lutheran reformation. All effort to get Luther to change his position failed. He was in conscience bound to adhere to the Word of God.

An edict of excommunication against Luther was issued by the pope in 1520. This edict was to go into effect 120 days after its publication. When Luther received a copy of it he defied the pope and publicly burned the document on the campus of the University of Wittenberg. This was on December 11, 1520. Here was the real break between Luther and the Romish Church.

And, now, when did Luther get married? At that time Luther had no thought of getting married. He advised others to marry and to found a Christian home. Some of his friends told him to follow his own advice and thus to prove his faith that marriage is honorable and as sacred and holy as is celibacy. Finally, at the age of almost forty-one years, Luther quite suddenly made up his mind to have his own home. His marriage to Katherine von Bora took place on June 13, 1525.

Now, did Luther leave the Roman Catholic Church in order to get married?

Our people should become better acquainted with the history of the Reformation. There are so many good books on the subject. Some of these books are brief and to the point, yet they contain all the real, essential facts. Enlighten yourself on the marvellous history of your church.

Family Relationship

I am puzzled about our Savior's words found recorded in Luke 12: 49–53. What does our dear Lord here want to teach us? Does this pertain only to family relation or also to other people?

The Revised Standard Version of the New Testament thus translates these verses: "I came to cast fire upon the earth; and would that it were already kindled! I have a baptism to be baptized with; and how I am constrained until it is accomplished! Do you think that I have come to give peace on earth? No, I tell you, but rather division; for henceforth in one house there will be five divided, three against two and two against three; they will be divided, father against son and son against father, mother against daughter and daughter against mother, mother-in-law against her daughter-in-law and daughter-in-law against her mother-in-law."

In figurative language Jesus here tells us that His coming and mission would bring about a great conflagration on earth, i.e., it would be the start of painful division and strife. Jesus divides humanity. How often we read, "And there was division among them." Some were for Him, passionately for Him, others were bitterly against Him. It is especially the cross of Jesus that causes the division. To some it is a stumbling block or foolishness, but to others it is the wisdom and the power of God unto salvation.

The "baptism" here referred to is the passion and death of the Savior, and this also describes the "fire" which was soon to be kindled, and which would set the world ablaze with strife, namely, in division and controversy about Him. If Jesus had not come, the world would have gone undisturbed on its way to perdition. But now He came to save mankind by the atoning sacrifice of His death in our behalf. If all would thankfully accept Him and trustfully look to Him for every blessing, all would be well. But while some cling to Him, depend on Him, and proclaim Him as man's only hope, others ignore Him, indifferently pass Him by, yes, even jeer and mock His holy name, and persecute His

145

followers. This sad and painful division reaches even into our homes, for it rends even the intimate blood ties of the family.

When Jesus says that in a family of five two shall be against three, and three against two, He, of course, does not mean that the division will never be four against one and one against four. He is simply predicting the sad state of affairs that shall exist in many a home because of His coming into this world.

Would it, then, have been better if He would not have come? God forbid! Far, far better that some be saved than that all should have gone on to eternal doom.

Jesus is the Prince of peace, He came to bring peace; He is our peace. All this is true. But when many reject Him and ignore His teachings, when they slight and thus trample upon the atoning blood, given in sacrifice for them, that causes painful strife on earth and will separate humanity into two divisions on the day of judgment and throughout eternity.

The Family Altar

Can a family that has no family altar be considered a Christian family? Is it a sin to have no family altar?

A true believer in Christ Jesus is a Christian. Such a person hears and heeds God's Word. "My sheep hear My voice . . . and they follow Me." "Blessed are they that hear the Word of God and keep it." A Christian family is a household of Christians, people who are disciples of Jesus Christ, who trust in His merits, pray in His name, and endeavor to walk in His footsteps. If they cease to do this they make shipwreck of their faith and are no longer of His discipleship. "If ye continue in My Word, then [and only then] are ye My disciples indeed," John 8:31.

Now, may we not imagine a family of which every member is a Christian, who has his private devotions and worships diligently with the assembled congregation in the house of God, and yet for some reason or other that family has never followed the blessed and commendable custom of having family devotion? Regular family devotion in every home is greatly to be desired, and we should do our utmost to introduce and foster it wherever possible. But I fear we should be going too far to claim that no household can be a Christian family without the custom which you refer to as the "family altar."

Any slight or neglect of the means of grace and indifference toward prayer and worship are, of course, sin, but please bear in mind that God has not prescribed to us any definite plan, form, or manner.

The Order of Marriage

May I ask whether it is possible to trace the origin of the marriage service?

Marriage is the oldest institution of society. It dates back to Paradise. No doubt, there has always been some ceremony connected with the marriage act. But we have no definite knowledge concerning this ceremony in the early centuries of the human family.

Of course, customs and forms changed from time to time and varied greatly in different parts of the world. Even today, among us here in America, there is a great variety of marriage services in use. To the Roman Catholic, since the days of Hildebrand (1073–1085), marriage is a sacrament, hence it must be performed by a priest and connected with a religious act. The state is interested in marriage, and the laws of the state concerning marriage are to be obeyed. The mere civil act of marriage demanded by the state is all that is necessary to perform a legal marriage. However, Christian people desire a religious service in connection with their marriage ceremony.

These various customs and forms of service in connection with marriage can doubtless be traced down through the centuries, but they vary greatly among the nations of the world.

Betrothal and Marriage

Please explain Deuteronomy 22:23–29. As I understand this, a betrothal (engagement) is equal to marriage. What if a girl breaks her engagement and marries another: whose wife would she be? St. Matthew 1:18–24 speaks of Joseph and Mary as "husband" and "wife" though they had not as yet been married. As I understand it, Mary was merely espoused to Joseph, yet she is called his wife.

Among the Jews of old betrothal was equal to marriage. In fact, the Jewish betrothal, which was a solemn promise before witnesses, was the marriage itself. No marriage ceremony followed—as is customary among us. There was, as a rule, an interval of time between the betrothal and the home-bringing of the bride to the house of her husband, but there was no religious ceremony at this later time, no additional exchange of vows. These Jewish customs were a part of the ceremonial law given to that particular people. They were, indeed, given by God and were, therefore, morally binding on Israel but cannot be imposed

147

upon us as though they were intended for all time and all people. If that were the case, the Mosaic laws of Deuteronomy 22:23–29 would also still have to be strictly enforced.

Our engagement is merely a promise to become husband and wife at some future time. That date, as a rule, is not chosen until some time later. The vows are not solemnly exchanged before witnesses until the wedding ceremony takes place. Then is when the engaged are "pronounced man and wife in the name of the Father, and of the Son, and of the Holy Ghost."

An engagement is something that should be regarded as sacred and solemn. It has to do with one of the most important steps in life. Only after prolonged and serious thought and much earnest prayer should one consent to become engaged. But engagement or betrothal among us is not marriage as it was among the Jews of old.

Remarriage after Divorce

Why do Lutherans permit divorced people to remarrry?

Doubtless, most of us are too lenient about the sin of divorce. But remember, all divorce is not forbidden. There may be an innocent party who suffers a divorce that is thrust upon him or her. Will you say that this innocent party has not a right to remarry? Moreover, Jesus told the faultfinding Pharisees of His day that "Moses because of the hardness of your hearts suffered you to put away your wives." Did Moses do this entirely on his own authority? Jesus does not charge Moses with having done wrong in *suffering* divorce under certain circumstances. Of course, someone has committed a terrible sin when a divorce takes place. The real offense has already been committed when the marriage vow is not faithfully kept. There are times when a person must choose the less of two evils. At any rate, individual cases will have to be left to the conscience and the best judgment of the local pastor and his congregation.

Premarital Promise

Do you think a Protestant does wrong if he repudiates the promise to rear his children as Roman Catholics which he made to the priest at the time of his marriage?

King Herod, when more or less intoxicated at the time of his birthday celebration, promised under oath that he would give the daughter of Herodias whatever she would ask. When she asked for the head of John the Baptist on a platter, he realized to his regret that he had made a mistake. To keep his rash promise he had to put to death the forerunner of the world's Redeemer. Should he or should he not have kept that hasty, thoughtless promise? I do not see how anyone can be in doubt as to what he should have done. He should have humbled himself and openly admitted that he had made a sad mistake. He did wrong in making such a reckless, far-reaching promise. Should he now commit a still greater wrong in order to keep a bad promise?

When a Protestant, in the presence of a priest, signs a printed promise to the effect that, should a kind providence make him a parent, he will rear his children in a faith in which he professes not to believe, that is a rash promise pressed upon him at a time when, as a rule, the youth little realizes the far-reaching consequences of his promise. The saying is true that love is blind, and to press from a young man or woman in that hour of infatuation such a far-reaching promise is certainly taking an undue advantage of that person. At the time few realize how much is involved in that promise.

Of course, if the so-called Protestant has no real convictions as to what is truth and what is error, it is a matter of indifference to him, and the religious training of his children will never weigh very heavily on his conscience. But suppose by God's grace he experiences a real change of heart. The enormity of his rash promise now begins to dawn upon him. He has pledged to rear his offspring in a faith which he now knows to be grossly false. He is to teach his child to believe that he can merit grace by works of penance imposed upon him by a priest instead of confidently depending solely on the grace of God as offered through the atonement which is ours in Christ Jesus, our divine Redeemer. He is to tell that dear child of his own bosom that after baptism he can find forgiveness only through the sacrament of penance administered by a properly ordained priest, and hence there is no salvation for him apart from a priest. He is to teach his child to pray to a departed human being and thus to commit what he knows to be nothing short of idolatry. Can he do this with a good conscience? When he awakens to the enormity of his youthful mistake he will humbly confess it before God and man, and to be true to his God and his conscience he cannot do otherwise than repudiate that careless promise, repent of it, and plead for pardon.

In this connection I think I should warn against mixed marriages, especially where there is such a vast difference as between a Roman Catholic and a Lutheran. Of course, if those who marry have no real convictions, if they are only nominal Christians, they may get along fairly well together. But if they are sincere in what they profess to believe concerning their soul's salvation they can never be one in the most essential thing of life, and it will bring about bitter strife and heartache, especially if children are born to them. And what will become of the children reared under such circumstances? About 20 per cent will faithfully follow either father or mother; the rest will, as a rule, be indifferent or even bitter against all religion and thus swell the great number of the unchurched who are on the broad road leading to perdition.

Communion of Children

Did Luther change the custom of giving the Lord's Supper to children of 6 and 7?

The Greek Catholic Church gives the Lord's Supper even to children that are quite small. This was the general custom before the Reformation. However, since about the time of the Reformation the Roman Catholic Church does not give Holy Communion until about the age of seven. Thus it is correct to say that it was the Protestant Reformers who corrected this sad mistake of giving the Lord's Supper to children who have not the least idea of what it means. Paul exhorts, "Let a man examine himself, and so let him eat of that bread, and drink of that cup." This self-examination certainly requires some knowledge concerning the fundamental truths of the Christian religion. One must have some understanding of "law" and "gospel," sin and grace. One must know something about the Savior and the need of this Savior and the object of this Holy Supper. Bodily food can bring nourishment to the child as well as to the adult; to the unconscious person, who does not even know that he is eating as well as to the one who has a good understanding as to what he is eating, and why he is eating. But it is not so with the spiritual food for the soul. The Lord's Supper is to bring us renewed peace, comfort, and hope in the assurance of pardon through the body that was broken for us and the blood that was shed for the remission of our sins. How can anyone secure these benefits if he has not even the least idea of what it is all about?

The Address, "Woman"

Will you please explain why Jesus always addressed His beloved mother Mary as "woman" instead of "mother"? See John 2:4 and John 19:26. This has always puzzled me, and I would like to hear your explanation.

Why Jesus should address His mother as "woman" has been a perplexing question to many Christian people. We are agreed that thereby He certainly did not wish to show any discourtesy or disrespect to His mother. We are told that this form of address would not seem as harsh to an Oriental as it does to us. Yet it certainly is far from the tender and affectionate term "mother." There must have been some weighty reason why on the cross Jesus did not say "mother" even as He did not thus address her at Cana.

Various explanations have been given. Some have suggested that Jesus avoided the term "mother" for fear that that tender way of address would have pained His dear mother's heart all the more. Others have supposed that Jesus did not want the cruel scoffers under the cross to know that this was His mother lest they ridicule her for having a criminal son. These explanations do not satisfy. They do not tell us why Jesus failed to use the term "mother" at Cana.

The real meaning lies deeper. While Mary was and always remained the dear mother who had given Jesus birth, yet when He entered upon His Messianic work as the Savior of sinners, this human, blood relationship was superseded by a higher, spiritual relationship. Mary henceforth must see in Jesus, not merely her son, but primarily her dear Redeemer and Savior from sin. This higher, spiritual relationship is the all-important thing for Mary as well as for all of us. God greatly honored Mary in permitting her to be the mother of the world's Redeemer. But her salvation rested, not on her motherhood, but on her discipleship. She was saved by grace through faith in the Lord Jesus just as you and I find pardon and salvation through Him as our Redeemer and Savior.

The last time we hear of Mary in Scripture she is with the disciples. She was one of the followers of Jesus, uniting with them in prayer, praise, and supplication in His name, trusting in His promises and looking forward to the time when He would also give them a blessed homegoing (see Acts 1:14). In this connection study also Matthew 12:46–50: "Who is My mother? and who are My brethren? And He stretched forth His hand toward His disciples, and said, Behold My mother and My brethren! For whosoever shall do the will of My Father which is in heaven, the same is My brother, and sister, and mother." What marvel of grace! Jesus picks up you and me and puts us on a level with His dear mother in this higher, spiritual relationship. "One is your Master, even Christ, and all ye are brethren." This includes also the Virgin Mary. In this we find the reason why Jesus, after He had entered upon His redemptive work, no longer addresses Mary as "mother."

PART FIVE

BELIEFS, CUSTOMS,
and TRADITIONS

Fatalism

People often express the fatalistic view, "If my number is up, I'll die." I don't like that expression. Can you give me information about it?

Here we have a question that puzzles many people. Is the length of man's life so fixed and determined by our Creator that man cannot change it? That is certainly not true. We do, indeed, read in Job 14:5: "Seeing his [man's] days are determined, the number of his months are with Thee, Thou hast appointed his bounds that he cannot pass." Here we are plainly told that man's earthly existence is fixed, "determined" by God, beyond which he cannot live. I take this to mean that God has allotted to each one a certain span of life, which he may live and enjoy if he so chooses. This is clearly the meaning of the words: "Thou hast appointed his bounds that he cannot pass."

This, however, cannot mean that the Lord has so definitely determined the length of man's life that, do what he will, he cannot change it. Was King Saul forced to thrust himself through with his own sword (I Samuel 31:4)? Could Judas not have lived longer (Matthew 27:5)? The Lord says: "Honor thy father and thy mother; which is the first commandment with promise; that it may be well with thee, and thou mayest live long on the earth," Ephesians 6:2, 3. This plainly tells us that an obedient, God-fearing person may live the full period of time allotted to him, whether his years be many or few. Time is to be measured not only by number of days but by what goes into those days. But these words also plainly imply that the wicked and disobedient may shorten their days, and usually do so, by their acts of violence and disregard of God's law.

It is wrong for a person to think that God has set a fixed time and determined a certain way in which each individual must die. Would all the men and the women who fell in the late war have died just at the moment they did had there been no war? God has created man with a free will. He can choose to act contrary to God's will. And though in the end God rules and overrules the acts of man He does not take from man his free will. Man can and only too often does in his ignorance or wilfulness choose the wrong. God has appointed that man will and must die sometime—unless he is still living when the Lord visibly returns to this earth—but the time and the manner of each man's death are largely determined by himself. Man can shorten his life by his carelessness and by disregard of the laws of health, and, alas, he can shorten the lives of others. Nothing can take place without the Lord's knowledge of it and His permission. That is, God suffers man to do wrong because he has been given the power of choice. But man is responsible for his actions and will have to give an account for them to his Maker.

The intelligent Christian is not a fatalist. It is a serious error for a person to think that whatever happens must happen. What may be avoided does not have to be. How often in our ignorance or wickedness we do that which is wrong, or for the same reason we fail to do what we ought to do!

Fortunetelling

Shall we have our fortunes told?

"Come on, and let's have our fortunes told." How common it is to be thus coaxed into having one's fortunes told! And certainly, there are plenty of chances to have one's fortune told. Who of us has not found on the doorstep or on the porch of his home cards telling of Madam ...., who is endowed with supernatural powers that enable her to penetrate the future? And we have all seen tents erected on the outskirts of the city or, perhaps, even well within the city where fortunetellers advertise their trade by means of a large painted hand with all its lines and markings. And advertisements such as the following are familiar to all of us: "Private reading, cards, etc., advice, tea served." "Diamond Tea Room. Lunch, tea, cards read by Mrs. Blank." "Psychology, Numerology, by expert; tea served." "Tea leaf reading free."

Now, when we remonstrate and say to those who would have us consult fortunetellers, "I don't think I should," we are assured, "It's all fun, just fun; there's nothing to it." Granted it is all "fun, just fun," should we even so have our fortunes told? Does what is done in fun always cause fun and invariably end in fun? I can still see the husband who called on a fortuneteller just for fun. The result of that call proved to be anything but funny, for the fortuneteller poisoned his mind with suspicions as to his wife's faithfulness. I know a group of girls who went to a fortuneteller just for fun. But while everything seemed funny to them at the time, there was nothing funny about the aftermath. One of the girls became ill just as the fortuneteller said she would, and when this happened, she lived in deadly fear that all the other unpleasant things which had been foretold would come true. No sooner did the other girls hear of her illness than they, too, were filled with fear and lived in fear until they could finally stand it no longer and sought relief by telling their parents about it.

Perhaps you will say, "Well, it just so happened that some of those things came true which the fortuneteller had predicted," or you may say, "There is really no such thing as the telling of fortunes." Are you positive that you are right in this assertion? Fortunes can be told, and they have been told. He has said, "Thou shalt not take the name of the Lord thy God in vain." And Luther interprets this command in this wise, "We should fear and love God . . . and not curse, swear, *conjure*"— which, among other things, means to tell fortunes and have them told. And has not God said in the plainest language possible, Deuteronomy 18:10-15: "There shall not be found among you any one that maketh his son or daughter to pass through the fire, or that useth divination, or an observer of times, or an enchanter, or a witch, or a charmer, or a consulter with familiar spirits, or a wizard, or a necromancer. For all that do these things are an abomination unto the Lord, and because of these abominations thy Lord doth drive them out from before thee. For these nations which thou shalt possess, hearkened unto observers of times and unto diviners, but *as for thee*, the Lord thy God hath not suffered thee so to do."

The Father in heaven, whose children we are, has cast a veil over the future, and His Word to us is, "Touch not this veil, and let no one meddle with it." Are joys in store for us? God will let us experience them in His hour. Are afflictions and sorrows to be our lot? God does not want us to reach over into the morrow and "drag in today" what is meant for tomorrow. Shall we have our fortunes told? No, not unless we want to sin against God, and not unless we want to walk about with a guilty conscience and a fearful spirit.

Halloween

What is the origin of Halloween? Why the witches, cats, false faces, etc.? I was of the opinion that these Halloween pranks were started by the Catholics in mockery of the Protestants. But, lo, I find the Protestants are as much for these Halloween frolics as are the Catholics. It seems to me we Protestants should be thankful for what happened on Halloween and celebrate the day differently than to mask, go wild, and tear up property.

The ancient Druids had a great autumn festival which commenced at midnight, October 31, and lasted throughout the following day, November 1. Among other things they believed that on this night the great lord of death, Saman, called together all the wicked souls that had been condemned within the past twelve months.

The Romans also had a festival about the first of November, which was in honor of Pomona, the patron goddess of tree fruits. Nuts and apples and other fruits, tokens of the winter store, were roasted before great bonfires and eaten amidst all manner of merrymaking. Thus it appears that the Druidic ceremonies and the Roman festivities were grafted one upon the other to become the origin of our present-day Halloween.

The name "Halloween" is of Christian origin and refers to the eve of All Hallows or All Saints' Day. The early Christians adopted the eve and the day following and gave new names and Christian observances to them.

Thus, you see, Halloween was observed centuries before the day of Luther. Why did Luther tack up his celebrated Ninety-five Theses on the Castle church in Wittenberg on the evening of October 31? Because the next day was All Saints' Day when the people would stream to church for the special services of that holy day. The observance of Halloween has nothing whatever to do with the posting of the important document that aroused all Europe and brought on the Reformation.

Santa Claus

Is it a sin for parents to tell their children that there is a Santa Claus?

I do not consider it a sin. When you tell your children a story, one which you have thought out yourself, or which you have heard or read some place, do you think that you are doing wrong? That story may be pure imagination, the persons you mention exist in your mind only, and the incidents you refer to are of your own invention. Would you say that you are sinning if you tell your children that story in order to amuse them or to teach them a lesson? Then the teaching by fables and even by parables would be wrong.

"Love is the fulfillment of the law." Then what is the opposite of love must be sin. Sin always injures or harms someone. Do we tell our children about a Santa Claus because we want to harm them? Is it not because we want to increase their happiness? Does love move us to do so or lack of love?

The essence of a lie is to deceive, and to deceive in order to harm. Now, I do not believe that children will be harmed because later in life they found out that there is no Santa Claus any more than I was harmed when I learned that the story of the Prodigal Son is a parable rather than an actual happening.

The wise parent will, of course, be discreet in what he tells his children about Santa Claus. And when those children are old enough, the parent will himself explain how Santa Claus is just a way of indicating the spirit of Christmas, and how the real spirit of Christmas centers in and comes from Jesus Christ, God's great gift of love to the world.

The Name of Christmas

Why is December 25 called "Christmas"?

"Christmas" is a compound of the two words "Christ" and "mass." "Mass" comes from the Latin word *missa*. The historical derivation of the word is this: In the ancient church only communicant members were present when the Lord's Supper was celebrated. After the sermon all the children, catechumens, and strangers were dismissed with the words: *"Ite, missa est,"* Go, you are dismissed. In this way the Holy Supper and the service immediately connected with it got to be known as the "Missa." In Old English that word is "Messe," and the holy service commemorative of Christ's birth, "Christ Messe." From this comes our present term "Christmas."

Change of Calendar

(1) I am told that a calendar change is being proposed, and that there is a bill pending in Congress urging that our nation sanction this change. I would be thankful to learn something about this proposed change. (2) Can we as Christian people conscientiously go along with this proposed change? I have a friend who is very much disturbed about it.

1. For a number of years a change in the calendar has been proposed and urged, especially by the commercial world. Our present arrangement, it is said, is very inconvenient when it comes to comparing profit

or loss month after month or quarter following quarter. The length of our months now varies from 28 days (leap year, 29 days) to 31 days. No regular sequence is followed in the present arrangement of the long and the short months. December and January follow each other, and each has 31 days. The same is true of July and August. Otherwise a long month is followed by a short one. This results in unequal quarters, varying from 90 to 92 days. The months contain a varying number of workdays, depending on the number of Sundays in the month. Such irregularities cause difficulties when it comes to comparative statistics. Months and quarters do not cover an equal length of time.

These difficulties could be largely overcome, we are told, by a change in the arrangement of the calendar. It is proposed that the year always begin with a Sunday, and that every quarter begin with a Sunday. Each of the four quarters is to contain 91 days. In each quarter there will be 78 workdays and 13 Sundays. The first month of each quarter is to have 31 days, each of the remaining two months of the quarter 30 days. Each month is to have 26 workdays, plus Sundays. The year is always to end on a Saturday. This can be brought about provided we drop out one day every regular year and two days every leap year. In other words, the "Edwards Perpetual Calendar" proposes that we have a 364-day-year arrangement, with one blank day following the end of December in regular years and an additional blank day between June and July in leap years. These blank days are not to be considered as a part of the week which precedes or follows them. They are simply extra days that we must have to fill out the solar year, that is, the length of time it takes the earth to make its circuit around the sun.

There is a World Calendar Association that is back of this movement, and, no doubt, we shall be hearing more about it in the near future.

2. I see no reason why we Christians cannot go along with this proposed change. We are not bound by God to any certain fixed day or to any definite period of time for our public worship. The people of God of Old Testament time were, of course, legally bound to the observing of the seventh day of the week. The Sabbath of the Jews began with sundown on the sixth day and ended with sundown on the seventh day of the week. From the clear teaching of Scripture we are convinced that the observing of the Sabbath was a part of the ceremonial law of Israel, from which we have been freed.

The inspired St. Paul calls that Christian "weak" in the faith who has religious scruples as to what he eats or drinks as though we were still under the ceremonial laws of the Old Testament concerning these things. The same is true of the Christian who esteems one day as more sacred than another as though Saturday were better than Monday or the first day of the week in itself more holy than some other day of the week. Another Christian esteems every day equally holy and sacred. That is the one whom the apostle commends because he knows his Christian liberty. "Happy is he that condemneth not himself in that thing which He [God] alloweth." See Romans, chapter 14.

Already at the very beginning of the Christian era the inspired apostles selected the first day of the week for public worship. Saturday was gradually dropped. There was no legislation regarding this. All was done in the spirit of Christian liberty.

The Word of God is to be diligently, publicly proclaimed, and the sacraments are to be administered. We are not to forsake the assembling of ourselves together for mutual edification. But we are not bound by God to any definite, fixed period of time. We worship God acceptably when we worship Him "in spirit and in truth," no matter where we are or what time of the day or of the week it may be. Whether the 25th of December comes a day earlier or a day later will not bother us in the least in the commemoration of our Savior's birth just as we now rejoice in the glorious resurrection whether Easter comes in March or in April. "Let no one pass judgment on you in questions of food and drink or with regard to a festival or a new moon or a sabbath. These are only a shadow of what is to come; but the substance belongs to Christ."

Origin of the Easter Egg

What is the origin of the Easter egg, the Easter rabbit?

The custom of presenting colored eggs to each other at Eastertime is of ancient origin. It prevailed among pagans even before the advent of Christianity. Doubtless the use of eggs in the spring of the year was originally symbolical of the revivification of nature, the springing forth of new life. It was a common policy of the early church, seeking to Christianize pagans, to endeavor to give a Christian significance to such pagan customs as could not be rooted out. This custom of exchanging pretty eggs, hiding and hunting them, etc., could easily be given a Christian significance. From the Christian point of view eggs are emblematic of the resurrection and of a future life.

The origin of the Easter rabbit, as I have heard it somewhere, is about as follows: A lady of wealth and nobility had moved into a little village of Germany many years ago. The children of that village knew nothing about colored Easter eggs. So this kind lady, who was a great lover of children, decided to give them some real joy on happy Easter day. Early on Easter morning, with a large basket filled with eggs of all colors of the rainbow, she stole out of the village, and here and there in the grass of the meadows, under the hedges and among the springing wild flowers, she hid her pretty eggs. Then the children were aroused and told to go on the hunt of them. Out they hurried as fast as their feet could carry them. When the little boy in the lead spied an egg and with a shout ran to get it, up jumped a rabbit and scampered away. Of course the boy concluded that the rabbit had laid it. We can imagine what a shouting and hurrying to and from there was as the excited happy children hunted for the Easter-rabbit eggs. From this the German parents learned the secret of preparing an innocent joy for their children on joyous Easter morning.

The Easter Lily

What is the meaning and significance of the Easter lily?

Flowers are beautiful and cheering, and they testify to the goodness of our God. They are, therefore, appropriate decorations of our places of worship. Flowers symbolize life and joy and are in honor of Him who is the "Rose of Sharon" and the "Lily of the Valley."

The white lily is especially appropriate for Easter. It is an emblem of life and purity and symbolizes the resurrection. As the bulb is planted in the ground, and in due time there springs from it a thing of beauty in newness of life, so the mortal body of man is consigned to mother earth, but it shall come forth again in the beauty, power, and glory of a new and perfect life.

Hands Folded in Prayer

How should a Lutheran fold his hands when praying?

The posture which we assume in prayer should indicate reverence and respect, but no definite posture is prescribed. To stand or kneel with folded hands and bowed head is an appropriate position. Jesus looked up toward heaven when in prayer He blessed the bread and the fishes before feeding the five thousand (Luke 9:16). But the penitent publican who went up into the Temple to pray, "standing afar off would not lift up so much as his eyes unto heaven, but smote upon his breast, saying, God, be merciful to me, a sinner," Luke 18:13. Thus the publican humbly *stood* with bowed head, but he did not fold his hands, for he used at least one, if not both of them, in beating upon his breast. Jesus knelt in prayer in Gethsemane. One artist pictures His hands as being folded. But for all we know, He may at times also have stretched them imploringly toward heaven. Thus no definite posture is prescribed. We may pray acceptably in any position. God looks upon the heart.

When the heart is right, the body will assume an attitude of reverence if at all possible to do so. From time immemorial folded hands have been considered an appropriate attitude of prayer. But should our hands be clasped with entwined fingers, or should our hands be held before us with palm against palm? That is entirely a matter of individual taste and custom. Among Lutherans I believe folded hands mean clasped hands with entwined fingers.

The Ringing of Church Bells

Some of our churches have the custom of ringing or tolling the church bell while the Lord's Prayer is being prayed in the morning service. What is the meaning and origin of this custom?

I do not know when this custom first came into vogue, but its meaning was explained to me thus in early childhood by my sainted grandmother. There are always some each Sunday or festival day who by force of circumstances are compelled to miss the public worship of God's house. These devoted souls are members of the fellowship of Christ, they are children of the household of God, though on that day they cannot assemble with their brethren in the holy sanctuary. They should be with them in spirit as much as possible, and when the petitions of the day culminate in the prayer Jesus Himself taught us, the church bell gives them notice of this, and they are expected to pause for a minute in what they are doing and join their assembled brethren in sending sacred petitions to the throne of grace. Who will not admit that this is a beautiful thought, and that if all the professed followers of Jesus would practice this custom, great blessing would result from it?

The Wearing of a Robe

Why is it that the Lutheran minister wears a robe?

This question was a very common one until recently. But in our day many churches that once ridiculed the German Lutherans for having preachers that looked like Catholic priests have themselves now not only a robed minister but also a vested choir and organist. Therefore to bring this question up to date it ought to be stated something like this: "Why is it custom in many churches of our day to have the minister, choir members, and organist robed?"

It is not because of any command of God. A man can preach the Word of God in truth and purity and administer the sacraments acceptably as instituted by Christ, whether he wears a special ministerial garb or not. A pastor can be a good Lutheran irrespective of the style of garments which he wears in the sanctuary or outside of it. And the orthodoxy of a Lutheran congregation is not judged by the custom which prevails in its midst as to robes and vestments. The Lord says: "Let all things be done decently and in order." Otherwise He leaves it entirely to our choice as to what we consider fitting, proper, and most suitable for the occasion. This is the position taken, therefore, also by our church. The use or nonuse of vestments, the order of service, church furnishings, church architecture, etc., are entirely a matter of Christian liberty.

Why, then, do Lutherans, as a rule, prefer to have their minister solemnly robed when he is officiating at the altar and in the pulpit? And why are more and more of the other churches introducing this custom? God designated the garments which the Old Testament priest was to wear when on duty. He described and prescribed in detail every particle of his clothing (see Exodus, chapter 28). But since the New Testament ministry and its work are equally as important and sacred as the Old Testament priesthood and its duties were, we certainly have a right to conclude that, though the Lord does not command the wearing of special solemn garments by the officiating minister in His sanctuary, He does approve them.

Why do the judges of all our higher courts wear a solemn, black robe while on duty? It is to impress upon the people in general the solemnity, the dignity, and the importance of their office and work. That is, no doubt, the chief object of robes and vestments used in connection with the services of God's house. It is to add beauty, reverence, dignity, and solemnity to the service. Nothing about the minister's clothing is to detract from the Scripture lesson which he reads, or the prayer which he offers, or the message which in the name of Christ he delivers. In the choir the poor man or lady is to be on equal footing with the more wealthy; no display of costly garments and fineries.

The Wood of Christ's Cross

Of what kind of wood was Christ's cross made?

I am unable to answer your question. You will have to ask one of those who claim to have a relic of the original cross on which the Savior died. You know it is claimed by some that Empress Helena, the mother of Constantine the Great, discovered the cross of Jesus. She built a church on the spot where this sacred relic was allegedly found. The greater part of the cross, it is reputed, she deposited in this church, the remainder she took to Constantinople. A part of this was later taken to Rome. Of course, many pilgrims came in wonder to gaze upon this sacred relic. It became a source of great revenue for Mother Church. Splinters of it could be purchased and taken along home. When some began to wonder how there could be so many particles of the original cross, "the proper authorities gave the world an assurance that the holy wood possessed the power of self-multiplication, and, notwithstanding the innumerable pieces which had been taken from it for the pleasure and service of the faithful, remained intact and entire as at the first" (*The Popular and Critical Bible Encyclopedia*).

Doubtless various kinds of wood are on display somewhere in the world, of each of which the claim is made that it is a part of the original cross on which Jesus was crucified.

Guardian Angels

My grandmother frequently speaks of her guardian angel. She believes that each child of God has an especially appointed protecting angel. Is there any Biblical proof for this belief?

It was a favorite opinion of the early Christians that every individual Christian is under the care of a particular angel, who is assigned to him at birth as a guardian. Artists have pictured for us the guardian angel watching over our little ones. Jesus said on one occasion: "Take heed that ye despise not one of these little ones; for I say unto you, That in heaven their angels do always behold the face of My Father which is in heaven," Matthew 18:10. This verse is usually referred to in proof of the idea of a guardian angel for each individual Christian and especially for every child. However, we fear that is putting into these words a thought that they do not contain. Christ warns against looking down upon even one of these little ones as though he were of minor importance, and we thus disregard and neglect him. He tells us that these little ones are so precious in God's sight that He delegates the angels to watch over them. This, however, does not necessarily say that each Christian person or each child has his own angelic companion and protector. God uses His angels as "ministering spirits, sent forth to minister for them who shall be heirs of salvation," Hebrews 1:14, and He often assigns an individual angel for some special duty. But at other times He sends them in pairs or in groups.

"It is his [Peter's] angel," said the people when that apostle stood knocking at the door of the home of Mary on the night when he was miraculously freed from prison by an angel (Acts 12). These words, too, are sometimes cited in proof of belief in a guardian angel. But

163

dare we use these words as the Biblical statement of a truth? Do they not rather state the superstitious idea of an alarmed people because of Rhoda's announcement, "Peter stands before the door" when they thought the apostle was still securely held in prison? The angels are, indeed, our guardian companions, but this does not say that each one has his guardian angel.

The Wings of Angels

Why do the artists always picture angels with wings?

The angels are spirits, but when these invisible beings of the upper world were sent to appear on earth they assumed a body in the likeness of man for the time being. We cannot conceive of shape or form without material substance, therefore we do not know what form or shape angels naturally have, or if they have any. Now when Gabriel appeared to Zacharias in the Temple or later to Mary at Nazareth, did the body in which he appeared have wings as well as a face, hands, and feet? I do not know, but I do not think so. Why, then, you are wondering, do the artists always picture angels with wings? I can give you only my private supposition.

The Bible speaks of the angels as having wings. Isaiah was given a vision of the Lord's glory. In it he beheld the seraphim: "each one had six wings; with twain he covered his face, and with twain he covered his feet, and with twain he did fly," Isa. 6:2. In the sixth verse of this same chapter Isaiah affirms: "Then flew one of these seraphim unto me." The artist has drawn these seraphim of Isaiah's vision for us, and each is, of course, represented as having six wings. The four cherubim, "living creatures," of Ezekiel's vision each had four wings and four hands (Ezek. 1). Why, then, do the artists usually represent the angels as having two wings? I suppose it is because the Lord Himself thus pictured them to Moses when He gave him instructions concerning the building of the Tabernacle (Exodus 25:18–22; see also I Kings 6:23–29).

The Crucifix

My children recently gave me a crucifix. Do you think it proper to hang it up in our home? If so, where should it be hung?

Why would you consider it improper for a Christian to display a crucifix in her home? Some people think it is Catholic to have a cross, crucifix, and statue of Christ. Fortunately, Christian people are getting away from that false notion more and more. Because some people misuse these symbols of Christianity is no reason that we should hesitate to use them as a confession of our Christian faith.

I am in no position to advise you as to the most suitable place for this crucifix in your home. I would suggest your bedroom. And may the thought of your gracious Savior give you peace and rest when you retire for the night and new courage and strength when you go forth to your work in the morning!

Statues of Christ

Is it not sinful to have statues of Christ when God tells us not to make any picture or likeness of anything that is in heaven above?

You must not tear these words out of their connection. The Lord says: "Thou shalt not make unto thee any graven image, or any likeness of any thing that is in heaven above, or that is in the earth beneath, or that is in the water under the earth: [and now comes the force of the command] thou shalt not bow down thyself to them, nor serve them." It is certainly a mistake to think that God here forbids the making of any likeness or picture of anything. There are those who think that it is sinful to have their photograph taken. This, however, cannot be the meaning of these words. Immediately after the giving of the commandments at Sinai the Lord gave Moses directions for the building of the Tabernacle. In the Holy of Holies of this sacred Tabernacle Moses was told to make two images of the cherubim, and the mercy seat was to be under the outstretched wings of these two angel images. Again the Lord said to Moses: "Thou shalt make the Tabernacle with ten curtains of fine twined linen, and blue, and purple, and scarlet: with cherubim of cunning work shalt thou make them," Exodus 26:1. Thus there were statues and pictures of angels in the Tabernacle of old, and they were there because the Lord Himself directed Moses to put them there. The same is true of the Temple of Solomon. Read the sixth chapter of II Kings. The angel images are minutely described. "And he [Solomon] carved all the walls of the house round about with carved figures of cherubim and palm trees and open flowers, within and without."

That which is forbidden is not the making of a picture or representation of something or the having of such a likeness, whether it be to beautify our homes or our churches; that which God forbids is the adoring and idolizing of these images. Neither does God want man to try to worship Him by means of, or through the aid of, some tangible likeness, for that leads astray, it tends toward idolatry.

165

The Wearing of a Cross

Is the wearing of the cross on the person a sign of Catholicism?

The Romish Church, doubtless, makes more extensive use of the symbol of the cross than does any other church as it does of other ecclesiastical ornaments, statuary, emblems, and vestments. But the cross is not an emblem or symbol of Catholicism but of the Christian religion. It is, therefore, perfectly in place and proper that it should be reverently used by any believer in Christ who with Paul will say: "God forbid that I should glory, save in the cross of our Lord Jesus Christ, by whom the world is crucified unto me, and I unto the world," Gal. 6:14.

The Meaning of I.H.S.

Does I.H.S. stand for "Jesus Hominum Salvator"? Does it stand for this in all denominations that use it? When did it originate? Is it true that it means, "In Hoc Signo"? Is it Greek for "Jesus"?

In *The Altar: Its Ornaments and Its Care*, by Rev. Henry Smart, D.D., we read: "I.H.S. This common symbol does not mean, 'I have suffered.' The three letters are the initials of JESUS HOMINUM SALVATOR; 'Jesus Savior of Men.' The original use of I.H.S. is derived from the first three letters of the Greek word for Jesus. I.H.S., being equivalent to I.E.S."

I.H.S.V. stands for *"In hoc signo vinces,"* "In this sign, or under this standard, thou shalt conquer." This symbol is used a great deal by the Knights Templars, but to my knowledge is never used by the Christian Church. And I feel sure that I.H.S. never stands for, "In This Sign."

PART SIX

HEALTH, SICKNESS, DEATH, and BURIAL

The Purpose of Sickness

Can you prove and illustrate from the Bible that sickness draws people closer to God?

It certainly ought not to be difficult to prove that sickness, pain, and distress tend to drive people to their divine Helper. If you are at all acquainted with the life of Jesus you will know how the sick, the crippled, the blind, etc., were continually coming to Jesus or being brought to Him. "Behold, there came a leper and worshipped Him, saying, Lord, if Thou wilt, Thou canst make me clean," Matthew 8:2. "When Jesus was entered into Capernaum, there came unto Him a centurion, beseeching Him, and saying, Lord, my servant lieth at home sick of the palsy, grievously tormented," Matthew 8:5, 6.

"Behold, happy is the man whom God correcteth; therefore despise not thou the chastening of the Almighty," Job. 5:17. "For whom the Lord loveth He correcteth; even as a father the son in whom he delighteth," Prov. 3:12. "Lord, in trouble have they visited Thee, they poured out a prayer when Thy chastening was upon them," Isa. 26:16.

God intends that His chastening hand of love should draw people closer to Him. But all do not yield to this fatherly chastening. They rebel and only harden themselves the more against God. Job doubtless was drawn closer to God by his awful suffering, but this is not true of his wife. She advised her husband to renounce his allegiance to God. "Curse God, and die," was her cynical remark. A God who permits such suffering to come upon a person is not worthy of allegiance, honor, and service, thought she. The malefactor to the right was drawn nearer to Jesus by his distress, but it had no such effect on the one to the left. Thus sickness, pain, and sorrow are intended to drive people to their

167

knees in repentance and to draw them to their divine Savior. But man in his wilfulness can and only too often does reject and rebel against the chastening hand of a kind, well-meaning Father, and thus that which was intended as a savor of life unto life gets to be a savor of death unto death.

Anointing the Sick

Does the Lutheran Church believe in anointing the sick with oil?

In the concluding chapter of his epistle St. James first warns the wicked rich of a terrible retribution that a just and holy God is sure to bring upon them. He then turns to the Christians, the "brethren" as he terms them, and exhorts them to exercise patience after the example of the suffering prophets and of Job. In verse 12 he pleads with them to abstain from all unnecessary oaths. The writer next turns to the prayer life of the believer. Verses 13 to 18 treat of this important subject. "Is any among you afflicted? let him pray. Is any merry? let him sing psalms."

No matter in what condition the Christian may find himself, let him turn his thoughts upward to God. Is he suffering? Has he sorrow or distress? Let him throw his burdens upon the Lord and look to Him for comfort, strength, and relief. Is he happy and cheerful because of the many blessings showered upon him? Let him not forget to sing praise unto his God, from whom cometh every good and perfect gift. Thus in good days and in evil days—and they make up our entire life—let the Christian walk close with his God and take everything to Him in prayer and praise.

Thus far we may say the writer refers to the shadow and the sunshine of life in general. But now he singles out three special conditions and gives instruction and exhortation concerning them. 1. If a Christian is sick, what should he do? 2. If one has distress of conscience because of sin, what then? 3. And if one err from the truth, whether in doctrine or in life, what should the brethren endeavor to do in such a case?

We are now especially concerned about the first distressing condition. "Is any sick among you? let him call for the elders of the church; and let them pray over him, anointing him with oil in the name of the Lord. And the prayer of faith shall save the sick, and the Lord shall raise him up; and if he have committed sins, they shall be forgiven him."

Is any sick among Christians, suffering from some painful and serious ailment, what should he do? Let him call for the elders of the congregation to which he belongs. All the brethren will, of course, be interested and intercede for the sufferer at the throne of grace. But let the sick one especially invite the leaders of the congregation, the pastors (there were usually two in that day), and let them pray for him and with him, having anointed him with oil (this is the more literal translation) in the name of the Lord. The prayer followed the anointing. Oil was seemingly usually used and carried about as a first aid. The Good Samaritan had oil and wine with him when he came upon the man who had fallen among thieves. When the Twelve were sent out by Jesus to heal the sick, to cleanse the leper, to cast out devils, etc., St. Mark relates, "And they cast out many devils, and anointed with oil many that were sick and healed them," Mark 6:13.

Why was this anointing done? It seems to have been a general custom of the day. The applying of the oil was, no doubt, soothing and refreshing and was, perhaps, also conducive to healing and relief. It would arouse the expectation and faith of the sick one and thus tend to put him in the right frame of mind. However, Jesus does not command the use of oil. In the above quoted passage Mark makes it plain that the apostles used it only at times. The emphasis is not on the anointing but on "the prayer of faith." It is this that shall "save the sick, and the Lord shall raise him up; and if he have committed sins, they shall be forgiven him."

We have here, however, no promise of a miraculous cure. The prayer of faith asks and expects no more than God promises. That prayer is always submissive and resigned to the will of Him who knows best. "Not my will, but Thine, be done." We dare not interpret James as here promising that God will invariably heal and restore the sick believer, and do so at once miraculously. True saints of God took sick and died of their ailments in the days of the apostles even as they do now. Poor Lazarus thus died at the gate of the rich man. St. Paul was never cured of "a thorn in the flesh," whatever affliction that may refer to. "Trophimus have I left at Miletum sick," Paul informs Timothy (II Tim. 4:20). Can you believe that Paul did not pray for him and with him, and was not their petition a prayer of faith?

There were physicians in the days of the apostles, and they prescribed remedies to the best of their knowledge. "They that are whole need not a physician; but they that are sick," says Jesus. Where did the Lord ever denounce the practice of medicine or the proper use of remedies? St. Luke was a physician. Paul calls him "the beloved physician," Col. 4:14. When Paul advised Timothy to "use a little wine for thy stomach's sake and thine often infirmities," he was suggesting a remedy (I Tim. 5:23). The Christians of James's day made use of physicians and their remedies, and the applying of oil by the elders or by any Christian brother when he visited his sick friend and prayed for him and with him is to be put on the same level with other remedies.

James considers it self-evident that the seriously ill will also call in a physician. But the Christian is concerned not only about the body. He has still greater concern about the welfare of his immortal soul. He craves the assurance of God's grace and love and the forgiveness of his sins. He knows also that on God's blessing depends the healing of his body. All healing is divine though God, as a rule, works according to the laws which He has laid down in nature. Therefore the Christian pleads for pardon, comfort, and peace, but he also asks God to guide and direct so that the proper remedy for his ailment may be found, and under His blessing, if it please Him, strength and health may be restored. The prescribing and the applying of the remedies for the body we leave to the medical profession; to men and women who have made that work a life's study. But as Christians, whether clergy or laymen, we pray God to give our physicians wisdom and skill, enable them to find the secrets of His laws in nature, and to add His blessing to their efforts.

The Gift of Healing

If St. Paul had the gift of healing, why did he leave Trophimus at Miletus sick? (II Timothy 4:20). His faithful helper, Timothy, also must have been troubled with "infirmities" (II Timothy 5:23). Certainly it would have been to the advantage of both for Timothy to have been strong and well. Why then, did Paul not heal him?

No mere mortal has the gift to heal except when God sees fit to grant him this power. And to no man did God ever grant the gift of healing in such a way that henceforth he was able to heal whenever and wherever he chose to do so. People got sick and died in the days of the apostles the same as now, and the apostles never thought of healing all or even a large proportion of them. The persons who received this miraculous power from Christ used it only when they received intimation from the Spirit of God that they should and could do so.

Paul healed many and even raised one from the dead, but he was unable to heal Trophimus and Timothy because he received no intimation from God that he should do so. And, lo, later on he could not heal himself though he desired it and earnestly and repeatedly asked God to grant him relief. But the answer of the Lord was: "My grace is sufficient for thee." God saw fit to have His faithful servant bear that painful "thorn in the flesh" the rest of his life.

Note that Paul does not reprove his fellow workmen, Trophimus and

Timothy, for lack of faith as if he could and would have healed them had they not lacked the necessary faith. The faith which the so-called divine healer insists on is simply the conviction that God will infallibly heal the sick one without means (medicine, medical care) if from the heart he asks God to do so. That is not Christian faith. The Christian believes that God loves him and in Christ Jesus is offering him every needful blessing, and that He will make all things (including sickness) work together for his good if he loves God (Romans 8:28). Faith cure expects of prayer what God never promised. No intelligent Christian expects God without fail to cure him of every ailment that may befall him. He prays, "Not my will, but Thy will be done" when asking for bodily and temporal blessings. Many a person lives closer to God and is more serviceable to God as a cripple or an invalid than he would be as a strong, healthy person.

The main function of Christian faith is not to free us of bodily ailments but to hold us to Christ as the Redeemer and Savior from sin.

Paul's Thorn in the Flesh

St. Paul asked God to relieve him of his terrible affliction. Was Paul an epileptic? I read an article on Paul which said he was under one of these terrible spells when Jesus appeared to him on the road to Damascus.

We are very much in the dark as to what is meant by that "thorn in the flesh" which so much distressed St. Paul. Prof. Goodspeed refers to it as "a bitter physical affliction." The idea that Paul had an epileptic fit when Jesus appeared to him at the gate of Damascus is silly in the extreme. An epileptic loses consciousness when a convulsion comes upon him, but he is not blind when consciousness returns. How would you explain the marvelous change that came over Paul in a few days? From being a bitter and most fanatic enemy of Jesus he suddenly became His most faithful follower and zealous advocate. This "thorn in the flesh" from all indications did not afflict Paul until late in life.

What Takes Place at Death

What happens when we die? Does the soul of the saved go directly to heaven, or does it sleep with the body until the last great day?

Our interest in these two questions never wanes. Especially when another dear one has been taken do we sit and ponder these questions.

The Bible gives us no uncertain answer to these questions, and we thrill in anticipation at the thought of what it tells us.

Bodily death is the separation of body and soul. From death until the day of judgment body and soul are not united. They do not sleep together in the tomb, nor does the soul sleep elsewhere while the body returns to its native elements in the grave. Jesus' dying words were: "Father, into Thy hands I commend My spirit." The lifeless (soul-less) body of the Master was buried in Joseph's new tomb. That was after the soul or spirit of Jesus had departed. Body and soul were not reunited until Easter morning. Thus it will be with you and with me and with all the blessed who die before the Lord's visible return. "Then shall the dust return to the earth as it was; and the spirit shall return unto God who gave it," Ecclesiastes 12:7.

To the penitent malefactor Jesus said: "Today shalt thou be with Me in paradise," Luke 23:43. Is it possible that the soul of this man is with Christ and all the blessed in paradise, but he is unconscious of this blessed fact because to this day he is still in a deep sleep? Stephen was the first Christian martyr. With his dying breath he prayed: "Lord Jesus, receive my spirit," Acts 7:59. His spirit then was certainly not carried to the grave with the body, neither is it tucked away somewhere in the heavenly Father's house in a deep sleep.

Enoch and Elijah did not die. They were taken directly and bodily to heaven (Genesis 5:24; Hebrews 11:5; II Kings 2:1–11). Are they there in a deep, unconscious sleep? Moses and Elijah appeared on the Mount of Transfiguration and talked with Jesus in the presence of Peter, James, and John (Matthew 17:1–8).

Desire for Death

Is it pious to wish to die?

That depends on the motive which creates the wish. Why should a person wish to die? To some, life seems unbearable, and so they wish themselves dead and even take their own life. They hope thus to snuff themselves out of existence. But in reality they thus only thrust themselves before a righteous God to give an account of their rebellion and murder. For that is what suicide is, rebellion against providence and self-murder. When discontent and rebellion against God's providential ways lead one to wish himself dead, no one but Satan himself is the father of that wish.

A workman who is always wishing for Saturday night is not the best kind of workman. The servant of God who thinks only of being relieved from toil and taken to the haven of rest is, I fear, not the best kind of servant. And his desire to die may thus rather be a sign of weakness than of true piety.

There is, however, a certain desire to die that is truly pious and, therefore, perfectly in place. Paul, writing to the Philippians, says that he has a desire to depart. What gave rise to this desire? He longed "to be with Christ." He wished for the time when, free from all sin, he might be face to face in undisturbed fellowship with his Lord and Savior. And that is a legitimate and natural desire, not for the unregenerated, but for the truly converted people of God.

But note well what Paul says. "I am in a strait betwixt two, having a desire to depart, and to be with Christ; which is far better: nevertheless to abide in the flesh is more needful for you." While Paul longed to depart and to be with his Savior he also desired to be of further service to his Lord and His brethren here on earth. He did not know which desire was uppermost in his heart. His supreme desire was that Christ might be magnified through him, "whether it be by life, or by death." (Study Philippians 1:19–26.)

Thus I would say that our supreme wish should always be that His will be done, and that all our desires may be in conformity with His desire.

Kinds of Death

In my Sunday school class yesterday the teacher repeatedly referred to spiritual death as being different from bodily death. I know that the Bible also speaks of "the second death" (Revelation 21:8). I am confused on this subject. Can you help me?

It is the plain teaching of Scripture that death is threefold in character. This fact must be kept in mind when studying the passages which treat of death.

1. *Bodily death.* When the Bible says: "It is appointed unto man once to die, but after this the judgment," Hebrews 9:27, it is evident that this refers to bodily death. From bodily death no mortal is exempt except those notable exceptions, Enoch and Elijah, and those who will still be among the living when the Lord visibly returns for the final judgment. "We shall not all sleep, but we shall all be changed," I Cor. 15:51.

Bodily death signifies the separation of the soul from the body. "Then shall the dust return to the earth as it was, and the spirit shall return unto God who gave it," Eccles. 12:7. This passage clearly says that bodily death is the dissolution of the union of the body and the soul, and that while the former is again claimed by the earth, the latter survives and returns to Him who gave it.

The death of the blessed is described as being gathered to their people (Genesis 25:8); as a departing in peace (Luke 2:29); as a turning away from the evils to come (Isaiah 57:1); as a sleep (Matthew 9:21).

2. *Spiritual death.* To the Christians at Ephesus Paul writes: "And you He made alive, when you were dead through the trespasses and sins in which you once walked," Ephesians 2:1, R.S.V. Of course, he means not bodily but spiritual death. They had been dead to God, outside of His kingdom. "We all . . . were by nature [in our natural, unregenerated state and condition] the children of wrath, even as others," Ephesians 2:3. We were born into the world endowed with natural, bodily life (we were not stillborn) but without spiritual life. This higher life is given to us by a second birth, by a birth from above. "Except a man be born again, he cannot see the kingdom of God," John 3:3. All, therefore, who have not been born from above by the Spirit of God, who alone can impart spiritual life, are still spiritually dead. We must become "new creatures" (Galatians 6:15) by reason of a spiritual birth, otherwise there is no hope for us. "To be carnally minded is death," Romans 8:6. To live without God and the Savior is spiritual death (the "first death") and through the portals of bodily death those who are in this "first death" will be transferred into that state and condition which is known as eternal death or the "second death."

3. *Eternal death.* By eternal death is not meant annihilation, utter destruction. It is the opposite of eternal life. To be cast into outer darkness (without hope), exiled from God, the source of all love, peace, and grace, is what is called eternal death or "the second death" (Revelation 20:14; 21:8). Bodily death transfers the spiritually dead into eternal death. For the spiritually living—the pardoned—bodily death is swallowed up in victory, for it leads to life everlasting.

Sudden Death

Is a sudden death necessarily an evil death?

By no means. There are those who dread the thought of being taken out of this world without a moment's warning—as many are in this day of frequent accidents. They feel that they would be better prepared to meet their God if at least a few hours were granted them for special preparation. The manner of our death is not left to our choice. We ought to be prepared at any time to receive the summons of our God, and one is if he is a child of God.

Paul says, "If a child, then also an heir." Why do you feel unsafe? Are you uncertain as to your standing with God? With the apostle you ought to be able to say with full assurance of faith: "I know whom I have believed, and am persuaded that he is able to keep that which I have committed unto Him against that day." "Give diligence to make your calling and election sure," but do not doubt the promises of your God. "The blood of Jesus Christ His Son cleanseth us from all sin." What more do we need? "He that believeth on Me hath everlasting life," John 6:47. It is significant that Jesus does not say, he will have eternal life at some future time, viz., after death. No, the true believer hath, is already in possession of, eternal life. Spiritual life is eternal life already begun. That is why a sudden death cannot harm a believer: he is in possession of the abiding life that continueth forever. He is vitally united with the ever-abiding Head, and bodily death cannot sever that union.

Memory of the Dead

Do the departed have memory, and do they know what is taking place on earth now since their departure?

The departed doubtless have memory. To the lost "rich man" in hell Abraham said: "Son, remember," Luke 16:25. He did remember his past life. He recognized poor Lazarus even across the "great gulf fixed." He knew that he had five brothers still living on earth. He understood what Abraham referred to when he spoke of "Moses and the prophets." Those in eternity will remember their past life in this world. The lost know why they are not among the blessed, and their bitter remorse for neglecting salvation is a gnawing worm that will not die, and a torturing fire that will not be extinguished. The saved in heaven will never cease to thank, to praise, and to serve God for His infinite grace in giving them a Redeemer and Savior.

However, we have no reason to believe that the departed know all about what is happening in this world since the day they were transferred into eternity. Isaiah says: "Doubtless Thou art our Father, though Abraham be ignorant of us, and Israel acknowledge us not; Thou, O Lord, art our Father, our Redeemer: Thy name is everlasting," Isa. 63:16. Abraham was dead and gone long before the time of Isaiah. The same is true of Israel, another name for Jacob. There was no use to appeal to these departed fathers concerning the needs of their descendants in the days of Isaiah. They were ignorant of their needs. The blessed know that a kind providence looks after and cares for those whom they have left behind. The lost may worry about the impenitent and unbelieving whom they have left behind, but the lost, too, are ignorant of what is taking place in this world since they left it.

Speaking with the Dead

Is it possible to speak with the dead, cf. I Sam. 28:14–20?

Can the living talk with the dead? There have always been those who claim that they can. Saul went to the witch of Endor because he thought that she would enable him to speak with the departed Samuel.

Various explanations of this account have been given. There are those who believe that the whole thing was a fraud and a delusion. Saul was in a weakened condition because of worry and in a nervous state of mind. A powerful enemy was in the land, and he feared for the worst. In deep anxiety and in this wrought-up state of soul Saul goes to this woman who had been recommended to him as one who is able to converse with the dead. It is at night when he goes to visit her, the most favorable time to perpetrate delusion and fraud. Saul asks the woman to bring him up Samuel. How she went about to do this we are not told. No doubt she resorted to some kind of mysterious rap, peep or mutter (Isaiah 8:19). And something must have happened. What seems to have happened is that the floor opened up before them, and the image of an old man appeared. Saul "perceived" that it was Samuel, we are told, and he bowed himself deeply before him. Does it mean that Samuel actually appeared bodily, or did it only seem to be so to the excited, expectant Saul? I am inclined to believe that Samuel actually appeared. Brought forth, however, not by the witch of Endor, but by the Lord Himself, to terrify the conjuror and to proclaim doom to the unfaithful king.

But if God did call up Samuel from the dead on this occasion for some specific reason, it is the only instance of its kind related in the Scripture, and it gives us no warrant to believe that there is any communication going on between the living and the dead. The fact that the angel Gabriel once appeared in human form to the Virgin Mary and spoke to her is no proof that there are people now who converse with the angels. Nor is it true that some can hear the angelic host singing nowadays because they sang over the fields of Bethlehem the night Jesus was born.

Why should we have a desire to speak with the dead? We have "Moses and the prophets," and no one less than Jesus affirms that if people "hear not Moses and the prophets, neither will they be persuaded, though one rose from the dead," Luke 16:31. We know all that is necessary concerning the life to come. This claim that some people are able to talk with the dead is unprovable. Some of the great magicians of our day have exposed the tricks and false claims of the mediums of Spiritualism again and again. These entertaining magicians have challenged the mediums to do anything that they cannot do.

Attempting to talk with the dead is an abomination unto the Lord. Many passages of Scripture condemn it in the severest terms. We shall refer to but one. "There shall not be found among you any one . . . that useth divination, or an observer of times, or an enchanter, or a witch, or a charmer, or a consulter with familiar spirits, or a wizard, or a necromancer. For all that do these things are an abomination unto the Lord," Deut. 18:10–12.

Recognition in Heaven

Shall we recognize each other in heaven?

There are those who consider this question a purely speculative one. They seem to think that the Bible gives us no definite information on this subject. I am convinced that they are mistaken. God has not left us in uncertainty; His Word speaks in no uncertain terms also on this question. We shall begin with the Old Testament. At the time of the death of each of the old patriarchs, Abraham, Isaac, and Jacob, it is stated, "He was gathered unto his people." This cannot mean that he was buried with his ancestors because Abraham was not buried with his ancestors. Moreover, the statement announcing his having been gathered unto his people always precedes the account of his burial.

When Jacob thought that some wild animal had killed his beloved son Joseph he said, "I shall go down to Sheol [the place of the departed] to my son, mourning," Genesis 37:35, RSV. What comfort would there be in this if he would not recognize his dear son in the life to come? Take also the case of David. He said after his child had died, "I shall go to him, but he will not return to me," II Samuel 12:23. What comfort would there be in being together again in eternity if they would not recognize each other?

Let us now turn to the New Testament. On one occasion Jesus said: "Many shall come from the east and west, and shall sit down with Abraham and Isaac and Jacob in the kingdom of heaven." Shall we fellowship with these old patriarchs and not even know them? The Holy Supper is not only a memorial feast that points backward to Christ's death in our behalf on Calvary; it also points forward to the time when we shall eat and drink with Him and all the blessed in the heavenly Father's house (Matthew 26:29). Shall the children of the household of God feast together with Jesus, their elder Brother, and they be strangers to each other? I am sure the prepared place Jesus tells us about would lose much of its charm, in fact, it could not be home if in its sweet company we should not recognize and hold converse with those "we have loved long since and lost awhile."

The rich man Jesus tells us about had no trouble in recognizing Lazarus in the company of Abraham. He knew him even across the "great gulf." He remembered that he had left in this world five brothers who were as indifferent about eternity as he had been. He understood what Abraham meant by "Moses and the prophets." Hence, those in eternity have memory. "Son, remember" (Luke 16:25). If we have no recollection of this life when we reach heaven, how can we intelligently join in the song, "Worthy is the Lamb that was slain"? The martyrs "who were slain for the word of God, and for the testimony which they held," are represented as saying: "How long, O Lord, holy and true, dost Thou not judge and avenge our blood on them that dwell on the earth?" They certainly had memory of their past life and cruel manner of death. And, note, they spoke as comrades who suffered together and were looking to God to avenge their wrongs.

When the penitent thief met Jesus in paradise, was there not mutual recognition? So shall there be between us. Jesus graciously promises: "I go to prepare a place for you. And if I go and prepare a place for you, I will come again and receive you unto Myself; that where I am there ye may be also," John 14:2, 3. Is it possible that Peter and John and Mary and Martha and all the rest will be there in the prepared home and not recognize each other, nor remember how they sat together at the feet of Jesus and walked and communed with Him and with each other in Judea and in Galilee?

Paul exhorts us not to sorrow greatly for those who have fallen asleep in Jesus, for when He returns to earth He will bring them with Him. And they who are alive and remain unto His coming "shall be caught up together with them in the clouds, to meet the Lord in the air: and so shall we [reunited] ever be with the Lord. Wherefore comfort one another with these words," I Thessalonians 4:13–18. The comfort Paul would have us lay hold on is the assurance that we have not lost those dear ones who have departed in the faith. We shall have them again and be reunited with them forever in the heavenly Father's house. Without recognition of our loved ones the whole argument of the apostle would be without foundation. Again, Paul writes in this same epistle to the Thessalonian Christians that, though he should not see them again in this world, they would be his "joy and crown of rejoicing" when he presents them blameless before the Lord at His coming

178

(I Thessalonians 2:17–20). How could this be if there were no recognition in the life to come?

So, readers, I am going to ask you to take this sweet thought of recognition in heaven out of the realm of speculation and put it where it belongs, in the realm of positive certainty. Heaven is just as real as earth, and the kiss of reunion above is just as real as was the parting kiss here below.

> We shall meet beyond the river,
> Where the surges cease to roll.

The Resurrection of the Saints

Will you please explain Matthew 27:52, 53: "And the graves were opened; and many bodies of the saints which slept arose, and came out of the graves after His resurrection, and went into the holy city, and appeared unto many"? I would especially like to know: How much time was there between the earthquake and the resurrection of these saints? What holy city is referred to? What happened to these saints? Where are they now?

If the question be asked, "Where were these saints from late on Good Friday until Sunday morning?" we can only reply: "We have to do here with glorified bodies. Jesus remained on earth for forty days; where was He in the intervals between His appearances?" The "holy city" doubtless means Jerusalem. After these resurrected saints appeared to many they were translated into heaven.

When the lips of Jesus were sealed in death, God spoke to humanity in a different way; a miraculous manner that struck terror to the hearts of His enemies, but that strengthened the faith and brought new assurance to His people. These various signs, here referred to, no doubt occurred simultaneously at the moment of our Savior's death.

Your inquiry is especially about the third sign, the coming forth of many of the saints from their graves and appearing to many in the holy city after the resurrection of Jesus. We have here no figurative language. This is an account of what actually took place. You understand, of course, the kind of tombs used in that day among the Jews. The stone before the opening of the tomb could easily have been rolled away by the earthquake. But why, then, should only graves of the saints have been opened? This opening of the tombs must have been a separate miracle of almighty God. Not all the saints but only a select number was raised.

When Christ died He slew death, and as proof of this some of the saints who slept in the tomb were raised. When Jesus arose majestically on the third day He gave unmistakable proof to the world that death and the grave were indeed conquered. Not only did he appear to many, but also many of the resurrected saints appeared. The opening of the tombs, the awakening of these saints, and the leaving of the tombs, all, no doubt, occurred at the same moment, namely, when Jesus died. They did not appear to anyone until after the resurrection of Jesus on Easter morning because their appearance was a sign-testimony to the resurrection of Him who had truly conquered death and the grave.

Order for the Burial of the Dead

What is the origin of the burial service? When did it originate?

The earliest burial of which we have any authentic record is that of Sarah, the beloved wife of Abraham. There was, no doubt, some kind of service connected with this burial as well as at every burial among the Israelites of Old Testament time. Customs and forms doubtless changed from time to time and were more or less elaborate. In the early days burials were more of a family affair. We are using the word family in the wider sense of comprising not only a father and a mother and children but the families of these married children, all living together as a clan and having their flocks in common. Later, of course, death and burial became more an affair of the community or village in which they took place.

We have reason to believe that the burial service among the Christians of the apostolic church was quite simple, but from the days of Constantine, when Christianity became the religion of the state, it became more elaborate.

The Death of Luther

Did Martin Luther on his deathbed ask for a priest and request the last rites of the Catholic Church? I am told that he did.

You make me smile, and if it were not so serious, I fear I would smile out loud. I quote the following from *The Life of Martin Luther*, by Julius Köstlin, page 487:

"After Cölius had yet given him [Luther] a spoonful of medicine, he again said: 'I depart, and will yield up my spirit,' and three times in quick succession he repeated the words: 'Father, in Thy hands I commend my spirit, Thou hast delivered me, O faithful God.' Then he became entirely quiet and closed his eyes without answering those who were applying the different remedies in his behalf and were addressing him. Jonas and Cölius, however, after his pulse had been rubbed with strengthening lotions, asked him the question loudly: 'Reverende Pater (reverend father), do you abide by Christ and the doctrine as you have taught?' He then answered with a distinctly heard 'Yes.' Then he turned upon his right side and went to sleep. He continued to lie thus for a quarter of an hour, his feet and his nose became cold, and he drew a deep and gentle breath and was dead."

Now, please look up any history or encyclopedia and see if you can find anything so absurd about Martin Luther as that told you by some neighbor.

Cremation of the Dead

Much discussion is going on in newspapers and church papers of other denominations about cremation of the dead. Since we have no records that the practice was ever used during the past history of the church, and since it seems as if this idea originated among unbelievers, how does the Lutheran Church stand on this question of cremating the body?

To my knowledge the Lutheran Church has never in a formal way announced its stand on the question of cremation. This does not say, however, that Lutheran theologians have given this subject no serious study, or that it would be a matter of mere speculation for me or anyone else to state what position our church would take were the question ever brought before our church body for formal decision.

Most of the nations of antiquity to some extent at one time or another practiced cremation. This custom, however, never obtained among the people of God, neither in Old Testament nor in New Testament time. The unbelievers of the time of the French Revolution tried to revive the custom of cremating the dead, but without success. About the middle of the last century freethinkers and rationalists in Europe again began to advocate cremation, this time with better success. The first crematory in the United States was built in 1876. Since that time this mode of body disposal has made rapid headway in most civilized countries.

I shall not mention the arguments advanced in favor of cremation, but shall endeavor briefly to tell you why Christians generally believe that we should ordinarily cling to the time-honored custom of placing our departed in mother earth. We do so, not because of any direct command of God. The Lord has given us no specific directions as to what disposal is to be made of the bodies of the dead. We cannot say, therefore, that God expressly forbids cremation, and that the practice of it in itself is sin. Peculiar local circumstances may even make it advisable.

But why, generally speaking, should we not cremate the dead? Because from the beginning of time God seems to indicate that the dead are ordinarily to be buried. We need but recall the burial of all the worthies of Old Testament time. Proper burial was ever considered honorable, but the burning of the body was even prescribed by the Lord in punishment of certain acts of immorality (see Lev. 20:14 and 21:9; also the case of Achan the thief, Joshua 7:25). The wicked people of Sodom and Gomorrah were cremated by fire that fell from the heavens. Jesus sanctified the grave by being imbedded there Himself. Of Moses it is said that he died in the land of Moab, and that the Lord buried him (Deut. 34:5, 6). To Adam God said: "In the sweat of thy face thou shalt eat bread till thou return unto the ground; for out of it wast thou taken," Gen. 3:19. To Abraham Jehovah gave the promise: "Thou shalt go to thy fathers in peace: thou shalt be buried in good old age," Gen. 15:5. Although these passages have not the force of a direct command they certainly do prove that the Lord sanctions, yea, ordinarily expects burial, a fact that cannot be proven from any portion of Scripture in respect to cremation.

The promise of the resurrection fits in best with burial. When Jesus affirms: "Marvel not at this: for the hour in coming in the which all that are in the graves shall hear His voice, and shall come forth," John 5:28, 29, does it not presuppose burial? Speaking of the body, Paul says: "It is sown in corruption; it is raised in incorruption: It is sown in dishonor; it is raised in glory," etc. I Cor. 15:42, 43. Would he have used this figure of speech had he not burial in mind? The same is true when the Bible refers to the dead as sleeping, and the blessed as resting from their labors. "Except a corn of wheat fall into the ground and die, it abideth alone: but if it die, it bringeth forth much fruit," John 12:24. Take away burial, and this striking symbol and illustration of the Master Teacher loses its meaning.

Since cremation of the dead has never been the practice of the people of God, we shall certainly have to conclude that the believers have never considered the burning of the body as in conformity with the wish and desire of the Creator. We shall close with the words of Pastor Brobst: "While there is no positive prohibition of cremation to be found in Holy Writ, the purpose and spirit of the Scripture seems to be quite clearly defined in favor of burial and not cremation. Were it immaterial by which mode the dead are disposed of, there would very likely have been some cases of cremation in the Bible. But there are none, hence we are led to conclude that cremation *is not in accord with Scripture.*"

Moreover, "to do so is to take our stand on the side of the unbelievers whose godless aim is to mock our hope of the resurrection and to shatter our faith. They would cremate the body seemingly in a spirit of defiance of the promises of God to raise the dead bodies. But the Christian will not let himself be dismayed by these scoffers; he will insist upon burial as a proof of his belief and hope. Thus burial becomes a matter of principle over against atheists."